Global Warming and the American Economy

NEW HORIZONS IN ENVIRONMENTAL ECONOMICS

General Editors: Wallace E. Oates, *Professor of Economics, University of Maryland, USA* and Henk Folmer, *Professor of General Economics, Wageningen University and Professor of Environmental Economics, Tilburg University, The Netherlands*

This important series is designed to make a significant contribution to the development of the principles and practices of environmental economics. It includes both theoretical and empirical work. International in scope, it addresses issues of current and future concern in both East and West and in developed and developing countries.

The main purpose of the series is to create a forum for the publication of high quality work and to show how economic analysis can make a contribution to understanding and resolving the environmental problems confronting the world in the twenty-first century.

Recent titles in the series include:

Spatial Environmental and Resource Economics
Selected Essays of Charles D. Kolstad
Charles D. Kolstad

Economic Theories of International Environmental Cooperation
Carsten Helm

Negotiating Environmental Quality
Policy Implementation in Germany and the United States
Markus A. Lehmann

Game Theory and International Environmental Cooperation
Michael Finus

Sustainable Small-scale Forestry
Socio-economic Analysis and Policy
Edited by S.R. Harrison, J.L. Herbohn and K.F. Herbohn

Environmental Economics and Public Policy
Selected Papers of Robert N. Stavins, 1988–1999
Robert N. Stavins

International Environmental Externalities and the Double Dividend
Sebastian Killinger

Global Emissions Trading
Key Issues for Industrialized Countries
Edited by Suzi Kerr

The Choice Modelling Approach to Environmental Valuation
Edited by Jeff Bennett and Russell Blamey

Uncertainty and the Environment
Implications for Decision Making and Environmental Policy
Richard A. Young

Global Warming and the American Economy
A Regional Assessment of Climate Change Impacts
Edited by Robert Mendelsohn

Global Warming and the American Economy

A Regional Assessment of Climate Change Impacts

Edited by

Robert Mendelsohn

Edwin Weyerhaeuser Davis Professor, School of Forestry and Environmental Studies, Yale University

In Association with the Electric Power Research Institute
NEW HORIZONS IN ENVIRONMENTAL ECONOMICS

Edward Elgar
Cheltenham, UK • Northampton, MA, USA

Published by
Edward Elgar Publishing Limited
Glensanda House
Montpellier Parade
Cheltenham
Glos GL50 1UA
UK

Edward Elgar Publishing, Inc.
136 West Street
Suite 202
Northampton
Massachusetts 01060
USA

A catalogue record for this book
is available from the British Library

Library of Congress Cataloguing in Publication Data
Global warming and the American economy : a regional assessment of climate change impacts / edited by Robert Mendelsohn.
        p. cm. — (New horizons in environmental economics)
    "In association with the Electric Power Research Institute."
    Includes bibliographical references and index.
        1. United States—Economic conditions—1981—Regional disparities. 2. Climatic changes—United States. I. Mendelsohn, Robert. II. Series.

HC106.8 .G594 2001
330.973'092—dc21

2001018972

ISBN 1 84064 593 8

Typeset by Manton Typesetters, Louth, Lincolnshire, UK.
Printed and bound in Great Britain by MPG Books Ltd, Bodmin, Cornwall.

I dedicate this book to my wife, Susan Mendelsohn, whose strength, courage, and affection I cherish and depend upon.

Contents

Figures

Tables

List of contributors

Richard M. Adams, Department of Agriculture and Resource Economics, Oregon State University, Ballard Extension Hall 330B, Corvallis, OR 97331-3601, USA

Megan Harrod, Stratus Consulting, P.O. Box 4059, Boulder, CO 80306-4059

Brian Hurd, Stratus Consulting, P.O. Box 4059, Boulder, CO 80306-4059

Nicholas D. Livesay, Industrial Economics Incorporated, 2067 Massachusetts Avenue, Cambridge, MA 02140, USA

Bruce A. McCarl, Department of Agricultural Economics, Texas A&M University, College Station, TX 77843, USA

Robert Mendelsohn, Yale School of Forestry and Environmental Studies, 360 Prospect Street, New Haven, CT 06511, USA

James E. Neumann, Industrial Economics Incorporated, 2067 Massachusetts Avenue, Cambridge, MA 02140, USA

Brent Sohngen, Department of Agricultural Economics, Ohio State University, 2120 Fyffe Road, Columbus, OH 43210-1067, USA

Joel B. Smith, Stratus Consulting, P.O. Box 4059, Boulder, CO 80306-4059

Acknowledgments

This project is a continued effort that was first conceived in 1993. The initial concerted effort focused on developing new methods and applying them to measure national impacts across the United States. The principal investigators of each chapter continued to develop these methods in this book and apply them to study regional impacts in this analysis. This entire effort has required close cooperation among a large group of people in order to make sure that regional boundaries, climate scenarios, economic assumptions and resource use are consistent across all the studies.

We are grateful to the Electric Power Research Institute and the California Energy Commission for funding this research. We owe specific thanks to the project directors, Tom Wilson and Larry Williams of EPRI, and to Guido Franco of CEC, for their direction, guidance, and emotional support. We also wish to thank Joel Smith, who has played an integral role in keeping this project on time and budget, providing keen perspective and insight, and exhibiting statesmanship and patience. In many ways, Joel deserves to be a co-editor of this volume.

We especially want to thank the authors and co-authors of each chapter for their dedication to this project and willingness to finish this effort. The authors should be acknowledged for their willingness to develop their individual chapters within the context of this project. Developing a multi-sector analysis that is consistent across the economy is a difficult task but one these authors handled without complaint.

The project benefited greatly from peer review. We want to thank the three reviewers, Gary Yohe, Richard Tol and John Reilly, for critically examining an early version of the manuscript and providing constructive suggestions.

Finally, the volume has been greatly improved by the professional editorial efforts of Christina Thomas from Stratus Consulting. Her thorough review of all the chapters has tightened and clarified the arguments and language throughout the book and helped improve the final product immensely.

My goal as editor has been to provide a clear explanation of what we think will happen to the economy in each region of the United States if climate changes. The effort has led to some clear insights about which regions are vulnerable and how impacts will be shared through the market place. We hope that readers find the methods, results and policy implications of this work enlightening and thought provoking. Climate change is a challenging issue not only because it affects the entire planet but also because of its long reach across time. This book answers but a few of the pressing questions about climate change and is as much a call for further research as it is a report on work completed.

Abbreviations

ASM	Agricultural Sector Model
BGC	Biogeochemistry Cycle model
BIOME	Biome model
CENTURY	Century model
CO_2	carbon dioxide
DOLY	Dynamic Global Phytogeography model
ENSOs	El Niño/Southern Oscillations
EPA	Environmental Protection Agency
ET	evapotranspiration
GCM	general circulation model
GDFL	Geophysical Fluid Dynamics Laboratory model
GDP	Gross Domestic Product
IPCC	Intergovernmental Panel on Climate Change
M&I	municipal and industrial (water uses)
MAPSS	Mapped Atmospheric Plant Soil System model
OSU	Oregon State University model
TEM	Terrestrial Ecosystem Model
UKMO	United Kingdom Meteorological Office model
VEMAP	Vegetation/Ecosystem Modeling and Analysis Project

1. Introduction

Robert Mendelsohn and Joel B. Smith

This book contributes to the growing field of assessments of impacts of climate change by discussing the regional distribution of market effects of climate change across the United States. Although there are now several estimates of the national impacts of climate change, there are no quantitative regional estimates in the literature. If the country experiences a few degrees of warming, what will happen in each region? What difference will it make to each region if the change in climate turns out to be more substantial? Are the effects about the same for everyone or are some regions more vulnerable than others? These are the questions that this book seeks to answer.

HISTORY

In the 1980s, as interest in climate change increased, researchers set out to identify what types of impacts climate change might cause. The first comprehensive assessment of impacts in the United States was compiled in a US Environmental Protection Agency (EPA) study (Smith and Tirpak 1989). This assessment found that scenarios of 3° to 5°C average global warming could cause adverse impacts to agriculture, forestry, energy, water, coastal resources, health and biodiversity.

Economists then used the EPA sectoral analyses and scattered other studies to value these impacts in the United States. After Nordhaus's (1991) pathbreaking estimate came a series of analyses (for example, Cline 1992, Titus 1992, Fankhauser 1995, Tol 1995). These analyses were then captured in the second assessment recent report of the Intergovernmental Panel on Climate Change (IPCC) in a chapter on climate change impacts (Pearce *et al.* 1996). The studies estimated the dollar magnitude of impacts to each climate-sensitive sector. These estimates included impacts to market sectors (agriculture, coastal resources, energy, forestry, and water) where there was substantial quantitative information and impacts to nonmarket sectors (aesthetics, ecosystem change, health, and recreation) where there was much less information. Although the analysts could not agree on the magnitude to assign each sector, their aggregate estimates suggested that a doubling of greenhouse gases would cause long-run net damages in the United States equal to about 1–2 per cent of GDP.

The second comprehensive empirical study of impacts on the United States was completed in 1999 (Mendelsohn and Neumann 1999). That study examined the potential impacts of climate change on market sectors of the US economy as a whole. It examined impacts on agriculture, timber, water resources, coastal resources, energy, commercial fishing, and recreation. This second analysis included the full potential of adaptation to minimize costs of climate change and provided a more comprehensive analysis of the sectors. This examination of a complete cross-section of sectors revealed beneficial impacts that had been overlooked in earlier studies. This study found that a relatively small amount of warming (1.5 to 2.5°C) would produce small net benefits to the US economy (see Figure 1.1). Specifically, there would be large benefits in agriculture and small benefits in forestry, and the total benefits would be larger than the total damages from water, energy and coastal impacts nationwide. With more substantial warming (5°C), these net benefits would be substantially reduced and even become negative (see Figure 1.1).

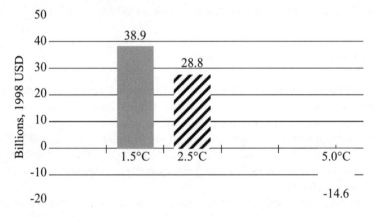

Source: Derived from Mendelsohn and Neumann 1999.

Figure 1.1   Estimated economic impacts of climate change in 2060 at three different temperature scenarios with no change in precipitation

HYPOTHESES

One of the interesting aspects of climate change is that impacts will not be uniform across sectors, across the world, or even within many countries (see, for example, Watson *et al*. 1998). Some areas could have benefits while others could have damages. Some sectors may see 'positive' impacts while other sectors may see 'negative' impacts. Impacts may also change as climate continues to change, changing the character and distribution of these impacts across sectors and regions. The EPA and other studies suggest that there could be substantial regional shifts in economic activity in the United States (for example, Smith and Tirpak 1989, Adams *et al.* 1999a, 1999b). These studies predict that southern areas of the nation are more likely to face adverse impacts than northern areas. Mendelsohn and Neumann (1999, p. 324) note: 'For the most part, these results support the intuitively plausible hypothesis that colder more northern states will enjoy higher than average benefits from warming.' Although the above studies provide broad predictions of regional impacts, they do not present quantitative predictions for each region and market sector.

This study uses the methods and scenarios developed in Mendelsohn and Neumann (1999) to examine the regional distribution of the market impacts of climate change in the United States. The empirical studies in Mendelsohn and Neumann suggest that the economic productivity of market sectors has a hill-shaped relationship with absolute temperature (Mendelsohn and Schlesinger 1999), implying that the impact of climate change for a location will depend on the initial temperature of that region. Cold places (on the left side of the hill) are more likely to have benefits from warming (climb the hill), whereas hot places (on the right side of the hill) are more likely to have damages (fall further down the hill). For a temperate country like the United States close to the top of the hill, there could be economic benefits[1] associated with small amounts of warming such as 1.5 to 2.5°C and damages associated with larger amounts of warming such as 5°C (see Figure 1.1).

Our regional hypothesis is that economic activities in colder northern regions are more likely to have economic benefits from climate change (or have less harm) and those in warm southern areas are more likely to be harmed (or have fewer benefits). We expect the Northeast, Midwest and Northern Plains to have economic benefits from warming. In contrast, we expect the Southeast, Southern Plains and Southwest to have economic damages from warming. The effects in the Pacific Northwest are more difficult to hypothesize because the region lies in northern latitudes but enjoys a relatively mild climate.

The difference in the impacts between the northern and southern region is expected to increase the more severe the climate scenario. Although early analyses recognized that impacts would most likely become more severe as the magnitude of climate change increased, they often assumed climate change would be harmful across all scenarios (Nordhaus 1991, Pearce *et al.* 1996). With low temperature change scenarios (increases of 1.5°C), however, the universal benefits of carbon fertilization from higher levels of CO_2 could dominate. The expected regional differences may appear only with higher temperature change scenarios.

Regional effects may also vary because of other differences across regions. Regions with more productive cropland, such as the Midwest, are likely to have larger agricultural impacts. Regions with important forestland, such as the Southeast, are likely to have larger timber impacts. Regions with more people and more economic activity, such as the Northeast, are likely to have more energy impacts. Regions with more people are also more likely to have larger consumer impacts if prices for food or wood products change because of climate. Regions that are drier, such as the Southwest, or which have more hydropower, such as the Northwest, are more likely to be sensitive to changes in water flows. Regions with more low-lying and developed coastline, such as the Southeast, will be more sensitive to sea level rise.

SECTORS

This study addresses the following market sectors of the United States:

- agriculture
- timber
- water resources
- coastal structures
- energy.

Mendelsohn and Neumann (1999) also examined commercial fisheries, which is also a market sector, but only in a sensitivity analysis. There have been few scientific studies on the effects of climate change on commercial fisheries, identifying how specific marine and estuarine areas would be affected, so biophysical estimates of the effects of climate change on commercial fisheries are limited. Further, because the entire sector is relatively small, it is not likely that fishery effects will be large. Commercial fisheries are consequently not included in this study.

Mendelsohn and Neumann (1999) addressed only selected nonmarket sectors: recreation and water quality. Since we are not able to provide reliable estimates of the impacts in several important nonmarket sectors such as aesthetics, ecosystem change, and health, we felt it was important to omit all nonmarket impacts. Note that these impacts are omitted solely because we have little confidence in the available estimates, not because we judge these sectors to be unimportant. The effect of climate change on the quality of life in each region and in the world at large is an important topic that we leave for future research.

METHODS

One of the most significant changes in the methods presented in Mendelsohn and Neumann (1999) concerns adaptation. The sector studies attempted to fully assess the potential for efficient adaptation to offset the negative impacts of climate change and take advantage of positive impacts. In the studies in this book, the costs and benefits of adaptation are also weighed, and adaptations are included only if their benefit exceeds their cost.

There is considerable controversy in the literature about whether adaptation will be efficient or not. Adaptation is likely to be efficient if the decision maker is the sole beneficiary of the action taken and there are no adverse effects of the decision maker's actions on other parties. In this book, we consequently assume rational economic behavior by individuals and firms when the incentives to adapt to climate change are private. Because this book is concerned only with climate impacts in market sectors, most of the adaptations considered fall into this category. In agriculture, for example, farmers are likely to pick new crops that will grow under the new climates they will experience. The forestry model assumes that timber firms will harvest trees in peril and plant new species adapted to warming. The energy model assumes that people will change their buildings as climate warms, decreasing insulation from the cold and increasing cooling capacity.

However, some of the adaptations in market sectors may depend on government action to perform activities that benefit many parties at once. When the incentives to adapt are shared across individuals, it is no longer obvious that rational economic behavior will be adopted. Examples of public adaptation include government agencies providing climate forecasts, building water facilities, reallocating water, or protecting coastal areas. All of these activities require coordinated engineering plans and social policies that will affect many people differently. In this book, we assume that these public actions will be efficient. For example, the water study assumed that water managers would reallocate water supplies to their highest valued use as water became scarce. The coastal study uses benefit–cost analysis to examine whether coastal property will be protected and what would be the optimal timing of adaptation measures, as opposed to assuming that all developed areas would be protected (as, for example, in Titus *et al.* 1991). Assuming that public adaptation is efficient may prove to be too optimistic. Whether public policy efficiently adapts to climate change is not clear. This is a controversial assumption and more research is needed to determine what to expect. Nonetheless, what is clear is that adaptation has the potential to substantially reduce costs and enhance benefits, is integral to impact assessment, and deserves careful policy analysis.

Measuring the impacts from climate change is very challenging. The climate since greenhouse gases began to accumulate in the atmosphere has increased 0.6°C over 100 years. Given the myriad other factors that have changed over this time period, it is not straightforward to isolate the impacts of climate using intertemporal data. This study consequently does not rely on longitudinal analysis but, in common with most of the impact literature, depends on two other approaches instead. First, many studies have conducted controlled experiments to isolate the effects of temperature and carbon dioxide. The results are then incorporated into simulation models that predict future consequences from specific climate scenarios. We rely on simulation models to capture effects in agriculture, coastal structures, forestry and water. Second, some studies have examined cross-sectional differences between one climate zone and another. We rely on these empirical models to estimate both agriculture and energy impacts.

Most of the studies in this book rely on only one approach. However, given the prominent role of agriculture effects in aggregate outcomes, we rely on both experimental-simulation and cross-sectional methods for that sector. Both methods have strengths and weaknesses; however, since the strengths and weaknesses of the two methods are quite different, the methods serve as good checks and balances of each other. The experimental method, for example, isolates the effect of each stimulus, be it temperature, precipitation or carbon dioxide. The cross-sectional method relies on natural experiments and so is vulnerable to charges of misinterpreting causal agents. The experimental method explicitly models cause and effect and so satisfies a desire for logical connections between the stimulus and the final response. The cross-sectional approach relies on correlation and so does not provide causal insights. The cross-sectional method, however, includes all the responses by the system to being in a different climate. The simulation approach includes only what the analyst models. The cross-sectional approach consequently includes unknown responses such as changes in insects and actual changes in farmer behavior whereas the simulation approach must guess at these unmeasured factors. Thus, the simulation approach, by not examining all of the changes and particularly the adaptations, may overestimate the negative effects of climate change. In contrast, the cross-sectional approach, by assuming that all behaviors change, may overestimate the positive effects of climate change. Note that for systems such as agriculture, neither approach examines the costs and feasibility of rapid adaptation.

The point of the above argument is not to suggest one approach is superior to the other but rather to argue that using both methods is superior to relying on just one approach. If the results disagree, it is apparent that there are still important factors that one or both methods are not yet taken into account. If the results are quite similar, however, it suggests that there may be consensus about impact estimates (given the scenarios used).

Another important improvement in recent impact studies is the attention being placed on dynamics. The early literature focused primarily on comparative equilibrium studies, comparing conditions today with equilibrium conditions in a doubled CO_2 world. For some sectors that can adjust relatively quickly, such as agriculture, such equilibrium comparisons may provide reasonable insights into the effects of climate change. However, comparative static analyses of sectors with substantial capital stocks, such as timber and coastal resources, can be misleading. For these sectors, the dynamic path of the change is critical. There is every reason to believe that the damages in these sectors are 'path dependent' (Schneider 1997). Very rapid changes would cause substantial damages in these sectors, but very gradual changes may be easy to adapt to. In this study, dynamic models are used to examine timber and sea level rise in order to capture the effects of both the pace and the level of climate change.

REGIONS

We define regions in the continental United States to be consistent with the US National Assessment (National Assessment Synthesis Team 2000). We excluded Alaska, Hawaii and the US territories because they represent entirely different systems that were not analyzed in Mendelsohn and

Table 1.1   Regional definitions

Region	States
Northeast	Connecticut, Delaware, Maine, Maryland, Massachusetts, New Hampshire, New Jersey, New York, Pennsylvania, Rhode Island, Vermont, West Virginia
Midwest	Illinois, Indiana, Iowa, Michigan, Minnesota, Missouri, Ohio, Wisconsin
Northern Plains	Kansas, Montana, Nebraska, North Dakota, South Dakota, Wyoming
Northwest	Idaho, Oregon, Washington
Southeast	Alabama, Arkansas, Florida, Georgia, Kentucky, Louisiana, Mississippi, North Carolina, South Carolina, Tennessee, Virginia
Southern Plains	Oklahoma, Texas
Southwest	Arizona, California, Colorado, Nevada, New Mexico, Utah

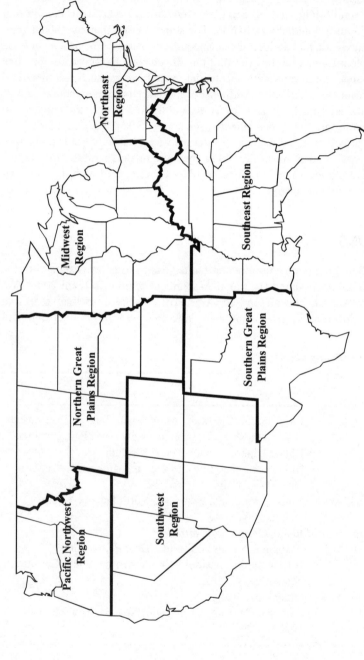

Figure 1.2   Seven regions used in this study

Neumann. We are specifically interested in comparing regions in the southern half of the country with those in the northern half so that we can explore our hypothesis concerning the relatively beneficial and harmful impacts in colder and warmer areas. However, these divisions are not perfect in this regard because parts of northern latitude regions, such as the Northwest, are somewhat mild and areas in the southern regions, such as the southern Rocky Mountains, can be cool relative to the rest of the country. The National Assessment regions divide the country between the north and south except for the Great Plains. We further divided the Great Plains region into Northern and Southern Plains, where the Southern Plains include Texas and Oklahoma. The National Assessment also divided Montana, Wyoming and Colorado between two regions. In some sectors, we cannot divide states into smaller areas because of the absence of information, and so we placed these states into the region where most of their area fell. The regions are displayed in Table 1.1 and Figure 1.2.

One of the main hypotheses of this book is that climate impacts will vary depending on initial climate. To understand what this might mean for each region, Table 1.2 presents current winter and summer temperatures and precipitation in each region. The table reveals that the three northern regions – the Northeast, Midwest and Northern Plains – are all currently relatively cool, whereas the three southern regions – the Southeast, Southern Plains and Southwest – are all currently relatively warm. The table also reveals that the

Table 1.2   Current regional climate

Region	Temperature (°C)		Precipitation (cm/month)	
	Winter	Summer	Winter	Summer
Northeast	−2.03	22.42	5.77	7.29
Midwest	−6.66	22.62	3.14	7.15
Northern Plains	−6.77	23.46	1.10	4.92
Southeast	5.25	26.05	7.20	9.52
Southern Plains	5.96	28.07	3.45	5.01
Northwest	0.45	22.76	7.96	5.16
Southwest	1.04	22.51	4.27	2.04
United States	−0.2	23.5	4.9	6.7

Note: Winter is December, January and February and summer is June, July and August. Climate variables are 30-year averages.

Source: Data from Mendelsohn et al. 1999.

Table 1.3   Regional characteristics

Region	Cropland (million acres)	Farm value (billion USD)	Timber supply (%)	Population (%)	GDP (%)
Northeast	22.2	56.6	5.7	27.4	25.0
Midwest	119.9	262.0	5.7	25.7	21.0
Northern Plains	115.5	132.51	1.0	3.0	6.0
Northwest	21.3	42.9	25.8	3.1	4.0
Southeast	59.0	129.6	55.5	20.9	21.0
Southern Plains	60.2	126.7	0.2	6.9	5.0
Southwest	25.6	116.2	6.1	13.2	18.0
United States	423.7	866.5	100.0	100.0	100.0

Note: All values are for 1990, except farm value, which is in 1998 USD.

Source: Data from Mendelsohn et al. 1999.

Southwest, Northern Plains and Southern Plains are also drier than the other regions. Given the initial temperature conditions, greater damages are expected in the southern regions and greater benefits are expected in the northern regions.

The magnitude of impacts in each region is also likely to be related to the region's characteristics. Table 1.3 provides some basic background measures for each region in this study: cropland, farm value, timber supply, population and percentage of GDP by region. Regions with more of these basic elements are likely to have larger effects in corresponding sectors.

For some purposes, these regions are too large. One cannot see important impacts within some of the regions. For example, some of the vegetation studies that are the basis for the forestry analysis show vegetation productivity in the upper Southeast (particularly Kentucky and Tennessee) increasing while productivity in the lower South is decreasing. These dramatic differences in local areas can balance out for the region as a whole. Just as national results mask underlying effects in each region, regional results may mask significant changes in local areas. Whenever possible, we attempt to provide qualitative discussion of important variation within regions. Readers should be cautious not to assume that region-wide findings necessarily apply at the state or local level: impacts can vary within regions.

BASELINE SCENARIOS

The early impact literature generally examined climate change impacts as though they would happen to a 1990 economy, although a few studies such as Rosenberg (1993) did project into the future. The advantage of using a 1990 economy is that it is well understood. With a well-defined economic baseline, the impact measurement appears more precise. Climate change, however, is predicted to unfold over the twenty-first century. By focusing on a 1990 economy, the conventional impact studies obtained an accurate measure of the wrong phenomena. What we want to measure is the effect of climate change on our future world. Unfortunately, since it is difficult to determine what the future will look like, we must settle for an impact analysis based on an uncertain future scenario. This approach increases the sources of uncertainty. Key socioeconomic factors such as population, income and technology will change, all of which are likely to affect how climate change will affect the United States. Although focusing on the future is more uncertain, estimates of future impacts consider what society needs to have measured.

Mendelsohn and Neumann (1999) developed a scenario of economic conditions in 2060 from background research on population projections and economic growth. They assume that in 2060 the US GDP will be $21.8 trillion (1998 USD) and the population will be 290 million. There is enormous uncertainty about the socioeconomic conditions in 2060. Who in 1940 could have imagined what life in 2000 would be like, with the information age, expanding service sector, declining manufacturing sector, globalization and modern government programs? We cannot accurately predict what life will be like in 2060, nor is it possible to know how future changes might affect each region. A baseline scenario is indeed a scenario, not a prediction. What is important to realize is that the economy will not resemble the current 2000 economy by the time that climate changes.

To get a sense of the importance of projecting forward, the sectoral studies in Mendelsohn and Neumann (1999) compared the climate impacts to both a 2060 economy and the 1990 economy. They found that the 2060 impacts were significantly larger than the 1990 impacts; however, the impacts as a fraction of GDP were the same. Baseline economic conditions consequently do matter. Further, under some scenarios of climate change, total welfare decreased with 1990 socioeconomic conditions but increased with 2060 socioeconomic conditions. In this study, we focus on the impacts to a projected 2060 economy. Readers should keep in mind that alternative baselines could affect the magnitude and possibly even the direction of the impacts.

CLIMATE CHANGE SCENARIOS

Mendelsohn and Neumann (1999) used uniform annual and national changes in temperature and precipitation. The same nine scenarios are used in this study and are displayed in Table 1.4.

Table 1.4   Climate change scenarios

Scenarios	
1	+1.5°C; 15% increase in precipitation
2	+1.5°C; 7% increase in precipitation
3	+1.5°C; 0% change in precipitation
4	+2.5°C; 15% increase in precipitation
5	+2.5°C; 7% increase in precipitation
6	+2.5°C; 0% change in precipitation
7	+5°C; 15% increase in precipitation
8	+5°C; 7% increase in precipitation
9	+5°C; 0% change in precipitation

Note: Scenario 1 is the mild scenario; scenario 5 is the central scenario; and scenario 9 is the harsh scenario.

Examining these scenarios is a sensitivity analysis. The analysis examines a range of outcomes that climate scientists think are plausible (Houghton *et al.* 1996). However, climate is not necessarily going to change uniformly across seasons and across the entire country. The IPCC predicts that there will be more warming in inland areas than in coastal areas, more warming in higher latitudes than in lower latitudes, more warming in winter than in summer and more warming at night than during the day. Precipitation is highly unlikely to change uniformly, because there will be variation by season and location. Actual changes in every region are not likely to be the same, even if we cannot predict how they will differ.

To address this problem, many studies of climate change impacts have used outputs from general circulation models (GCMs) because they provide plausible (although certainly not accurate) estimates of regional and monthly variation from climate change (for example, Smith and Tirpak 1989, National Assessment Synthesis Team 2000). There are three problems with using a limited set of GCM runs for impact assessment. First, it is difficult to compare results across models. It cannot be determined which of the many climate variables are responsible for observed effects, whether the average level of the variables are important or whether the distribution of these variables over space and season is the most critical factor. The second problem is that each new GCM run produces a new set of results, displacing previous GCM runs. Impact studies based on old GCM outputs can quickly become out of date. Third, using such a small sample of GCM outputs does not necessarily provide a representative sample of climate outcomes.

Instead of relying directly on GCM outputs, this study examines a set of uniform climate change scenarios. Within each scenario, every location and every season is expected to experience the same climate change from their current condition. Mendelsohn and Neumann (1999) developed these uniform scenarios to examine a broad range of plausible changes. The scenarios capture a temperature range from 1.5°C to 5.0°C and a precipitation change from 0 per cent to 15 per cent (see Table 1.4). The temperature range compares closely with the range predicted by the IPCC for the twenty-first century of between 1.5°C and 4.5°C (Houghton *et al.* 2001), although warming in the United States may well be somewhat greater than global average warming (Wigley 1999).

These climate scenarios do not capture the full range of plausible climate changes that could occur over the coming century. The uniform scenarios do not permit regional variation in climate, nor do they allow the climate change to vary across seasons. In a recent comparison of the national impacts from the climate predictions of 14 GCMs, Williams *et al.* (1998) demonstrated that regional and seasonal differences lead to a wide range of impact estimates. The uniform scenarios do not reflect this range of outcomes; they do not project changes in interannual or diurnal variation. They show only the effect of average temperature and precipitation changes across a plausible range of climates.

The studies add these uniform changes to current climate as observed over a period of 20 to 30 years. Thus, as with many GCM-based studies, studies using uniform scenarios do not account for changes in climate variance, particularly the frequency and intensity of extreme events.

There are many advantages to using the uniform climate change scenarios. First, the scenarios are transparent and understandable. Unlike GCM output, the uniform scenarios translate easily to all locations and seasons. Second, the scenarios permit analysis of the sensitivity of the impacts to changes in temperature and precipitation. The effects of increasing temperature alone can be determined by examining results holding the change in precipitation constant (for example, at +7 per cent), and the effects of increasing precipitation can be determined by examining results when the change in temperature is held constant (for example, at +2.5°C). Third, the method makes it relatively easy to compute how the sector responds across climate outcomes. One can estimate climate response functions to changes in average annual temperature and precipitation from the results of the detailed studies (Mendelsohn and Schlesinger 1999). Fourth, the scenarios will stand the test of time. Researchers in the future can use these impact results to estimate the consequences of new GCM predictions. The results are no longer tied to specific climate models and so they are more robust.

Of course, if the focus of future concerns becomes variations in climate outcomes across seasons or regions, the uniform scenarios would not be helpful. Because climate scientists do not yet agree upon how greenhouse gases affect climate variability (Houghton *et al.* 1996), the study did not examine the impact of climate variability. If climate scientists predict that greenhouse gases will change these features of the climate, these effects will have to be added to the results in this book.

It is possible that individual regions will be more sensitive to regional temperature change than to national temperature change. A benign (adverse) temperature change may be amplified if the climate changes were region specific and not national. For example, if a region enjoyed a warming that increased agricultural production and this warming did not occur nationally, prices might not fall. The welfare gain from the regional climate change would be larger than if the change were national. Welfare responses, for both good and ill, might be larger for regional climate variations.

For agriculture and timber, we consequently examined the sensitivity of individual regions to changes in their climate. We assumed that the entire nation would have a 2.5°C increase in temperature and a 7 per cent increase in precipitation (scenario 5, or the central scenario). Regions were examined separately and were assumed to be exposed to a scenario of +1.5°C and 15 per cent increase in precipitation (scenario 1, which is relatively mild and wet) and a scenario of +5.0°C increase in temperature and no change in precipitation (scenario 9, which is relatively hot and dry). We examined whether regional climate sensitivity exceeds national sensitivity and whether regional sensitivities vary.

STRUCTURE OF THIS BOOK

This book systematically measures the sectoral impacts in each region of the United States to the nine climate scenarios outlined above. Chapters 2 through 7 of this book consider the regional impacts of climate change on market sectors in the United States, following the format in Mendelsohn and Neumann (1999). Chapters 2 and 3 examine agriculture using an experimental-simulation approach and a cross-sectional approach. Chapter 2, by Richard Adams and Bruce McCarl, uses an agronomic-economic general equilibrium modeling approach, and Chapter 3, by Robert Mendelsohn, uses a cross-sectional empirical approach. Chapter 4, by Brent Sohngen and Robert Mendelsohn, begins with ecological forecasts of changes in biomes and productivity and then uses a dynamic economic model to predict harvest, planting and management intensity. This model then estimates the welfare effects in timber markets over time. In Chapter 5, by Brian Hurd and Megan Harrod, economic models allocate water-given changes in runoff due to climate change. The welfare effects of these changes are measured for selected watersheds and then extrapolated to each region. James Neumann and Nicholas Livesay use an intertemporal economic model to examine the economically efficient response to sea level rise over time and the resulting damages in Chapter 6. In Chapter 7, Robert Mendelsohn uses cross-sectional analysis to estimate short-run and long-run changes in residential and commercial energy expenditures. The chapter then calculates the welfare effects from climate change in the energy sector.

Chapter 8 covers the potential effectiveness of adaptation to ameliorate the negative effects of climate change or to enhance the positive effects. This topic was addressed in each sector in Mendelsohn and Neumann (1999) but was not discussed as a whole, as we do here. It is critical not only for understanding the vulnerability of US market sectors to climate change but also to provide information to policy makers on what types of adaptations should be encouraged to reduce risks to climate change. The chapter makes the critical distinction between private adaptation (where the benefits of the change accrue to the person making the change) and public adaptation (where there are many people affected by the adaptation). The chapter discusses what actions government must take to encourage more efficient public adaptation.

Finally, Chapter 9 synthesizes the results. We examine the overall benefits and damages that occur across the United States under alternative warming scenarios. We focus on how these impacts are distributed across the regions and across sectors. We specifically test whether northern regions benefit more than southern regions and how these regional results are affected as temperatures warm. Finally, we note the importance of including impacts on consumers as well as producers, because the market spreads impacts across people from every region.

NOTE

1. Note that this study does not consider potential damages to natural ecosystems, endangered species, coastal wetlands or human health. This book evaluates only market sectors; a complete evaluation of climate change must include both market and nonmarket effects.

REFERENCES

Adams, R.M., B.H. Hurd and J. Reilly (1999a), Agriculture & Global Climate Change: A Review of Impacts to US Agricultural Resources, Arlington, VA: Pew Center on Global Climate Change.

Adams, R.M., B.A. McCarl, K. Segerson, C. Rosenzweig, K.J. Bryant, B.L. Dixon, R. Conner, R.E. Evenson and D. Ojima (1999b), 'Economic effects of climate change on US agriculture', in R. Mendelsohn and J.E. Neumann (eds), *The Impact of Climate Change on the United States Economy*, Cambridge, UK: Cambridge University Press, pp. 18–54.

Cline, W.R. (1992), *The Economics of Global Warming*, Washington, DC: Institute for International Economics.

Fankhauser, S. (1995), *Valuing Climate Change: The Economics of the Greenhouse*, London: Earthscan Publications Ltd.

Houghton, J.T., Y. Ding, D.J. Griggs, M. Noguer, P.J. van der Linden, D. Xiaosu and K. Maskel (eds), 2001, "Climate Change 2001: The Scientific Basis", Cambridge, UK: Cambridge University Press.

Mendelsohn, R. and J.E. Neumann (eds) (1999), *The Impact of Climate Change on the United States Economy*, Cambridge, UK: Cambridge University Press.

Mendelsohn, R. and M. Schlesinger (1999), 'Climate response functions', *Ambio*, 28, 362–6.

Mendelsohn, R., W. Nordhaus and D. Shaw, 1994, "The Impact of Global Warming on Agriculture: A Ricardian Analysis", *American Economic Review* 84 (4): 753–71.

National Assessment Synthesis Team (2000), Climate Change Impacts on the United States: The Potential Consequences of Climate Variability and Change, Report for the US Global Change Research Program. Cambridge, UK: Cambridge University Press.

Nordhaus, W.D. (1991), 'To slow or not to slow: The economics of the greenhouse effect', *Economic Journal*, 101, 920–37.

Pearce, D.W., W.R. Cline, A.N. Achanta, S. Fankhauser, R.K. Pachauri, R.S.J. Tol and P. Vellinga (1996), 'The social costs of climate change: Greenhouse damage and the benefits of control', in J.P. Bruce, H. Lee and E. F. Haites (eds), *Climate Change 1995: Economic and Social Dimensions of Climate Change*, Cambridge, UK: Cambridge University Press, pp. 179–224.

Rosenberg, N.J. (1993), 'Towards an integrated impact assessment of climate change: The MINK Study', *Climatic Change*, 24, 1–173.

Schneider, S. (1997), 'Integrated assessment modeling of global climate change: Transparent rational tool for policy making or opaque screen hiding value-laden assumptions?' *Environmental Modeling and Assessment*, 2, 229–49.

Smith, J.B. and Tirpak, D. (eds) (1989), *The Potential Effects of Global Climate Change on the United States*, EPA-230-05-89-050, Washington, DC: US Environmental Protection Agency.

Titus, J.G. (1992), 'The costs of climate change to the United States', in S.K. Majumdar, L.S. Kalkstein, B. Yarnal, E.W. Miller and L.M. Rosenfeld (eds), *Global Climate Change: Implications, Challenges, and Mitigation Measures*, Philadelphia: Pennsylvania Academy of Science, pp. 384–409.

Titus, J.G., R.A. Park, S.P. Leatherman, J.R. Weggel, M.S. Greene, P.W. Mausel, S. Brown, C. Gaunt, M. Trehan and G. Yohe (1991), 'Greenhouse effect and sea level rise: The cost of holding back the sea', *Coastal Management*, 19, 171–204.

Tol, R.S.J. (1995), 'The damage costs of climate change toward more comprehensive calculations', *Environmental and Resource Economics*, 5, 353–74.

VEMAP (1995), 'Vegetation/Ecosystem Modeling and Analysis Project (VEMAP): Comparing biogeography and biogeochemistry models in a continental-scale study of terrestrial ecosystem responses to climate change and CO_2 doubling', *Global Biogeochemical Cycles*, 9, 407–37.

Watson, R.T., M.C. Zinyowera and R.H. Moss (eds) (1998), *The Regional Impacts of Climate Change: An Assessment of Vulnerability*, Cambridge, UK: Cambridge University Press.

Wigley, T.M.L. (1999), The Science of Climate Change: Global and US Perspectives, Arlington, VA: The Pew Center on Global Climate Change.

Williams, L., D. Shaw and R. Mendelsohn (1998), 'Evaluating GCM output with impact models', *Climatic Change*, 39, 111–33.

2. Agriculture: Agronomic–economic analysis

Richard M. Adams and Bruce A. McCarl

INTRODUCTION

The economic impact of climate change on agriculture is one of the most important effects identified in earlier climate change analyses (Adams *et al.* 1989, 1990, 1999, Reilly *et al.* 1996). In this chapter, we report regional-level effects of the previously examined uniform climate change assumptions employed in Mendelsohn and Neumann (1999). We also examine additional climate change scenarios, which contain regional differences in temperature and precipitation. The additional scenarios represent possible climate extremes in each region, holding the changes in all other regions constant. This tests the sensitivity of the earlier evaluations to regional climate assumptions. It can also suggest regions that are particularly important to the measurement of national level effects.

This analysis is based on the Agricultural Sector Model (ASM), a spatial equilibrium model of the US agricultural sector. The ASM is the basis for many of the national level quantitative estimates of the economic impacts of climate change found in the literature. The focus here is on regional rather than national impacts. To be consistent with the other sectors in this book, the ASM was adapted to report the impacts in the seven regions defined in Table 1.1 in Chapter 1, instead of the 10 regions used in some of the earlier analyses (see Figure 2.1 in Adams *et al.* 1999). This involved combining the Corn Belt and Great Lakes regions into one region, the Midwest, combining the Northern Great Plains with some states from the Mountain region (forming the Northern Plains) and combining the Appalachian region with the Northeast (labeled as the Northeast). This aggregation does not affect total crop acreage, total production or resource inventories within the ASM; it simply changes how the results are tabulated and reported by region.

OVERVIEW OF THE AGRICULTURAL SECTOR MODEL

The ASM has been used in many analyses of the interaction between agriculture and the environment, including the work by Adams *et al.* (1989, 1990, 1995 and 1999) on climate change. It allows for disaggregate analysis of regional impacts of change, with endogenous price adjustments.

The ASM represents production and consumption of primary agricultural products, including both crop and livestock products. Processing of agricultural products into secondary commodities is also included. The production and consumption sectors are assumed to be made up of a large number of individuals, each of whom operates under competitive market conditions. This leads to a model that maximizes the area under the demand curves less the area under the supply curves. The area between baseline supply and the demand curves equals the baseline economic welfare. Similarly, the area between the supply and demand curves after a posited climate change equals the new economic welfare. The difference between these two areas equals the change in economic welfare, equivalent to the annual net income lost or gained by agricultural producers and change in welfare to consumers as a consequence of global climate change. Both domestic consumption and foreign consumption (exports) are included.

The model integrates a set of micro- or farm-level crop enterprises for multiple production regions which capture agronomic and economic conditions with a national (sector) model. Specifically, producer-level behavior is captured in a series of technical coefficients that portray the physical and economic environment of agricultural producers in each of the 63 homogeneous production regions in the model, encompassing the 48 contiguous states. Here, these production regions are then aggregated to the seven regions. As in earlier studies, irrigated and nonirrigated crop production and water supply relationships are included in the analysis. Availability of land, labor and irrigation water is determined by supply curves defined at the regional level. Farm-level supply responses generated from the 63 individual regions are linked to national demand through the objective function of the sector model, which features demand relationships for various market outlets for the included commodities (see Chang and McCarl 1993 for details of ASM).

Several changes were made to ASM in Adams *et al.* (1999). First, citrus and tomatoes (a proxy for vegetable production in general) were added to the model. Incorporating these crops allows an analysis of the effect of climate change on selected high-valued fruits and vegetables that might benefit from temperature increases. Second, climatic-based data were added to the analysis to simulate the effects of climate change on:

1. potential migration of crops (northward) into other production areas

2. farmer adaptations in the form of changing varieties, planting dates and crop mixes
3. livestock performance due to animal physiology arising from changes in temperature and in feed supplies
4. ground and surface water availability
5. exports of US agricultural commodities based on supply changes in the rest of the world arising from climate change.

The procedures used to implement these changes in ASM are described in Adams *et al.* (1999). Finally, a dynamic component was added, allowing simulations into the future (for the 2060 analysis).

With these changes, the ASM was then used to simulate the impacts of alternative climate change scenarios on the agricultural sector. Before the ASM can be run, several exogenous inputs must be prepared using a variety of sources. The climate change and economic scenarios must be chosen. The estimated impacts on the yields of crops and forage must be determined (including the role of technological change in future yields). Animal grazing requirements and performance must be estimated. Crop migration potentials have to be calculated, and changes in water resource availability must be estimated. These inputs are described in detail in Adams *et al.* (1999).

REGIONAL RESULTS FROM PREVIOUS ANALYSES

The results reported in Adams *et al.* (1999) focused primarily on national level effects of the various uniform climate change scenarios. The more recent US National Assessment (Reilly *et al.* 2000) also provides national level effects arising from an application of the ASM. Those national (or aggregate) level effects reflect changes in regional crop yields, crop revenue and welfare and in most cases show gains to agriculture from modest warming. In this section, we focus on the regional level effects for each of the seven regions (Table 1.1 in Chapter 1) associated with the original climate scenarios evaluated in Mendelsohn and Neumann (1999). Specifically, we provide regional results for the nine original climate scenarios (Table 1.4 in Chapter 1). These scenarios encompass the full range of temperature (1.5 to 5.0°C) and precipitation (0 to 15 per cent) scenarios found in the original set of 64 scenarios (see Adams *et al.* 1999 for a complete listing). The remaining scenarios in Adams *et al.* also examined variations in CO_2 levels.

Here we focus on two types of regional outcomes. First, we examine changes in total economic welfare in each region under each scenario. Economic welfare in the ASM is calculated as economic surplus, or the sum of consumer and producer surplus. Economic surplus is a widely accepted meas-

Table 2.1 Changes in regional economic welfare under uniform climate changes (billions 1998 USD)[a]

Scenario	Region						
	NE	MW	NP	NW	SE	SP	SW
1 (1.5°C, +15%)	5.85	10.30	3.51	1.62	6.44	6.17	2.33
2 (1.5°C, +7%)	6.75	9.56	3.80	1.29	7.22	4.74	2.40
3 (1.5°C, 0%)	5.90	8.37	3.74	1.29	7.49	3.99	2.43
4 (2.5°C, +15%)	5.29	10.11	1.27	1.65	5.81	6.07	2.03
5 (2.5°C, +7%)	6.83	8.76	1.16	1.51	7.28	4.54	2.36
6 (2.5°C, 0%)	5.75	8.02	2.31	1.35	7.15	4.07	2.20
7 (5.0°C, +15%)	3.66	5.96	–1.59	1.92	4.76	5.35	0.46
8 (5.0°C, +7%)	3.30	4.11	0.33	1.71	5.13	3.76	–0.11
9 (5.0°C, 0%)	3.71	2.44	–0.40	1.24	4.63	2.04	–0.70

Note: a. Changes in welfare measured against 2060 ASM without climate change (base case).

ure of economic well-being in applied economics. These changes in economic surplus are reported in Table 2.1.

The results in Table 2.2 are changes from the base case, which comes from a run of ASM constructed for 2060 in the absence of any climate change (i.e., run under a repeat of 1995 climate). As is evident from the table, nearly all regions experience an increase in welfare under the climate change scenarios (the exceptions are the Northern Plains and the Southwest under the highest temperature scenarios). These welfare increases are driven by the underlying yield changes from warming, increases in precipitation and the assumed increase in atmospheric CO_2. As discussed in Adams *et al.* (1999) and elsewhere, increases in atmospheric CO_2 have the potential to increase plant growth, and ultimately crop yields, because of a 'fertilizer' effect. In the yield projections used here, atmospheric CO_2 levels in 2060 are assumed to be 530 ppm, or about 180 ppm higher than current levels. Changes in temperature, precipitation and CO_2 cause crop yields to vary from very small changes to increases of more than 40 per cent. These changes in crop yields drive the changes in economic welfare generated in ASM.

The increases in national yield reduce national prices. The lower prices, in turn, increase consumer surplus. The consumer surplus effects are concentrated in regions with more population, not necessarily more farmland. The producer surplus, in contrast, is concentrated in regions with more farmland. The net effect of regional yield changes on regional producer surplus is complicated because it depends on how much yields increase *versus* how much prices fall.

The results in the table follow some expected patterns. The largest change in absolute welfare from climate change occurs in the Midwest, the region with the largest amount of agricultural activity. The three regions with the largest population, the Midwest, the Northeast and the Southeast, also have large absolute welfare effects. The findings also support earlier studies that show that precipitation increases can offset or soften some of the negative effects of rising temperatures. For example, with a 5°C warming, an increase in precipitation increases the welfare change (or reduces the losses) in every region.

Table 2.2 provides estimates of changes in producer welfare only under the climate scenarios in Table 2.1. The results in Table 2.2 can be viewed as measuring the changes in producer profits in each region. As the results indicate, producers in some regions always gain under climate change (the Midwest, the Northern Plains and the Northwest) while other regions always experience reductions in producer welfare (the Northeast and the Southeast). The Southeast and Southern Plains show a mixed pattern, although many scenarios result in reductions in producer welfare. This regional pattern of gains in northern latitudes and reductions in southern areas is consistent with other studies that focus on producer welfare (for example, see Chapter 3).

Because consumer surplus is included in Table 2.1, the regional patterns there differ from those in Table 2.2. Producer profits can be adversely affected when prices fall because of increased production, whereas consumer

Table 2.2   Changes in regional producer welfare under uniform climate changes (billions 1998 USD)

	Region						
Scenario	NE	MW	NP	NW	SE	SP	SW
1 (1.5°C, +15%)	−2.12	2.80	3.30	0.45	−1.53	2.57	−3.25
2 (1.5°C, +7%)	−1.05	2.21	1.94	0.45	−5.90	2.88	−3.06
3 (1.5°C, 0%)	−0.94	1.91	1.52	1.29	7.49	3.99	−2.43
4 (2.5°C, +15%)	−2.61	2.69	3.22	0.51	−2.1	0.37	−3.49
5 (2.5°C, +7%)	−0.96	1.43	1.74	0.38	−0.52	0.25	−3.08
6 (2.5°C, 0%)	−0.96	1.71	1.52	0.37	0.44	1.65	−2.50
7 (5.0°C, +15%)	−2.41	0.25	3.12	1.04	−1.32	−2.30	−3.79
8 (5.0°C, +7%)	−1.10	−0.63	1.96	0.98	0.11	−0.26	−3.61
9 (5.0°C, 0%)	−0.47	−1.49	0.54	0.64	0.44	−0.90	−3.62

welfare will increase under a price reduction. With the declining national prices, the changes in Table 2.1 are always more positive because of rising consumer surplus effects. As discussed above, the regional effects in Table 2.2 are larger in regions with more agriculture and in regions that are more climate sensitive, such as the Southwest.

The effects of the climate scenarios on regional crop production are reported in Table 2.3. This table contains the percentage change in crop production within each region from the 2060 scenario without climate change (base case). Production is measured as an index number, where physical units of production (bushels or tons) are weighted by unit prices. The base case index is 100; the numbers in Table 2.3 are changes from that base. As is evident from the table, almost all regions experience an increase in crop production under climate change (and the effect of increases in CO_2 on yields). The only exceptions are a few regions under the highest temperature increase. Some of the largest percentage changes in crop production occur in areas with heat-tolerant crop mixes, such as the Southeast or Southwest. (Any increases in Southwest crop production will depend on availability of irrigation water, given this region's dependence on irrigation.) The Northern Plains also experience a large increase in crop production from the base case. In some regions, the increase in crop production is associated with a reduction in producer welfare, as reported in Table 2.2. The reduction in producer welfare in the Southwest and Northeast is due largely to the sharp reduction in prices associated with the increase in production. An adverse effect on the livestock sector is also felt across several regions.

Table 2.3   Percentage changes in regional crop production[a]

	Region						
Scenario	NE	MW	NP	NW	SE	SP	SW
1 (1.5°C, +15%)	24.2	24.2	46.8	36.0	55.3	27.5	41.5
2 (1.5°C, +7%)	21.8	17.5	22.2	7.0	48.2	17.4	25.2
3 (1.5°C, 0%)	25.8	22.3	32.0	21.9	52.4	16.4	34.5
4 (2.5°C, +15%)	16.6	17.4	57.8	34.6	45.6	25.3	39.1
5 (2.5°C, +7%)	16.2	11.2	31.9	6.5	43.1	19.9	21.8
6 (2.5°C, 0%)	18.0	15.9	44.6	20.7	47.0	19.2	30.8
7 (5.0°C, +15%)	–3.8	–3.1	53.2	12.3	25.7	11.1	22.5
8 (5.0°C, +7%)	–18.3	–12.1	19.8	6.7	25.0	3.9	6.9
9 (5.0°C, 0%)	–1.7	–6.1	36.9	3.3	26.2	8.5	15.1

Note: a. Changes in value measured against 2060 ASM without climate change (base case).

ANALYSIS OF DIFFERENTIAL CLIMATE EFFECTS IN REGIONS: SCENARIOS AND PROCEDURES

The analysis above and in Adams *et al.* (1999) involved national uniform temperature and precipitation changes. In this section, we examine the sensitivity of agriculture to regional climate variation. We assume that the national climate changes according to the central scenario (2.5°C and 7 per cent precipitation increase). We then examine each region sequentially and assume that this specific region experiences either a mild scenario (+1.5°C and +15 per cent precipitation) or a harsh scenario (+5°C and no change in precipitation). This results in 14 additional scenarios (seven regions by two climate changes for each region).

As with earlier climate assessments using ASM, the primary effect of changes in climate is assumed to be on crop yields. Changes in temperature and precipitation affect crop productivity and yields by altering plant physiology, irrigation water needs through crop evapotranspiration (ET) and irrigation water supplies. These are projected with a combination of crop and hydrological modeling. In turn, the resultant changes in yields, water requirements and water supplies are entered into ASM to obtain estimates of economic consequences for that climate scenario. The forecast yield and water requirements used under the harsh and mild scenarios and for the central scenario were those generated in the original analysis. Adams *et al.* (1999) provide a detailed description of the crop modeling procedures. The water supply data were those used in Hurd *et al.* (1999). When ASM is solved under each set of yield and water changes corresponding to the climate change assumptions represented in the 14 scenarios, a set of model results or outputs unique to each scenario is generated. As with results reported earlier in this chapter, these differences in model outputs are then used to measure the economic consequences of the regional change assumptions examined here.

REGIONAL SENSITIVITY RESULTS

Table 2.4 provides the changes in economic welfare generated by the ASM for each of the 14 scenarios. These changes are reported in billions of 1998 USD and are measured relative to the central scenario solution (the 2060 ASM specifications under 2.5°C warming and a 7 per cent increase in precipitation). As was the case in Adams *et al.* (1999) (and in all solutions of ASM), the measure of economic welfare reported in Table 2.4 is economic surplus, or the sum of producer and consumer surplus.

The third column of Table 2.4 reports the total economic surplus associated with the central scenario and each of the 14 regional scenarios. These

Table 2.4   Changes in welfare from central scenario (billions 1998 USD)

Scenario	Region	Total surplus	Welfare change	% change
1 (2.5°C, +7%)	—	33.42	No change	No change
2 (1.5°C, +15%)	Northeast	33.96	0.54	1.62
3 (5°C, 0%)	Northeast	30.18	−3.23	−9.68
4 (1.5°C, +15%)	Midwest	35.59	2.17	6.50
5 (5°C, 0%)	Midwest	25.70	−7.72	−23.09
6 (1.5°C, +15%)	Northern Plains	33.59	0.17	0.50
7 (5°C, 0%)	Northern Plains	33.05	−0.37	−1.09
8 (1.5°C, +15%)	Northwest	33.49	0.07	0.21
9 (5°C, 0%)	Northwest	33.94	0.52	1.55
10 (1.5°C, +15%)	Southeast	35.38	1.96	5.86
11 (5°C, 0%)	Southeast	30.70	−2.71	−8.12
12 (1.5°C, +15%)	Southern Plains	34.47	1.05	3.14
13 (5°C, 0%)	Southern Plains	32.40	−1.02	−3.04
14 (1.5°C, +15%)	Southwest	34.36	0.94	2.82
15 (5°C, 0%)	Southwest	32.13	−1.29	−3.85

Note: Scenario 1 is Central scenario.

estimates range between approximately $26 and $36 billion. However, this amount represents a very small percentage or fraction (less than 2 per cent) of the overall economic value reported for the 2060 base case economic model. This is consistent with other ASM-based climate change evaluations that show that global warming is likely to have only a small economic effect on the US agricultural sector. However, as indicated by the fourth and fifth columns of Table 2.4, the effect of changing the climate assumptions in a given region is more dramatic. For example, under scenarios 6 and 7, the Midwest region shows gains (from the benign case) and losses (from the adverse case) of approximately $2 billion and $8 billion, respectively. These amount to approximately 7 and 23 per cent of the change in total economic surplus reported for the central scenario (of $33.4 billion). Thus, if climate change in this region differs from other regions of the United States, then the treatment of regional climate can have a substantial effect on total national consequences. All other changes in welfare (from the uniform central scenario) are more modest, given that these other regions represent substantially less agricultural acreage and crop value than does the Midwest region (as defined here). However, as a percentage of total welfare, changes of almost 10 per cent are observed in the Northeast and the Southeast.

Table 2.5　Regional index numbers for total value of crop production

Scenario	Region						
	NE	MW	NP	NW	SE	SP	SW
1 (central) (2.5°C, +7%)	118.0	115.9	144.6	120.7	147.0	119.2	130.8
2 (1.5°C, +15%)	128.4	116.4	142.2	120.6	147.0	118.7	131.0
3 (5°C, 0%)	82.8	113.5	147.5	119.0	143.6	122.9	131.8
4 (1.5°C, +15%)	119.1	116.5	142.7	120.4	157.3	109.8	131.7
5 (5°C, 0%)	116.4	112.9	137.6	119.9	118.5	136.1	131.3
6 (1.5°C, +15%)	117.4	127.3	144.0	120.9	146.5	117.2	131.5
7 (5°C, 0%)	127.3	91.01	146.0	121.8	144.4	124.3	129.0
8 (1.5°C, +15%)	115.6	114.1	142.7	118.7	143.6	122.3	130.1
9 (5°C, 0%)	120.5	116.7	130.2	120.5	147.6	120.8	132.2
10 (1.5°C, +15%)	118.0	115.2	144.4	120.9	143.8	130.4	131.2
11 (5°C, 0%)	118.2	115.8	143.3	119.9	146.6	98.2	130.5
12 (1.5°C, +15%)	117.8	115.4	145.7	118.7	146.1	116.6	140.9
13 (5°C, 0%)	117.8	115.4	143.0	121.8	146.7	128.4	113.6
14 (1.5°C, +15%)	117.7	115.3	144.9	128.1	146.3	120.9	130.4
15 (5°C, 0%)	118.1	116.1	144.6	106.9	147.1	119.8	132.1

The changes in total welfare are driven by changes in crop production and value within each region. Table 2.5 reports index numbers for total value of crop production by region, as estimated by ASM. The crop values in Table 2.5 are weighted by crop price and are measured as Fisher Price Indices. Table 2.6 reports the percentage changes in the value of crop production (index numbers) in each region between the central scenario and the scenario of interest. As evident from Table 2.6, the primary changes in value of crop production occur in the region experiencing a change in temperature and precipitation distinct from the central scenario assumption. However, some minor changes in crop production and value are also observed for the other six regions because of the general equilibrium nature of the ASM and its component regions. That is, as climate change alters yields and hence the comparative advantage of one region's crops and crop mixes, national prices are altered, which in turn causes changes in profitability and crop mixes in competing regions.

An examination of diagonal elements in Table 2.6 confirms the expectation that changes in climate in a given region will largely be measured in that region's value of crop production. For example, the two scenarios affecting the Midwest region result in changes in crop value for this region of +11.0 and −25.0 per cent, respectively. The changes in crop value in other regions for those two scenarios are generally quite small. Regions that produce simi-lar mixes of crops, however, are affected by changes in Midwest production,

Table 2.6 Percentage change in regional value of production from the central scenario

Scenario	Region						
	NE	MW	NP	NW	SE	SP	SW
1 (central) (2.5°C, +7%)	0.00	0.00	0.00	0.00	0.00	0.00	0.00
2 (1.5°C, +15%)	10.40	0.50	−2.40	−0.10	−0.10	−0.50	0.20
3 (5°C, 0%)	−35.20	−2.50	2.94	−1.70	−3.50	−0.37	−0.10
4 (1.5°C, +15%)	1.00	0.50	−1.90	−0.30	10.20	−9.20	0.80
5 (5.0°C, 0%)	−1.70	−3.10	−6.90	−0.80	−28.50	16.90	0.40
6 (1.5°C, +15%)	−0.70	11.35	0.15	0.20	−0.60	−0.20	0.60
7 (5°C, 0%)	3.30	−24.80	1.40	1.15	−2.70	5.10	−1.90
8 (1.5°C, +15%)	−2.40	−1.80	3.10	−2.10	−3.40	−1.90	−0.80
9 (5°C, 0%)	2.50	0.70	−14.30	−0.30	0.50	1.60	1.40
10 (1.5°C, +15%)	−0.10	−0.80	−0.20	0.30	3.30	11.20	0.30
11 (5°C, 0%)	0.10	0.20	−1.30	−0.90	−0.40	−21.00	−0.40
12 (1.5°C, +15%)	−0.30	−0.60	1.10	−2.10	−0.90	−3.00	10.10
13 (5°C, 0%)	−0.20	−0.60	−1.60	1.10	−0.30	9.20	−17.30
14 (1.5°C, +15%)	−0.40	−0.60	0.30	7.30	−0.70	1.70	−0.40
15 (5°C, 0%)	0.10	0.10	1.15	−13.90	0.10	0.60	1.30

as expected. When Midwest crop yields increase (decrease), the similar crops in these other regions decrease (increase). In some cases, a reduction in supply in one region, such as the decline in the Southeast (of 28 per cent) under the 5°C increase with no change in precipitation, triggers a large increase in production in a competing region (for example, the 17 per cent increase in the Southern Plains). These changes in crop production in other regions are the result of the interaction between crop production (supply) and prices within the structure of ASM. This shows the importance of modeling price effects in the context of environmental or policy changes that affect a large geographical area or influence a substantial proportion of total output.

Changes in regional climate have the potential to alter resource use, particularly the amount of cropland required to produce given levels of output. This is because the primary effect of climate change is reflected in crop yields. Thus, if crop yields increase because of climate change (or any other factor such as improvements in technology), then the amount of land in production will decline, unless there is a simultaneous increase in demand. Table 2.7 contains changes in two categories of cropland (irrigated and dryland) used under each scenario. These changes are in national or aggregate totals associated with the central scenario and the regional climate changes. The sum of irrigated and dryland makes up the third column in the table (total cropland).

Table 2.7   Changes in national crop acreage, by type, under regional
climate change assumptions

Scenario	Region	Percentage change in total acreage		
		Irrigated	Dryland	Total cropped acreage
1 (2.5°C, +7% precipitation across all regions)	—	10.34	−2.33	0.28
2 (1.5°C, +15% precipitation)	Northeast	10.50	−2.57	−0.12
3 (5°C, 0% precipitation)	Northeast	7.64	−2.15	−0.13
4 (1.5°C, +15% precipitation)	Midwest	13.77	−2.76	0.65
5 (5°C, 0% precipitation)	Midwest	8.15	−3.15	−0.82
6 (1.5°C, +15% precipitation)	Northern Plains	12.57	−5.58	−1.84
7 (5°C, 0% precipitation)	Northern Plains	9.37	−1.52	0.72
8 (1.5°C, +15% precipitation)	Northwest	10.08	−2.36	0.20
9 (5°C, 0% precipitation)	Northwest	10.19	−2.03	0.49
10 (1.5°C, +15% precipitation)	Southeast	11.16	−2.70	0.15
11 (5°C, 0% precipitation)	Southeast	6.79	−2.70	−0.74
12 (1.5°C, +15% precipitation)	Southern Plains	11.25	−2.83	0.07
13 (5°C, 0% precipitation)	Southern Plains	10.01	−2.88	−0.22
14 (1.5°C, +15% precipitation)	Southwest	11.08	−2.51	0.29
15 (5°C, 0% precipitation)	Southwest	10.56	−2.32	0.34

Note: Scenario 1 is Central scenario.

As the results in Table 2.7 demonstrate, the use of cropland varies with scenario and type of cropland. In the central scenario, a uniform change in temperature and precipitation results in a 10 per cent increase in irrigated land but a reduction in dryland and a very small overall increase in cropland. For perspective, it should be noted that irrigated cropland is about 20 per cent of total US cropped acreage. Irrigated lands typically have higher yields, so the contribution of irrigation to total value of crop production exceeds its proportion of land use. It should also be noted that for the Northeast, Southeast and Midwest regions, irrigated cropland is currently a small proportion of total cropped acreage. Most cropland in these regions is rainfed (farmed without irrigation). As one moves west, the proportion of irrigated land as a total of all cropland increases. The arid Southwest has the highest percentage of irrigated cropland. This distribution of types of land, in the aggregate and by region, is important to keep in mind when evaluating the percentage change in each type of land.

The total amount of land in production does not vary substantially under any scenario, in contrast to the results in Chapter 3. The greatest percentage change in total cropland in production is less than 2 per cent (associated with one climate change assumption in the Northern Plains). All other changes in total cropland are less than 1 per cent. Eight of the scenarios result in increases in total cropland, while six show reductions. The effects of the regionalization of temperature and precipitation assumptions on land use are tied to the absolute quantities of cropland in a region and to the relative importance of each type of land in the affected region. For example, larger percentage changes across assumptions are noted in irrigated cropland when changes occur in the regions where irrigation is a small component of land use. However, where the potential for expansion is high, such as in the Midwest and Northern Plains, the differences in irrigated acreage between climate scenarios are fairly large. Conversely, the percentage change in irrigated acreages between scenarios is smallest when the climate change scenario is imposed on a region with a large proportion of irrigated land, such as the Southern Plains, Southwest and Northwest. In these regions, the changes in acreage relative to the base are fairly stable: they are all similar to the change in the uniform or central scenario, or approximately 10 per cent.

CONCLUSION

Within the climate impacts literature in the United States, there are three general approaches to measuring the climate sensitivity of a sector. One approach (and the most common) is to begin with a GCM-based climate forecast and simulate what will happen to crop yields and markets. One difficulty with GCM-based forecasts is the sparse number of nodes or forecast points within the GCM grids; most studies rely on fewer than 50 sites to represent the entire United States. Another concern is the accuracy of the regional forecasts. A second approach (see Chapter 3) is to examine cross-sectional evidence across climate zones and use this to forecast the impact of climate change. A third approach is to use a historical climate analogue believed to be representative of climate under warming (see Easterling *et al.* 1993). With the last two variants, assumptions must also be made concerning carbon dioxide effects, since these effects are not captured by these approaches. By comparing the regional implications of climate changes, the analysis conducted here extends the earlier Adams *et al.* (1999) analysis in two ways. First, it examines the regional implications of the nationally uniform climate change scenarios (such a regional comparison was not provided in Adams *et al.* 1999). Second, this evaluation explores the effects of regional deviations from the uniform national climate scenarios.

As the results in Table 2.1 demonstrate, the effects of climate change on total economic welfare vary across regions. Almost all regions benefit from climate change because of predicted increases in aggregate production that reduce crop prices and increase consumer surplus. The largest effects occur in areas with the largest population, including the Northeast, Midwest and Southeast, a finding consistent with the recent US National Assessment (Reilly *et al.* 2000). Table 2.1 reports the sum of changes in consumer and producer well-being. Table 2.2 shows the effects of climate change on producer welfare only. The largest effects on producer welfare occur in the regions with strong agricultural production. Some regions gain but others lose under climate change, with farmers in northern regions generally gaining and farmers in southern regions losing. As the results in Table 2.5 indicate, regional variations of climate changes have the potential to alter the changes in total welfare in a substantial way. For example, for one region (the Midwest), the imposition of a more severe climate change assumption resulted in a 23 per cent reduction in welfare (from the central scenario). Changes in two other regions resulted in approximately 8 and 10 per cent reductions in welfare.

The changes in welfare are linked to changes in crop production experienced in each region under the various scenarios. As shown in Table 2.6, changes in the regional value of crop production were also noteworthy in some regions. For example, the Northeast and Southeast experience nearly a 30 per cent reduction in crop production under the harsh climate change scenario.

These results suggest that regional climate assumptions are important in the US agricultural sector. This finding supports previous studies that have also found regional patterns of climate change to be important (see Adams *et al.* 1995, 1999, Williams *et al.* 1998). Despite their importance, regional climate forecasts may not improve the overall validity of the analysis, because current regional climate forecasts are highly uncertain and vary across GCMs. Finally, including regional climate variation is not likely to change the general consensus of this chapter and other assessments. The increases or reductions in agricultural productivity from climate change are a small proportion of agricultural output.

REFERENCES

Adams, R.M. (1989), 'Global climate change and agriculture: An economic perspective', *American Journal of Agricultural Economics*, 71, 1272–9.

Adams, R.M., R. Fleming, B.A. McCarl and C. Rosenzweig (1995), 'A reassessment of the economic effects of climate change on US agriculture', *Climatic Change*, 30, 147–67.

Adams, R.M., B.A. McCarl, K. Segerson, C. Rosenzweig, K.J. Bryant, B.L. Dixon, R. Conner, R.E. Evenson and D. Ojima (1999), 'Economic effects of climate change on US agriculture', in R. Mendelsohn and J.E. Neumann (eds), *The Impact of Climate Change on the United States Economy*, Cambridge, UK: Cambridge University Press, pp. 18–54.

Adams, R.M., C. Rosenzweig, R.M. Peart, J.T. Ritchie, B.A. McCarl, J.D. Glyer, R.B. Curry, J.W. Jones, K.J. Boote and L.H. Allen, Jr. (1990), 'Global climate change and US agriculture', *Nature*, 345, 219–24.

Chang, C.C. and B.A. McCarl (1993*), Documentation of the ASM: The US Agricultural Sector Model*, Texas A&M University, Texas: Department of Agricultural Economics.

Easterling, W., P. Crosson, N. Rosenberg, M. McKenney, L. Katz and K. Lemon (1993), 'Agricultural impacts of and response to climate change in the Missouri–Iowa–Nebraska–Kansas (MINK) Region', *Climatic Change*, 24, 23–61.

Hurd, B.H., J.M. Callaway, J.B. Smith and P. Kirshen (1999), 'Economic effects of climate change on US water resources', in R. Mendelsohn and J.E. Neumann (eds), *The Impact of Climate Change on the United States Economy*, Cambridge, UK: Cambridge University Press, pp. 133–77.

Mendelsohn, R. and J.E. Neumann (eds) (1999), *The Impact of Climate Change on the United States Economy*, Cambridge, UK: Cambridge University Press.

Reilly, J. and 22 authors (1996), 'Agriculture in a changing climate: Impacts and adaptations', in R.T. Watson, M.C. Zinyowera, R.H. Moss and D.J. Dokken (eds), *Climate Change 1995: Impacts, Adaptations and Mitigation of Climate Change: Scientific-Technical Analyses*, Cambridge, UK: Cambridge University Press, pp. 427–67.

Reilly J. and 17 authors (2000), Changing Climate and Changing Agriculture, Report of the Agricultural Sector Assessment Team, US National Assessment, http://www.nacc.usgcrp.gov/sectors/agriculture/draft-report/.

Williams, L., D. Shaw and R. Mendelsohn (1998), 'Evaluating GCM output with impact models', *Climatic Change,* 39, 111–33.

3. Agriculture: A Ricardian analysis

Robert Mendelsohn

INTRODUCTION

The impacts of warming on agriculture could well be the most important market effect of climate change. The possibility that changing climates could damage large agricultural zones has motivated considerable research on this topic (Reilly *et al.* 1996). Agricultural research has followed two major approaches: experimental simulation and cross-sectional studies. The simulation models begin with basic agronomic results showing crop yields changing under various climatic conditions. These results are then fed into an agro-economic model that predicts how farm production and prices will change. Chapter 2 presents an example of this approach applied regionally to US agriculture. Cross-sectional models follow an empirical approach to this same problem. They examine farm outcomes across space and measure the correlation between climate and farm value. Using these empirical relationships, the approach then predicts how farm welfare will change under alternative climate scenarios. This chapter explores the cross-sectional approach for a regional analysis of US agriculture.

The cross-sectional approach was first suggested by Mendelsohn *et al.* (1994), who examined counties across the United States. That study regressed value per acre on a number of climates and control variables, and discovered that the climate variables had a quadratic relationship with farm value and that climate could be captured by seasonal measures from four evenly spaced months. The study also discovered that it was important to control for other variables that could explain spatial farm values. Some of these effects could be dealt with by including a battery of control variables capturing soil and economic effects. However, weighting was also required to capture heteroskedasticity and to remove the undue influence of cities on farm values. Two types of weights were explored. One approach focused on land use and used the percentage of land in crops as a weight. The other approach focused on production and used the magnitude of crop gross revenue as the weight. These two weights for counties yield different results. The cropland model predicts that higher temperatures are harmful, whereas the crop revenue model predicts that moderate increases in temperature are beneficial.

The technique was further expanded in Mendelsohn *et al*. (1996). Instead of using farm value per acre as the dependent variable, this study relied on aggregate farm value per area of land in a county. This change in the dependent variable allowed this later study to explore the effect of climate not only on the value of existing farms but also on the probability that land would be farmed. The results indicated that more land was farmed in counties in more favorable climates. As climate became too warm, farms would be restricted to locations within a county with access to water or more favorable growing conditions.

Mendelsohn *et al*. (1999) explored including additional climate variables in the regressions, such as interannual temperature and precipitation and diurnal temperature variation. The results suggested that interannual variation and diurnal variation are generally harmful to crops. Further, the results suggested that interannual temperature effects were more important than interannual precipitation effects, which was surprising given the traditional emphasis in agriculture on droughts. The only seasons in which variation is beneficial are winter, when farmers can take the variation into account before planting, and fall, when diurnal variation apparently signals crops to begin ripening.

Including the climate variation terms in the regression model also changed some of the coefficients of the climate normal variables. To a certain extent this was expected since climate variation variables are correlated with climate normals. In general, with the variation terms included, the normal temperature coefficients changed, suggesting that warming was more beneficial to crops compared with the normal coefficients in the models where variation terms are omitted. Cross-sectional models that do not explicitly include climate variation variables implicitly capture some of the effect of climate variation in the climate normals.

The Ricardian technique has since been extended to developing countries. One study applied the cross-sectional approach to farms in India (Dinar *et al*. 1998), and another study extended the approach to farms in Brazil (Sanghi 1998). These studies reveal that agriculture in both of these regions is also sensitive to seasonal climates and has a quadratic functional form. These additional studies consequently support the application of this empirical methodology to agriculture.

In this study, we estimate the climate sensitivity of American agriculture by regressing both farm value per acre and aggregate farm value per area of county on climate and other control variables. We then calculate the impacts of a set of climate scenarios on each county in the United States using these regression results. We aggregate these counties into the seven regions of this study (see Table 1.1 in Chapter 1). The analysis provides a distinct pattern across the United States. Small warming tends to be beneficial in most of the United States. However, as warming becomes severe, more regions become damaged, starting with the warmer southern regions. The less precipitation, the more severe these effects become.

METHODOLOGY

This cross-sectional analysis of farming in US counties explores two dependent variables. In the first regression, farmland value per acre is regressed on climate and control variables. By examining just existing farmland, this model holds the aggregate amount of farmland constant. In the second regression, aggregate farm value in the county divided by land in the county is the dependent variable. The aggregate regression allows the amount of land that is farmed to vary. The aggregate regression thus examines how climate affects both the probability that land is farmed and its market value per acre.

The analysis relies on a quadratic equation of the following form:

$$V = \sum a_i N_i + \sum b_i N_i^2 + \sum d_j Z_j + e, \qquad (3.1)$$

where N_i are climate variables, Z_j are socioeconomic variables and e is an error term. Climate is measured using seasonal temperature and precipitation normals (30 year average measures in January, April, July and October). Weather is not included in the analysis.

To facilitate interpretation of the climatic coefficients, we subtracted the mean from all climate variables. The linear climate coefficient can consequently be interpreted as the marginal impact of that variable on farmland evaluated at the US mean climate. Without demeaning the climate variables, the linear term would have reflected the marginal impact of the climate variable when it was equal to zero. The coefficient on the squared term reflects the shape of the relationship, with a positive term implying a U shape and a negative term implying a hill shape.

The control variables remove a host of influences that affect farm values, including key soil and economic impacts. Careful accounting of control variables is especially important in cross-sectional analysis because the approach relies on a natural experiment with many uncontrolled variables. These uncontrolled variables can be confused with climate effects if they are spatially correlated, leading to biased climate coefficients. By including these variables explicitly in the regression, the analyst can control for these unwanted influences.

The observations in the two sets of regressions are weighted using percent-age of cropland and crop revenue as weights. These weights also help control the regression by focusing attention on areas with agriculture, not areas with high farm values, such as urban locations. Regions such as the Midwest get weight from both measures because it has a lot of cropland and it produces much crop revenue. However, regions with vast acreage but low production such as the Northern and Southern Plains get more weight with the cropland measure and productive southern regions get more weight with the crop revenue model. The productive southern regions have crops that do well in warm weather, whereas the northern regions, and especially the Northern Plains, favor cool weather crops. The two weights consequently give two different measures of climate sensitivity.

A number of criticisms have been leveled at the Ricardian approach. Some of these critiques raise issues about the method in general and some are specific to the actual applications that have been applied to date. Perhaps the most general concern is that cross-sectional evidence may not apply to future changes over time. The approach assumes that the way that farmers respond to alternative climates over space is the same way that farmers will respond in the long run to those same climates over time. However, if a study has mistakenly associated effects with climate that are actually due to some other factor that varies across the geography, this assumption may not hold. One of the key issues in these cross-sectional analyses is whether the authors have done a good job controlling for unwanted variation. Specifically, the question is whether important variables that are likely to be correlated with climate have been omitted.

One variable that has not been properly measured in existing applications of the Ricardian technique is the aggregate supply of water (Darwin 1999, Hanemann 2000). Water supplies were omitted because of limited available data. Although there are careful studies of irrigation in selected watersheds such as the Colorado River basin, information about the entire country is quite limited (see Hurd *et al.* 1999). By omitting aggregate water supply as a factor, the Ricardian estimates assume that the only limiting factor to agriculture is the climate in the county being examined. In fact, many irrigated counties obtain water from upriver counties. How much water a particular county can have also depends on water allocations. The Ricardian applications have overlooked the importance of climate and water from other counties. To test the importance of including irrigation in the Ricardian framework, Mendelsohn and Nordhaus (1999b) include the percentage of land that is irrigated in the Ricardian model. Some of the results for the crop revenue model are sensitive to including irrigation but, interestingly, the cropland models were not affected.

The issue of water cannot be handled properly without using a sophisti-cated hydrological-economic model. The model would connect other counties

through the water supply to the county growing the food. Climate change
scenarios could then predict changes in runoff. The hydrological-economic
model would then predict how water allocations would change since proportional reductions are often not the most efficient response to runoff reductions.
Adding sophisticated hydrological-economic models to agricultural models
of climate change is a clear priority for new research.

Another criticism that has been leveled against the Ricardian approach is
that it assumes prices are held constant (Cline 1996). Clearly, if one were
examining a purely local phenomenon, this would be a reasonable assumption. However, global warming is pervasive enough that it may well change
the global supply of crops and thus change prices. By holding prices constant, the Ricardian model underestimates damages and overestimates benefits.
Because the likely changes in supply are relatively small (for example, less
than 25 per cent), the absolute size of this bias is likely to be small (Mendelsohn
and Nordhaus 1996). Nonetheless, holding prices constant remains a flaw of
the technique. Unfortunately, the only way to properly take prices into account is to build a global agricultural model. This is quite difficult. Constructing
and verifying a global agricultural model cannot be done with accuracy at
present, so it remains very uncertain what the global supply effect from
warming will be and what the resulting price changes should look like.

Another general criticism is that the technique provides only an overview
of the net impact on farmers. Detailed information concerning how farmers
are adjusting to climate is missing. There is no information concerning planting dates, tilling practices, which crops are grown, and which varieties are
being used. Examining farm values does in fact shortcut through this im-
mense wealth of adjustments, and the Ricardian technique is vulnerable to
this criticism. In principle, however, the cross-sectional approach could be
generalized and these important details examined. That is, analysts can examine how climate affects planting and harvest dates, which crops are grown,
which tilling practices are most profitable, and other detailed aspects of farm
choices. This is an important area of climate research that needs to be
explored.

Finally, the Ricardian technique has been criticized for assuming that
farmers can foresee all changes. The Ricardian studies have emphasized that
the cross-sectional approach has been useful as a way of including adaptation
in the analysis. Critics feel that perhaps the Ricardian approach has included
too much adaptation and has made farmers too all seeing (Fankhauser *et al.*
1999; Quiggin and Horowitz 1999; Hanemann 2000; Schneider *et al.* 2000).
These critics complain that farmers would be slow to adjust to changing
climate and that their adjustments would be very expensive. After all, farmers
would have to understand that climate is changing, abandon growing their
current crops, and shift to entirely different crops. The Ricardian model may

be too optimistic in assuming that these changes will occur at all and that they will be relatively inexpensive.

We argue that these criticisms about adjustment costs apply to some other sectors, but probably not agriculture. Agriculture is likely to adapt to climate change relatively easily (Mendelsohn and Nordhaus 1999a). First, American farmers have demonstrated that they are adept at changing when new opportunities arise either from changes in agricultural policies or from new technologies. For example, farmers across the country have quickly adopted the new genetically altered crops. Second, if farmers simply adapt to the climate change they have already observed, their adjustments will probably be fast enough. Schneider *et al.* (2000) compare farmer adjustments with a 20-year lag to perfectly forward-looking farmers. For a large change in climate, the two measures get almost identical results. Third, climate change will be spread over an entire century. Although the climate changes will not necessarily follow a linear progression, farmers will have time to get used to the difference between today's condition and future equilibriums. Most of the capital that farmers own is short-lived, with an average life expectancy of about 5 years. From now through 2060, farmers will replace that equipment approximately 12 times. The Ricardian model assumes that over this time period, farmers will take advantage of this natural replacement to change crops. Although this may involve some premature retirement of equipment, the costs of adjustment are likely to be quite small given these multiple opportunities to adjust without cost.

EMPIRICAL RESULTS

The multiple regressions are displayed in Table 3.1. The dependent variable in the first and second regressions is the aggregate value of farmland in a county divided by the total area of the county. The dependent variable in the third and fourth regressions is the value per acre of existing farms. The third and fourth regressions hold the land in farms constant. The first and third regressions use cropland as a weight, and the second and fourth regressions use crop revenue as a weight.

One can draw a number of hypotheses about the regional consequences of warming from Table 3.1. First, because the overall climate sensitivity is quadratic, it is likely that regions that are currently warm will suffer damages and that regions that are currently cool will enjoy benefits. It is also likely that as warming increases, it will become more harmful. Because of the beneficial effects of precipitation, it is likely that regions with more precipitation will benefit. Finally, it is expected that regions with more cropland will have larger effects. That is, the magnitude of aggregate effects will increase

Table 3.1   Multiple regression on farm values

Independent variables	Aggregate		Per acre	
	Percentage cropland	Crop revenue	Percentage cropland	Crop revenue
January temp.	−213.0	−242.0	−159.7	−287.2
	(16.32)	(20.44)	(9.95)	(13.21)
Jan temp sq.	−2.20	−2.56	−1.34	−2.68
	(12.91)	(17.66)	(6.41)	(10.04)
April temp.	54.6	108.0	−32.1	24.4
	(3.23)	(8.29)	(1.55)	(1.02)
Apr temp sq.	−1.93	−3.49	−4.90	−6.69
	(3.60)	(9.21)	(7.43)	(9.61)
July temp.	−307.0	−278.0	−279.0	−157.8
	(19.58)	(22.43)	(14.51)	(6.92)
July temp sq.	−4.82	−3.92	−2.96	−0.30
	(9.38)	(13.03)	(4.69)	(0.54)
October temp.	364.0	392.0	345.4	390.1
	(14.32)	(16.73)	(11.09)	(9.06)
October temp sq.	5.82	9.08	6.63	12.35
	(7.64)	(17.17)	(7.10)	(12.73)
January rain	50.2	87.9	85.1	279.7
	(2.81)	(5.63)	(3.88)	(9.77)
Jan rain sq.	1.6	−1.5	2.7	−10.8
	(0.70)	(0.91)	(0.95)	(3.71)
April rain	89.3	53.1	103.8	82.8
	(4.64)	(2.81)	(4.40)	(2.38)
Apr rain sq.	−9.3	1.7	−16.2	−62.1
	(1.36)	(0.28)	(1.92)	(5.63)
July rain	−23.8	16.1	−34.6	−115.6
	(2.22)	(1.57)	(2.63)	(6.17)
July rain sq.	27.6	8.7	51.9	57.0
	(6.14)	(2.34)	(9.41)	(8.35)
October rain	−171.0	−87.3	−50.0	−124.1
	(9.37)	(5.00)	(2.23)	(3.90)
October rain sq.	−26.1	8.3	2.1	170.9
	(2.35)	(1.28)	(0.16)	(14.43)

Table 3.1   continued

Control variables	Aggregate		Per acre	
	Percentage cropland	Crop revenue	Percentage cropland	Crop revenue
Constant	724.0	820.0	1329.0	1451.0
	(40.21)	(49.00)	(60.18)	(47.22)
Income *per capita*	51.3	24.4	71.1	–48.5
	(13.51)	(5.99)	(15.25)	(6.48)
Density	67.0	30.0	130.0	153.0
	(1.17)	(0.66)	(18.51)	(18.47)
Density sq.	–0.81	–0.53	–1.72	–2.04
	(3.09)	(3.65)	(5.31)	(7.61)
Solar radiation	–83.0	–26.1	–90.6	–105.6
	(6.88)	(2.52)	(6.12)	(5.52)
Altitude	–134.0	–65.3	–167.0	–163.0
	(5.98)	(3.53)	(6.10)	(4.80)
Salinity	–654.0	–176.0	–683.0	–582.0
	(3.91)	(1.46)	(3.33)	(2.63)
Flood prone	–137.0	–191.0	–164.0	–663.0
	(3.89)	(4.62)	(3.41)	(8.75)
Wetland	–334.0	–546.0	–58.0	762.0
	(3.34)	(5.90)	(0.48)	(4.48)
Soil erosion	–1060.0	–1730.0	–1260.0	–2690.0
	(6.42)	(9.86)	(6.21)	(8.37)
Slope length	25.7	66.7	17.3	54.0
	(5.27)	(14.41)	(2.90)	(6.35)
Sand	–55.0	–175.0	–138.0	–288.0
	(1.32)	(4.72)	(2.72)	(4.24)
Clay	109.0	78.3	86.4	–7.9
	(6.36)	(4.13)	(4.09)	(0.23)
Water capacity	0.59	0.38	0.38	0.21
	(18.55)	(13.25)	(9.69)	(3.89)
Permeability	–1.6e-3	–5.5e-3	–2.5e-3	–12.8e-3
	(0.85)	(4.47)	(1.07)	(5.68)
Adj r sq.	0.772	0.802	0.779	0.837
Observations	2938	2938	2938	2938

Note: Dependent variable is farm value per area in the aggregate regression and value per acre in the per acre regressions. Observations are weighted as stated and values in parenthesis are t-statistics.

Table 3.2   Regional agricultural characteristics

Region	Cropland (million acres)	Crop revenue (millions 1998 USD)	Farm value (billions 1998 USD)	Farm value (1998 USD/acre)	Percentage irrigated
Northeast	22.2	3.9	56.6	1,446.0	0.8
Midwest	119.9	21.0	261.2	1,758.0	0.8
Northern Plains	115.5	9.0	133.0	513.0	4.9
Northwest	21.3	3.8	43.0	1,089.0	11.3
Southeast	59.0	12.3	130.0	1,263.0	3.2
Southern Plains	60.2	6.0	124.0	747.0	4.9
Southwest	25.6	11.8	116.0	800.0	9.9
US	423.7	67.7	864.0	1,245.0	5.0

with cropland acreage. The magnitude of the climate coefficients for the aggregate regressions is larger than the coefficients for the per acre regressions. This increased climate sensitivity implies that the aggregate model will yield more dramatic results.

To anticipate how climate change might affect each region, it is helpful to know the characteristics of each region. Table 3.2 displays the current agricultural attributes of each region. The Midwest and Northern Plains enjoy the largest amount of cropland, each having about one-fourth of American cropland. The Southeast and Southern Plains contribute another eighth each. The remaining regions have only a 5 per cent share each. The Midwest also has the largest share (31 per cent) of the national crop revenue. The Southeast and Southwest are the next two largest regions, with about 17 per cent of crop revenue each. Note that cropland does not produce the same revenue in every region (see Table 3.2).

Another way to measure the magnitude of agriculture is to sum the value of farmland. The Midwest comes first in this dimension, enjoying 30 per cent of the aggregate value of American farmland. The Northern Plains, Southeast, Southern Plains and Southwest come in a distant second, with about 14 per cent each of total value (Table 3.2). The Midwest is the most valuable region because it has the most cropland and because the value per acre is the highest. The Northeast and Northwest have valuable cropland on a per acre basis but very small amounts of land available. The Southeast is also valuable per acre and this makes up for its small share of land. Agriculture in the remaining regions has a low per acre average value but much land.

One of the reasons that the value per acre varies across regions is climate. The winter and summer climates in each region are shown in Table 1.3 in Chapter 1. Regions that are dry (the Southwest, Northern Plains and Southern

Plains) tend to have lower values per acre; cold winters appear to contribute to value. The other reason that values vary is because of control variables. For example, regions with more population (Northeast and Midwest) have higher values. Regions with good soils such as the Midwest also have higher values.

CLIMATE SIMULATIONS

The impacts of climate change on national agricultural values are shown in Table 3.3. Each of the regressions in Table 3.1 is used to calculate an impact. There are consequently four impact calculations for each climate scenario. In general, the crop revenue scenarios are more optimistic than the cropland scenarios, especially with warmer scenarios. In all scenarios, benefits are maximized with a 1.5°C warming. The crop revenue per acre model predicts an increase in value per acre of about 23 per cent, whereas the aggregate farm value model predicts about an 83 per cent increase. The aggregate model prediction is much larger because the model predicts a substantial increase in crop acreage in northern regions from warming. In the crop revenue scenarios, benefits continue to be positive as temperatures warm further, but the magnitude of the benefits falls. That is, the cumulative benefits relative to

Table 3.3   National results from Ricardian agriculture analysis[a] (billions 1998 USD/yr)

		Temperature		
	Precipitation (%)	1.5°C	2.5°C	5.0°C
Aggregate cropland	0	11.8	2.5	−7.1
	7	11.6	2.4	−7.2
	15	11.4	2.4	−7.2
Aggregate crop revenue	0	15.5	13.4	9.9
	7	16.5	14.5	10.9
	15	17.8	15.3	12.1
Per acre cropland	0	2.2	−1.6	−7.8
	7	2.6	−1.2	−7.4
	15	3.3	−0.6	−6.8
Per acre crop revenue	0	4.6	4.2	4.1
	7	4.9	4.3	4.3
	15	5.4	4.7	4.6

Note: a. Annualized with a real interest rate of 4%.

current conditions are positive even though further warming beyond 1.5°C is marginally harmful. With the cropland model, the benefits of a 1.5°C warming are more modest, 13 per cent in the per acre model and 58 per cent in the aggregate model. According to the cropland model, however, effects rapidly become damages as temperatures warm beyond 1.5°C. With a 2.5°C warming, the value per acre has fallen below current levels. However, aggregate acreage still increases, so the overall effect remains beneficial. Warming must reach 5°C before the cumulative effect becomes harmful.

Whether cropland can expand as much as the models above suggest is an important question. Only about 25 per cent of the land in farming counties is currently used for cropland. Although the most optimistic picture increases cropland by almost one-third, the total amount of land in crops would still be only 32 per cent of the land in farming counties. There appears to be enough land to support this expansion. A more likely constraint is water. In semi-arid places that currently depend on irrigation, the aggregate supply of water is likely to be a constraint on the expansion of cropland. For example, in the Southwest and eastern Northwest, where over 10 per cent of cropland is irrigated, water constraints will most likely limit aggregate cropland expansion. However, much of the projected expansion in cropland in the Midwest and Northern Plains is rainfed and may well be possible.

The impacts across regions from climate change are displayed in Table 3.4. In most regions, warming effects were more harmful when precipitation increases were low. The crop revenue model predicted more beneficial impacts than the cropland model. Warming effects become more harmful the more severe the temperature increase.

Some of the calculations in Table 3.4 exhibit clear regional differences. For example, with the per acre crop revenue model, warming is beneficial except in the Northwest and the Southwest. These two regions happen to have the narrowest disparity between summer and winter temperatures. The impacts are largest in the Midwest and Northern Plains, which happen to have the widest disparity between winter and summer temperatures. In the Midwest and Northern Plains, both small and large temperature increases lead to large benefits, of about $2 billion per year per region. Warming benefits are also significant in the Southeast ($0.7 billion per year). In the Northeast, the benefits are small because there is little cropland. The Southern Plains also exhibit small benefits from warming, probably because the region is already quite warm. The benefits in the Southeast, Northeast and Southern Plains all decline as temperature increases. Warming causes damages in the Northwest and Southwest that are worse as temperature increases. The results for the Northwest may seem counterintuitive. On the one hand, the region is clearly in the north, and yet it behaves like a southern region. The answer lies in the peculiar climate of the Northwest. Because of warm Pacific air, the region

Table 3.4 *Regional results from Ricardian agriculture analysis[a] (millions 1998 USD/yr)*

		Temperature		
	Precipitation (%)	1.5°C	2.5°C	5.0°C
Region: Northeast				
Aggregate cropland	0	775	63	−736
	7	631	−53	−794
	15	476	−172	−850
Aggregate crop revenue	0	1,175	1,077	894
	7	1,318	1,208	1,010
	15	1,503	1,384	1,166
Per acre cropland	0	32	−152	−479
	7	65	−119	−450
	15	111	−74	−406
Per acre crop revenue	0	72	32	−1
	7	17	13	1
	15	30	26	22
Region: Midwest				
Aggregate cropland	0	3,634	2,302	−152
	7	3,583	2,248	−207
	15	3,548	2,210	−245
Aggregate crop revenue	0	4,799	4,855	4,852
	7	4,944	5,001	4,994
	15	5,137	5,193	5,184
Per acre cropland	0	823	−107	−1,801
	7	958	28	−1,666
	15	1,155	225	−1,468
Per acre crop revenue	0	1,980	1,954	2,063
	7	1,988	1,961	2,069
	15	2,069	5,043	2,150
Region: Northern Plains				
Aggregate cropland	0	3,411	1,724	−116
	7	3,322	1,656	−151
	15	3,234	1,590	−184
Aggregate crop revenue	0	4,180	3,980	3,585
	7	4,194	3,993	3,599
	15	4,221	4,021	3,627

Table 3.4   continued

		Temperature		
	Precipitation (%)	1.5°C	2.5°C	5.0°C
Region: Northern Plains				
Per acre cropland	0	1,161	248	–1,188
	7	1,145	231	–1,201
	15	1,148	235	–1,201
Per acre crop revenue	0	2,105	2,051	2,110
	7	1,929	1,877	1,936
	15	1,769	1,716	1,776
Region: Northwest				
Aggregate cropland	0	144	338	–749
	7	102	–388	–806
	15	48	–453	–869
Aggregate crop revenue	0	157	–4	–262
	7	251	89	–182
	15	365	199	–79
Per acre cropland	0	–52	–254	–591
	7	–25	–227	–568
	15	9	–194	–537
Per acre crop revenue	0	–123	–196	–284
	7	–98	–171	–260
	15	–64	–137	–227
Region: Southeast				
Aggregate cropland	0	1,252	–813	–2,521
	7	1,556	–525	–2,452
	15	1,968	–123	–2,290
Aggregate crop revenue	0	2,137	1,496	371
	7	2,630	1,985	838
	15	3,242	2,594	1,428
Per acre cropland	0	73	–570	–1,687
	7	295	–378	–1,472
	15	585	–58	–1,187
Per acre crop revenue	0	427	327	232
	7	681	579	486
	15	1,029	928	834

Table 3.4   continued

		Temperature		
	Precipitation (%)	1.5°C	2.5°C	5.0°C
Region: Southern Plains				
Aggregate cropland	0	1,082	−831	−2,004
	7	814	−996	−2,021
	15	502	−1,161	−2,041
Aggregate crop revenue	0	1,562	929	−169
	7	1,641	1,009	−94
	15	1,750	1,118	12
Per acre cropland	0	146	−543	−1,532
	7	145	−543	−1,520
	15	153	−533	−1,502
Per acre crop revenue	0	184	119	85
	7	195	129	96
	15	238	175	139
Region: Southwest				
Aggregate cropland	0	1,542	393	−812
	7	1,566	432	−772
	15	1,599	483	−725
Aggregate crop revenue	0	1,450	1,110	630
	7	1,529	1,188	709
	15	1,622	1,277	802
Per acre cropland	0	−17	−236	−546
	7	−5	−221	−530
	15	12	−202	−510
Per acre crop revenue	0	−33	−57	−60
	7	−31	−54	−57
	15	−26	−48	−52

Note: a. Annualized with a real interest rate of 4%.

enjoys a moderate climate that resembles the southern regions. However, the region is not quite like the Southwest, because it also enjoys far more precipitation.

With the per acre cropland model, benefits are seen in the same regions as the crop revenue model predicts with a 1.5°C increase. These benefits, however, are smaller than with the crop revenue model, for example, amounting to less than $1 billion in the Midwest and Northern Plains. Further, the benefits fall precipitously as temperatures rise above 1.5°C. For example, the Midwest and Northern Plains begin with almost a $1.2 billion benefit with 1.5°C warming, but this impact turns into only a $118 million gain at 2.5°C warming and over a $1.2 billion loss at 5°C warming. The Southeast and Southern Plains also respond harshly to larger temperature increases, with about a $236 million gain at 1.5°C warming, a $472 million loss at 2.5°C and a $1.42 billion loss at 5°C. The effects in the remaining regions are smaller but they follow similar patterns.

The predictions of the aggregate model in Table 3.4 follow the same patterns as the per acre crop model but the effects are stronger. More warming results in fewer benefits and eventually damages. However, the aggregate model captures the powerful effect that climate has on the acreage of crops planted. The expansion of cropland is especially evident in the Northern Plains and Midwest. With a 1.5°C warming, the aggregate model predicts benefits in these regions of between $3.5 and $4.7 billion each. This benefit declines rapidly at higher temperatures according to the cropland model but remains high according to the crop revenue model. Large positive effects of over $1 billion are seen in the Southeast, Northeast, Southern Plains and Southwest at 1.5°C as well. With the crop revenue model, these impacts fall as temperatures warm but they remain beneficial. With the cropland model, these large benefits turn into damages at 5°C. With the Southeast and Southern Plains, for example, these damages rise to between $2 and $2.5 billion. The southern regions thus get hurt more by these severe scenarios than the northern regions.

In Table 3.5, we examine the effect of temperature increases on the value of an average acre in each region. This frees the regional comparisons from the size of the agricultural sector in each region. To focus on temperature, we examine just cases where precipitation increases by 7 per cent. We further examine only the two regressions in Table 3.1 that hold crop acreage constant. The results make clearer some of the findings in Table 3.4. The crop revenue model continues to be more optimistic about warming than the cropland model. More severe temperature increases generally increase damages. Warmer southern regions generally suffer more damages than cooler northern regions and cooler regions benefit more than warmer regions. The biggest gains occur in the Midwest and Northern Plains. The crop revenue model predicts $17/acre gains in both regions, whereas the cropland model predicts smaller benefits of $8–$10/acre, which become damages as temperature increases above 2.5°C. The Southeast, Southern Plains and Northeast enjoy smaller gains on a per acre basis, but these shrink rapidly as temperatures rise. The Northwest is surprisingly the most vulnerable to warming on a per acre basis. The Northwest has both a cool summer and a mild winter, and

Table 3.5   Regional changes in value per acre with three temperature scenarios[a] (1998 USD/acre/yr)

Region	Temperature		
	1.5°C	2.5°C	5.0°C
Weight: Cropland			
Northeast	2.94	−5.37	−20.28
Midwest	7.99	0.24	−13.89
Northern Plains	9.91	2.01	−10.40
Northwest	−1.16	−10.66	−26.71
Southeast	5.00	−5.89	−24.96
Southern Plains	2.42	−9.02	−25.25
Southwest	−0.17	−8.63	−20.67
US	6.09	−2.82	−17.49
Weight: Crop revenue			
Northeast	7.45	2.72	4.13
Midwest	16.58	16.36	17.26
Northern Plains	16.71	16.25	16.77
Northwest	−4.59	−8.04	−12.23
Southeast	11.54	9.82	8.25
Southern Plains	3.22	2.14	1.58
Southwest	−1.19	−2.10	−2.23
US	11.40	10.50	10.30

Note: a. Estimates include a 7% increase in precipitation.

warming may make both seasons less productive. The Southwest also suffers consistent damages from warming. With the cropland model, all the southern regions suffer large damages on a per acre basis when warming becomes severe.

To understand why the aggregate model predicts much larger effects in the northern regions, we regress the fraction of land in cropland on climate and other control variables. This regression has the same pattern of coefficients as found in Table 3.1. Warmer temperatures increase crop acreage up to a point and then cause acreage to shrink. These regressions are used to explore the impact of alternative climate scenarios on crop acreage. The results are shown in Table 3.6. Warming of 1.5°C would dramatically expand crop acreage in the United States by between 80 and 100 million acres, or about 19 to 24 per cent. Half of this expansion would occur in the Midwest and Northern Plains,

Table 3.6   Regional changes in cropland under three temperature scenarios[a] (millions of acres)

Region	Temperature		
	1.5°C	2.5°C	5.0°C
Weight: Cropland			
Northeast	4.6	0.9	−5.8
Midwest	23.8	18.6	7.1
Northern Plains	26.3	17.6	0.2
Northwest	1.9	−1.3	−6.5
Southeast	5.8	−6.3	−25.8
Southern Plains	7.5	−5.0	−25.2
Southwest	12.8	4.6	−6.6
US	82.7	29.1	−62.6
Weight: Crop revenue			
Northeast	9.2	11.9	15.1
Midwest	22.6	27.3	33.2
Northern Plains	28.4	33.8	40.2
Northwest	4.8	6.2	7.7
Southeast	5.4	5.5	3.5
Southern Plains	13.5	12.5	9.1
Southwest	18.9	23.1	27.1
US	102.8	120.3	135.9

Note: a. Estimates include a 7% increase in precipitation.

in both cases increasing acreage by about one-fourth. Although this is a dramatic increase, there is substantial land that is not in cropland in these regions. If farming gets more productive, currently marginal lands may become profitable for growing crops. Another dramatic expansion would occur in the Southern Plains and Southwest. The acreage in the Southern Plains would increase by almost three times and the acreage in the Southwest would increase by 75 per cent. As discussed before, the expansion in the southern regions may be problematic because the model does not consider aggregate water supplies.

CONCLUSION

This study relies on cross-sectional evidence to predict the impact of warming on regional agriculture in the United States. A variety of regressions that use alternative weighting schemes and different definitions of farm value are explored. The conventional Ricardian study uses farm value per hectare as the dependent variable. The enhanced regression uses aggregate farm value per land in the county as the dependent variable. Both regressions capture the effect of climate on existing farms. The second regression also captures how climate will change crop acreage.

All the regressions demonstrate that climate has an important effect on farm values. Climate affects both the value per acre of cropland and how much land is devoted to cropland. The study finds that temperature and precipitation have a quadratic relationship with farm value. The study specifically finds that farm value has a hill-shaped relationship with temperature. For areas that are cool, warming will increase farm values. However, once farms exceed the temperature that yields the highest value, further warming is harmful.

The study reveals that the magnitude of the results depends on the dependent variable used in the model and the weighting of observations. The crop revenue model is more optimistic than the cropland model about warming. The aggregate model exhibits more dramatic effects than the per acre model. However, all the models suggest that national farm values will maximize at 1.5°C warming. The crop revenue models then predict benefits will shrink but stay positive. The cropland model predicts benefits will shrink more rapidly and become damages when warming reaches 5°C.

These results are consistent with the agro-economic results reported in Chapter 2. The simulation model also finds that mild warming is beneficial but severe scenarios would harm US crops. The primary difference in the national results between the two approaches in this book is that the simulation model reflects a steeper hill-shaped relationship with temperature. That is, the simulation model predicts a larger rise with little warming and a larger fall with more warming. The cross-sectional approach suggests this same hill, but it is flatter.

These national results do not appear to agree with Smith and Tirpak (1989), who suggested agriculture would suffer either a $10 billion gain or a $10 billion loss. Nor do they agree with most of the analyses, based on Smith and Tirpak, that predicted losses in US farming (Cline 1992, Fankhauser 1995, Tol 1995 or Pearce *et al.* 1996). There are, however, several explanations why these numbers do not agree. First, the Smith and Tirpak results are based on a 1990 economy. They would be substantially larger if they had been extrapolated to 2060. Second, the $10 billion damage estimate cited in Smith and

Tirpak occurs when no carbon fertilization is assumed. However, hundreds of experimental studies have confirmed that carbon fertilization will occur on crops (Reilly *et al.* 1996). Finally, the current studies allow crop migration to more productive zones and they include warm weather crops.

The cross-sectional models also predict dramatic regional effects. We find that the Midwest and the Northern Plains will have the largest benefits from warming. This is partly because both regions are currently cool and so will gain much per acre from warming. Both regions also have a large acreage of cropland so that any increase in productivity will lead to large economic consequences. Finally, the aggregate model also predicts that both regions will gain large amounts of new cropland from warming. According to the crop revenue model, the Midwest and Northern Plains could gain the most from warming. The Southeast, Southern Plains and Northeast would all benefit as well with modest warming but the amounts would be much smaller and they would decline as temperatures rose. The models generally also predict small damages in the Northwest and Southwest.

Even though the agro-economic simulation results lead to larger national numbers, the cross-sectional results indicate greater differences across regions. The cross-sectional model envisions more dramatic increases in farmland in regions that are becoming more productive, specifically the Midwest and Northern Plains. Although the simulation model also predicts an increase in farmland in the Midwest and Northern Plains, it anticipates a much smaller response.

These results assume that farmers will adapt to climate change if it increases their profits. The analysis projects that the adaptation farmers have made to current climate would also be applied to future climates. The added profits from changing crops, planting dates, varieties, irrigation, and tilling practices are all assumed to occur in the future. The empirical estimates capture and reflect these adaptations. The results do not capture long-run investments in new research and development. It is likely that potential new varieties, new cropping techniques, and new crops will be invented by agricultural research in the future. However, these technological solutions are not reflected in these estimates. Future farmers are simply assumed to be as knowledgeable as existing farmers. The costs of engaging in different types of farming are assumed to be the same as today. Given that farmers are being given a century to adapt, we expect a gradual change will occur in agriculture as climate slowly changes. As with the migration of farms westward over the nineteenth and twentieth centuries, we expect the migration polewards to occur so slowly that most farmers and experts will not even realize the adaptation has occurred.

The cross-sectional results do not capture the fertilization effect of future increases in carbon dioxide. The cross-sectional evidence is all being measured at the single current level of carbon dioxide. There is no way to discern the influence of carbon dioxide on crop productivity with the cross-sectional data. Our only hope to include carbon dioxide effects comes from assessments of laboratory experiments. These experiments have shown that carbon dioxide consistently increases crop productivity. The magnitude of these effects varies across crops. However, virtually every crop tested has shown these carbon fertilization results. According to Reilly *et al.* (1996), carbon fertilization increases crop productivity by an average of 30 per cent. Given our assumption that prices will not change, a 30 per cent increase in productivity should result in a 30 per cent increase in net revenue. Multiplying the cropland value in each region by 4 per cent provides an estimate of annual net revenue. Multiplying this by 30 per cent yields the fertilization estimates in Table 3.7. For the United States as a whole, the fertilization benefit is an additional \$10.4 billion per year. These fertilization estimates should be added to the cross-sectional results in Tables 3.3 and 3.4.

Combining the results from this study and the carbon fertilization effects, it is highly likely that American agriculture will not suffer large damages from climate warming over the twenty-first century. In fact, with mild climate scenarios, warming will most likely lead to large benefits in the agricultural sector. These benefits will not be evenly spread across the United States but rather will be concentrated in the Midwest and Northern Plains. Further, some regions, especially the Northwest and the Southwest, are likely to suffer damages from warming. As temperatures increase to 5°C, however, most regions will not benefit from warming and many may suffer damages. The final impact in agriculture depends on which climate scenario occurs. However, it would appear that American agriculture is not likely to suffer large losses from the climate scenarios now projected for the twenty-first century.

Table 3.7   Effect of carbon fertilization on annual net revenue (billions 1998 USD/yr)

Region	Revenue change
Northeast	0.68
Midwest	3.14
Northern Plains	1.58
Northwest	0.52
Southeast	1.56
Southern Plains	1.49
Southwest	1.39
United States	10.36

This study focused on a limited set of climate scenarios that climate scientists think are likely for the twenty-first century. One of the great uncertainties about these projections concerns whether climate variation might also change. The climate scientists have been reluctant to predict changes in climate variation because some climate models see increases while other models see declines in climate variation. However, it is important to note that both agronomic and cross-sectional empirical research have identified the importance of climate variation to agriculture. Droughts from loss of precipitation have been a concern to farmers for centuries. Increases in interannual variation in temperature or precipitation will increase expected damages in agriculture. Cross-sectional research indicates that American farm values are particularly sensitive to temperature fluctuations. If interannual temperature fluctuations increased by 25 per cent, farm values would fall by one-third (Mendelsohn *et al.* 1999). If diurnal temperature variation decreased by 25 per cent, farm values would increase between 25 and 45 per cent. Interannual precipitation appears to be less important. A 25 per cent increase in interannual precipitation would result in only a 6 per cent decline in farm values. Potential changes in climate variation are important and certainly contribute to the range of possible effects in agriculture over the next century. However, analysts must realize that except for diurnal variation, it is not yet clear how greenhouse gases will affect climate variation.

REFERENCES

Cline, W. (1992), *The Economics of Global Warming*, Washington DC: Institute for International Economics.

Cline, W. (1996), 'The impact of global warming on agriculture: Comment', *American Economic Review*, 86, 1309–12.

Darwin, R. (1999), 'Comment on "The impact of global warming on agriculture: A Ricardian analysis"', *American Economic Review*, 89, 1049–52.

Dinar, A., R. Mendelsohn, R. Evenson, J. Parikh, A. Sanghi, K. Kumar, J. McKinsey and S. Lonergan (eds) (1998), 'Measuring the Impact of Climate Change on Indian Agriculture', World Bank Technical Paper No. 402, Washington, DC.

Fankhauser, S. (1995), *Valuing Climate Change – The Economics of the Greenhouse*, London: Earthscan.

Fankhauser, S., J.B. Smith and R.S.J. Tol (1999), 'Weathering climate change: Some simple rules to guide adaptation decisions', *Ecological Economics*, 30(1), 66–78.

Hanemann, W.M. (2000), 'Adaptation and its measurement', *Climatic Change*, 45, 571–81.

Hurd, B.H., J.M. Callaway, J.B. Smith and P. Kirshen (1999), 'Economic effects of climate change on U.S. water resources', in R. Mendelsohn and J.E. Neumann (eds), *The Impact of Climate Change on the United States Economy*, Cambridge, UK: Cambridge University Press, pp. 133–77.

Mendelsohn, R. and W. Nordhaus (1996), 'The impact of global warming on agriculture: Reply', *American Economic Review*, 86, 1312–15.

Mendelsohn, R. and W. Nordhaus (1999a), 'Reply to Darwin', *American Economic Review*, 89, 1053–5.

Mendelsohn, R. and W. Nordhaus (1999b), 'Reply to Quiggin and Horowitz', *American Economic Review*, 89, 1046–8.

Mendelsohn, R., W. Nordhaus and D. Shaw (1994), 'The impact of global warming on agriculture: A Ricardian analysis', *American Economic Review*, 84, 753–71.

Mendelsohn, R., W. Nordhaus and D. Shaw (1996), 'Climate impacts on aggregate farm values: Accounting for adaptation', *Agriculture and Forest Meteorology*, 80, 55–67.

Mendelsohn, R., W. Nordhaus and D. Shaw (1999), 'The impact of climate variation on agriculture', in R. Mendelsohn and J.E. Neumann (eds), *The Impact of Climate Change on the United States Economy*, Cambridge, UK: Cambridge University Press, pp. 55–74.

Pearce, D., W. Cline, A. Achanta, S. Fankhauser, R. Pachuari, R. Tol and P. Vellinga (1996), 'The social costs of climate change: Greenhouse damage and the benefits of control', in J. Bruce, H. Lee, and E. Haites (eds), *Climate Change 1995: Economic and Social Dimensions of Climate Change*, Cambridge, UK: Cambridge University Press, pp. 183–244.

Quiggin, J. and J.K. Horowitz (1999), 'Comment on "The impact of global warming on agriculture: A Ricardian analysis"', *American Economic Review*, 89, 1044–5.

Reilly, J. and 22 authors (1996), 'Agriculture in a changing climate: Impacts and adaptations', in R. Watson, M. Zinyowera, R. Moss and D. Dokken (eds), *Climate Change 1995: Impacts, Adaptations, and Mitigation of Climate Change: Scientific-Technical Analyses*, Cambridge, UK: Cambridge University Press, pp. 427–67.

Sanghi, A. (1998), Global Warming and Climate Sensitivity: Brazilian and Indian Agriculture, PhD Dissertation, Department of Economics, University of Chicago, Chicago, IL.

Schneider, S., W. Easterling and L. Mearns (2000), 'Adaptation: Sensitivity to natural variability, agent assumptions, and dynamic climate changes', *Climatic Change* 45, 203–21.

Smith, J. and D. Tirpak (1989), The Potential Effects of Climate Change on the United States: Report to Congress, EPA-230-05-89-050, Washington, DC: US Environmental Protection Agency.

Tol, R.S.J. (1995), 'The damage costs of climate change toward more comprehensive calculations', *Environmental and Resource Economics*, 5, 353–74.

4. Timber: Ecological–economic analysis

Brent Sohngen and Robert Mendelsohn

INTRODUCTION

This study estimates the regional effects of climate change on US timber markets. Two analyses are developed. The first analysis disaggregates the results of Sohngen and Mendelsohn (1999) into estimates of regional effects.[1] The second analysis presents the sensitivity of regional effects to region-specific climate change. In this second analysis, the baseline scenario is the central scenario of a 2.5°C warming and a 7 per cent increase in precipitation. Each region is then individually exposed to a harsher and a milder climate scenario. This second analysis examines regional climate variation, whereas the first experiment examines the impact of climate predictions from a single GCM. Both analyses rely on the methods developed in Sohngen and Mendelsohn (1998, 1999).

REGIONAL EFFECTS FROM NATIONAL CLIMATE SCENARIOS

Methods

The model in Sohngen and Mendelsohn (1999) is used here to estimate regional changes in consumer and producer surplus arising from climate change for six regions in the United States.[2] The original model contained only four timber types within the United States, based on the existing distribution of timber species used heavily for industrial purposes: southern pines, northern mixed pines, western conifers and pacific northwestern conifers. These timber types are found in specific regions under current climate conditions but were predicted to move with climate change by the ecosystem model (see Vegetation Ecosystem Modeling and Analysis Project, VEMAP 1995). The timber model was designed to capture these predicted shifts in boundaries during climate change. For example, southern pines begin in the southeastern United States, but then migrate to the Northeast, Midwest and

Great Plains in response to warming. In the earlier model, because the focus was on national impacts, the total quantity of both natural and managed migration was monitored, but not the specific quantity of each species in each region. This regional analysis monitors the specific migration of species from one region to the next.

Sohngen and Mendelsohn (1998, 1999) point out the importance of capturing the entire time path of changes for measuring welfare effects rather than just steady-state comparisons before and after a change. For instance, even though the northeastern United States may gain timber production in the long run, the overall economic effects in that region may be negative because the region loses timber production in early periods when northern species are dying back and the region is expending resources regenerating southern species as the climate changes. These early losses may or may not be compensated by future gains from a more productive forest in the Northeast dominated by species from the south. The effects, however, depend on the extent of ecological changes, the time path of the adjustment and the time path of price effects.

This chapter captures these spatial and temporal effects by carefully tracking the four timber species in the six regions and all relevant age classes (the exact number of age classes depends on the specific timber type and the region) in the baseline case (2060 without climate change) and the climate change scenarios. Note that some of the species may not remain in a region in the climate change scenarios. For example, an acre of northern forests in the Northeast region may convert to southern forests during climate change. The model would predict the loss of the existing northern forest (through either dieback and salvage in the dieback model or harvest in the regeneration model) and the replanting of the southern type in the Northeast. Future harvests of the new acres of southern forest planted in the Northeast would then be counted in the Northeast region.

The original models were reprogrammed to include a set of procedures that track harvests, replanting and ecological effects by region. The models were then re-estimated along the optimal pathways originally predicted and presented in Sohngen and Mendelsohn (1999). The solutions in this chapter are entirely consistent with the national results reported in Sohngen and Mendelsohn. The only difference in the model runs is that regional effects are calculated throughout. The model assumes perfect foresight both with and without climate change. As discussed in Sohngen and Mendelsohn, if foresters are slow to adapt to climate change, benefits will shrink and damages will increase.

The original model maximized the present value of net market surplus for the US softwood market (equation 5.6 in Sohngen and Mendelsohn 1999):

$$\underset{H_i(t),G_i(t)}{Max} \int_0^\infty e^{-rt} \left\{ \int_0^{Q^*} D(Q(H_i(t)),t)dQ - \sum_i \beta_i G_i(t) - \sum_i R_i(t)X_i(t) \right\} dt \quad (4.1)$$

where $D(\cdot)$ is a national demand function, $H(t)$ is the area of timberland harvested, $Q(t)$ is the quantity of timber harvested, $G(t)$ is the area of land regenerated, β is the regeneration cost per acre, $X(t)$ is the total area of land in forests and $R(t)$ is land rent. The subscript i represents the four timber types used. The total quantity of land in forests is measured with a stock constraint that measures the change in forest area in each period as the loss of forests from harvests and the gain in forests from regeneration:

$$\dot{X_i} = -H_i(t) + G_i(t). \quad (4.2)$$

The solution for this model can be found in Sohngen and Mendelsohn (1998, 1999).

To calculate welfare effects for each region, consumer and producer surplus was estimated by region for the baseline and the climate change scenarios. For this analysis, the subscript i includes the six regions instead. In any particular year, national consumer surplus is given as the area underneath a national demand function less price times quantity:

$$\int_0^{Q^*} D(Q(H_i(t))dQ - P(t)Q(t). \quad (4.3)$$

National producer surplus is then:

$$P(t)Q(t) - \sum_i \beta_i G_i(t) - \sum_i R_i(t)X_i(t). \quad (4.4)$$

Regional consumer surplus is estimated by assuming each region gets a share of national consumer surplus. Regional shares are given as any particular region's share of US GDP. These shares presented in Table 1.3 of Chapter 1 are taken from the National Income and Product Accounts maintained by the US Department of Commerce. The regional shares are assumed to remain constant over time even though the economy is growing. Regional producer surplus is then estimated with the following equation:

$$P(t)q_i(t) - \beta_i G_i(t) - R_i(t)X_i(t). \quad (4.5)$$

Regional producer surplus is total revenue from harvesting trees in region i, less the costs of replanting and renting forests in that region. A single equilibrium national price of timber is assumed, and regional quantities are quality adjusted as discussed in Sohngen and Mendelsohn (1999).

Scenarios

Regional welfare effects are estimated for 90 scenarios. The original analysis contained five climate change scenarios, nine combinations of ecological scenarios in VEMAP (1995) and two transient ecological change scenarios (dieback and regeneration) described in the earlier paper. One complicating factor in the timber analysis is that the climate scenarios used in the original analysis did not follow the same protocol as the other sectoral studies in Mendelsohn and Neumann (1999). The ecological modelers in VEMAP (1995) used spatially disaggregated (0.5 × 0.5 grid cells) predictions of climate effects from general circulation models (GCMs) rather than average uniform changes for the entire country. Sohngen and Mendelsohn (1999) used the US predictions from the GCMs to translate the available ecological predictions into a set of five climate change scenarios roughly consistent with the climate scenarios in Mendelsohn and Neumann (1999) and this book. The relevant matrix showing how the GCM models relate to average temperature and precipitation scenarios for the United States is shown in Table 5.4 of Sohngen and Mendelsohn (1999). The timber study consequently does not rely on uniform regional temperature and precipitation changes. The climate scenarios in the timber study vary by region and season depending on the GCM prediction.

The ecological models were derived from VEMAP (1995). Because the ecological models are static in nature, two transient ecological change models were developed to capture a range of potential ways in which the natural ecological adjustment to climate change could occur. These were called dieback and regeneration. The dieback scenario predicts that existing trees die when the underlying climate changes enough to support a new species of trees. The regeneration scenario assumes that existing trees can continue to live and grow in a region where climate changes the optimal species, but the original species cannot regenerate itself there. Thus, new species will slowly migrate into a region (or quickly be regenerated by human efforts) as climate changes.

EFFECTS FROM REGIONAL CLIMATE SCENARIOS

The regional climate analysis uses the central climate scenario (2.5°C, +7 per cent precipitation) that is 0.5 times the United Kingdom Meteorological Office (UKMO) scenario for the country as a baseline. The central scenario is the average impact from the 18 different ecological scenarios. The regional climate study compares how individual regions adjust to milder and harsher climate change scenarios when the rest of the country is experiencing the central scenario. The regional scenarios are based on the average ecological effects predicted across all the VEMAP models.

To develop the scenario, the ecological predictions of the ecological models were first averaged for the 2.5°C, +7 per cent precipitation scenario (UKMO × 0.5).[3] Thus, average predictions for dieback, regrowth of new forests and changes in ecological production for each region were calculated from the nine underlying combinations of ecological models. The average effects were used to make a new prediction of the economic effects of climate change. This new model run was not part of the original Sohngen and Mendelsohn (1999) analysis.

Regional effects for a harsh and a mild climate change scenario were then developed. The mildest available scenario is the 1.5°C, +7 per cent precipitation scenario (Geophysical Fluid Dynamics Laboratory model (GFDL) × 0.33). With this scenario, we averaged the nine VEMAP model combinations to determine regional ecological effects. The harshest scenario available is the UKMO prediction (5°C, +15 per cent precipitation). Although the Oregon State University (OSU) model appears to have a more harsh outcome of 5°C, +7 per cent precipitation, the UKMO model was selected because it predicts significant relative drying in important commercial timber species regions such as the South. The UKMO scenario is consequently the harshest climate scenario of the three GCM models for the timber sector. The nine VEMAP model outcomes were averaged for the UKMO scenario to produce the regional ecological effects. The economic model assumes that demand grows at 1.5 per cent per year and population grows at 1.0 per cent per year. Demand for wood products is assumed to grow more slowly than GDP (see Chapter 1). The discount rate used is 5 per cent. The welfare effects reflect the change in welfare between the climate scenarios and the baseline case. Welfare is consumer plus producer surplus, as estimated by equations (4.3) and (4.5).

RESULTS

The net present value of baseline consumer, producer and net surplus for the different regions is presented in Table 4.1. It is clear that the regions are not all alike. Production is heavily concentrated in the Southeast and to a lesser extent in the Northwest. Consumption varies with GDP and so it is heavily concentrated in the Northeast, Southeast and Midwest.

The timber model is a dynamic model. The model assumes a path of climate change with temperature changing gradually over the next 60 years from

Table 4.1   Baseline regional timber surplus (billions 1998 USD)

Region	Consumer surplus	Producer surplus	Net surplus
Northeast	67.50	6.31	73.81
Midwest	58.41	6.31	64.72
Great Plains	30.22	1.36	31.57
Northwest	10.35	28.74	39.09
Southeast	59.63	61.70	121.33
Southwest	49.62	6.76	56.38
Total US	275.72	111.18	386.90

Note: Present values calculated from 1990 to 2140.

current conditions to the new equilibrium associated with the doubling of greenhouse gases. In this chapter, it is assumed that the climate system reaches equilibrium in 2060. That is, the application does not explore the effects of continued increases in greenhouse gases beyond doubling. Timber species and forest productivity change over this time period, gradually moving toward the new equilibrium. The scenarios consider only a gradual warming.

The economics of the model are dynamic as well. Investments are made gradually in a changing economic environment. Prices are assumed to change over time in response to both changing demand and changes in supply. The model is explicitly forward looking, anticipating these changes and making rational economic choices to harvest and plant along the way.

Tables 4.2 and 4.3 present the average and percentage change in consumer, producer and net surplus for each region for each of the five climate scenarios averaged across the nine ecological scenarios. Separate results are shown for the dieback and regeneration scenarios. The range of results across the ecological models is also presented in Tables 4.2 and 4.3. Specific regional effects for net surplus and producer surplus for each of the climate and ecological scenarios are shown in Appendices A and B.

The climate change results in Tables 4.2 and 4.3 suggest that net surplus generally increases in each region, with the largest gains in the Northeast and Midwest, followed closely by the Southwest and the Great Plains. Consumer surplus rises in all regions because of lower prices with climate change than without. These four regions in particular account for 63 per cent of consumption in this model, and therefore receive the lion's share of the consumer benefits of lower prices. Although producer surplus declines in some scenarios for these regions (in many scenarios for the Midwest), producer surplus is not all that large to begin with in these regions. In aggregate, the losses to producers tend to be smaller than the gains to consumers.

Table 4.2   Dieback scenario: Present value of surplus changes averaged across ecosystem changes (billions 1998 USD)

Region	Surplus	(1) 5°C, 15% (UKMO × 1.0) $	Percent	(2) 5°C, 7% (OSU × 1.0) $	Percent	(3) 2.5°C, 15% (GFDL × 0.65) $	Percent	(4) 2.5°C, 7% (UKMO × 0.5) $	Percent	(5) 1.5°C, 7% (GFDL × 0.33) $	Percent
Northeast	CS	5.95	8.8	7.69	11.4	5.90	8.7	3.22	4.8	3.29	4.9
	PS	1.75	27.7	(0.19)	-3.0	1.11	17.5	3.04	48.2	2.27	35.9
		0.34–2.83		(0.48)–0.26		(0.07)–2.43		1.58–6.23		1.35–4.62	
	NS	7.69	10.4	7.52	10.2	7.01	9.5	6.27	8.5	5.56	7.5
		3.38–12.20		4.02–10.02		4.41–10.53		2.43–8.37		3.73–7.08	
Midwest	CS	5.14	8.8	6.66	11.4	5.11	8.7	2.80	4.8	2.84	4.9
	PS	0.25	3.9	0.09	1.4	(0.09)	-1.5	(0.01)	-0.2	(0.48)	-7.7
		(0.61)–1.24		(0.42)–0.77		(1.80)–1.27		(1.01)–1.26		(1.85)–0.79	
	NS	5.39	8.3	6.75	10.4	5.02	7.7	2.77	4.3	2.36	3.6
		1.50–9.64		3.63–11.48		1.92–8.68		0.17–4.59		0.31–4.72	
Great Plains	CS	2.67	8.8	3.45	11.4	2.64	8.7	1.44	4.8	1.48	4.9
	PS	0.44	32.4	1.09	80.1	1.81	133.7	0.83	61.4	1.39	102.8
		(0.13)–1.04		0.38–1.77		1.11–2.64		(0.04)–2.07		0.91–1.92	
	NS	3.10	9.8	4.53	14.3	4.45	14.1	2.28	7.2	2.87	9.1
		0.17–6.08		2.91–6.91		3.30–5.95		0.17–3.58		2.03–3.80	
Northwest	CS	0.91	8.8	1.18	11.4	0.91	8.7	0.50	4.8	0.51	4.9
	PS	(0.50)	-1.7	(0.64)	-2.2	(0.94)	-3.3	(0.45)	-1.5	(0.26)	-0.9
		(1.39)–0.55		(1.64)–0.01		(1.44)–(0.63)		(1.20)–0.32		(0.67)–0.01	
	NS	0.42	1.1	0.54	1.4	(0.04)	-0.1	0.05	0.1	0.25	0.6
		0.20–0.70		(0.20)–1.14		(0.72)–0.55		(0.64)–0.73		(0.12)–0.64	

Southeast	CS	5.25	8.8	6.80	11.4	5.22	8.7	2.86	4.8	2.90	4.9
	PS	(3.85)	-6.2	(3.96)	-6.4	(2.66)	-4.3	(1.58)	-2.6	(0.33)	-0.5
		(5.81)–(1.78)		*(5.97)–(1.98)*		*(4.57)–(0.80)*		*(3.34)–0.13*		*(2.01)–2.19*	
	NS	1.42	1.2	2.83	2.3	2.56	2.1	1.27	1.0	2.58	2.1
		(1.75)–5.16		*1.49–4.81*		*0.87–4.65*		*(0.13)–2.99*		*1.46–4.46*	
Southwest	CS	4.37	8.8	5.66	11.4	4.33	8.7	2.37	4.8	2.42	4.9
	PS	(0.34)	-5.1	(0.54)	-8.0	0.13	1.9	0.40	6.0	0.53	7.8
		(0.80)–0.12		*(0.78)–(0.37)*		*(0.47)–0.57*		*(0.21)–1.26*		*(0.07)–1.09*	
	NS	4.02	7.1	5.11	9.1	4.46	7.9	2.77	4.9	2.94	5.2
		0.34–7.92		*2.97–7.06*		*2.71–7.06*		*0.32–4.24*		*1.76–4.14*	
US	CS	24.30	8.8	31.45	11.4	24.10	8.7	13.18	4.8	13.44	4.9
	PS	(2.25)	-2.0	(4.17)	-3.7	(0.65)	-0.6	2.24	2.0	3.12	2.8
	NS	22.04	5.7	27.28	7.1	23.45	6.1	15.42	4.0	16.56	4.3

Notes: Real interest rates of 5%; ranges in italics; present values calculated from 1990 to 2140; * CS = consumer surplus; PS = producer surplus; NS = net surplus.

Table 4.3   Regeneration scenario: Present value of surplus changes averaged across ecosystem changes (billions 1998 USD)

Region	Surplus	(1) 5°C, 15% (UKMO × 1.0) $	Percent	(2) 5°C, 7% (OSU × 1.0) $	Percent	(3) 2.5°C, 15% (GFDL × 0.65) $	Percent	(4) 2.5°C, 7% (UKMO × 0.5) $	Percent	(5) 1.5°C, 7% (GFDL × 0.33) $	Percent
Northeast	CS	6.74	10	8.92	13	6.88	10	3.93	6	3.86	6
	PS	2.61	41	0.24	4	2.82	45	5.42	86	3.58	57
		0.78–4.93		*(0.59)–0.83*		*1.52–5.10*		*2.29–11.08*		*1.78–6.41*	
	NS	9.35	13	9.17	12	9.70	13	9.35	13	7.45	10
		5.73–15.30		*6.68–13.15*		*6.79–13.25*		*6.24–13.76*		*5.07–10.28*	
Midwest	CS	5.83	10	7.72	13	5.95	10	3.40	6	3.34	6
	PS	(0.96)	−15	(0.20)	−3	(0.50)	−8	(0.78)	−12	(0.67)	−11
		(1.94)–(0.31)		*(1.14)–1.09*		*(2.34)–1.43*		*(1.53)–0.25*		*(2.31)–1.05*	
	NS	4.87	8	7.53	12	5.45	8	2.63	4	2.67	4
		2.58–8.80		*4.35–12.40*		*2.21–9.20*		*0.01–4.40*		*0.57–5.02*	
Great Plains	CS	3.01	10	4.00	13	3.08	10	1.76	6	1.72	6
	PS	0.28	21	0.80	60	1.78	132	0.91	67	1.59	118
		(0.25)–0.79		*0.20–1.76*		*1.04–2.88*		*0.33–2.11*		*0.51–2.35*	
	NS	3.29	10	4.80	15	4.86	15	2.67	9	3.32	11
		1.69–5.72		*3.42–6.56*		*3.35–6.45*		*1.01–3.50*		*2.12–4.14*	
Northwest	CS	1.03	10	1.37	13	1.05	10	0.60	6	0.59	6
	PS	0.07	0	(0.33)	−1	(1.09)	−4	(0.30)	−1	(0.35)	−1
		(0.35)–0.74		*(0.78)–0.18*		*(2.57)–0.02*		*(1.69)–0.68*		*(1.12)–0.12*	
	NS	1.11	3	1.04	3	1.09	0	0.31	1	0.24	1
		0.54–1.83		*0.48–1.97*		*(1.74)–1.09*		*(1.27)–1.58*		*(0.67)–0.68*	

		(1)		(2)		(3)		(4)		(5)	
Southeast	CS	5.95	10	7.88	13	6.08	10	3.48	6	3.41	6
	PS	(3.93)	-6	(4.61)	-8	(3.63)	-6	(3.21)	-5	(1.57)	-3
		(5.79)–(2.16)		*(7.17)–(2.42)*		*(6.41)–(1.45)*		*(5.48)–(0.57)*		*(3.94)–(0.14)*	
	NS	2.02	2	3.27	3	2.44	2	0.26	0	1.84	2
		1.30–5.61		*0.76–5.58*		*0.94–4.73*		*(3.76)–2.62*		*0.48–3.89*	
Southwest	CS	4.96	10	6.56	13	5.06	10	2.89	6	2.83	6
	PS	(0.34)	-5	(0.54)	-8	0.55	8	0.85	13	0.97	14
		(1.00)–0.21		*(0.87)–(0.26)*		*(0.33)–1.53*		*0.08–2.42*		*(0.15)–2.24*	
	NS	4.60	8	6.02	11	5.62	10	3.74	7	3.80	7
		2.63–8.12		*3.91–9.33*		*3.61–7.81*		*1.55–4.89*		*2.35–5.30*	
US	CS	27.51	10	36.45	13	28.10	10	16.07	6	15.76	6
	PS	(2.27)	-2	(4.64)	-4	(0.05)	0	2.89	0	3.54	3
	NS	25.24	7	31.81	8	28.05	7	18.96	5	19.30	5

Notes: Real interest rates of 5%; ranges in italics; present values calculated from 1990 to 2140; * CS = consumer surplus; PS = producer surplus; NS = net surplus.

Unlike other estimates found in the literature (Perez-Garcia *et al.* 1997, McCarl *et al.* 2000), producer surplus rises in many regions under a number of scenarios despite lower price predictions. There are at least two reasons for this in this model. First, this model allows producers to adapt by transplanting new species better adapted to a changing climate. In many cases, these transplantations involve faster growing species that are more productive than the species landowners previously used. This enhances producer welfare by shortening rotations. In particular, in Tables 4.2 and 4.3, this effect generates the positive producer outcomes for northern regions like the Northeast, Midwest and Great Plains. Some negative producer effects occur when producers spend considerable sums regenerating new species early in the transition period, or when prices are lower, such as in the regeneration scenarios. Second, annual growth for all species is changing. In some cases, the annual change in timber growth may provide enough benefits in terms of wood quantity to offset lower prices. For any particular region, this depends empirically on the effects of all changes in timber growth and species distribution on prices as well as the change in growth rates for the particular region.

Given the potential loss of existing species, it is somewhat surprising that northern regions do not do worse during climate change. The main reason is that short-term losses imposed by dieback when it occurs are offset by long-term gains in overall productivity. These gains occur as fast-growing southern species move north into regions previously occupied by slower-growing northern species. Thus, northern areas tend to experience fairly substantial long-term gains in overall productivity.

Despite this, the Midwest region does experience some losses in producer surplus during climate change. These losses result from the combination of lower prices for existing forests, and planting costs in early periods as the region shifts its stock of trees to more southerly types. The negative producer effects are larger in the regeneration scenario because price levels in early periods are lower, thus reducing the value of existing timber resources. This study models a stumpage market and therefore does not include capital adjustments in the timber processing sector. Because the changes are gradual, we assume that the processing sector adjusts capital over time at little or no cost. No additional adjustment costs in sawmills or pulpmills are considered. Log transport costs and processing capital investment decisions would need to be modeled to estimate impacts under more rapid climate change.

The economic effects of the northern shift of southern species during climate change are nonetheless limited. Southern species shift dramatically northward only in the 2.5°C, +7 per cent precipitation and the 5°C, +15 per cent precipitation scenarios. Relatively less dieback and relatively less shifting of species northward occur in the other scenarios. Also, the movement of southern species into the Midwest region is minimized by the mask used in the original analysis to limit movement of southern species into productive agricultural lands. Much of the gain in productivity due to shifts in southern species actually occurs in the Southern Plains.

The Southeast and the Northwest gain net surplus, but the overall effects there are limited by losses to producers. Producer effects are negative in the Southeast because that region has considerable producer surplus to begin with, and those producers experience lower prices in early periods. In some ecological and climate scenarios, these economic losses are compounded because existing forest production is lost when some areas are no longer able to support forests.

In the 2.5°C, +15 per cent precipitation scenario, the losses to producers are larger than the gains to consumers in the Northwest, and the net effect is negative. As in the Southeast, forests in the Northwest contribute substantial production to US markets, and lower prices during climate change cause existing producers to lose welfare. The Northwest also expends some resources on planting in early periods, developing new areas of less productive western conifers in response to warming. Because these are longer rotation species, the region must wait many years to reap the gains of these efforts.

The largest percentage gains in net surplus occur in the Northeast, Great Plains and Midwest, followed by the Southwest. Relatively smaller gains in net surplus occur in the Southeast and Northwest. Percentage changes in consumer surplus are the same for each region because the methods used for calculating consumer surplus simply allocate total consumer surplus among the regions according to regional GDP (in the baseline and in the climate change cases). The largest proportional gains in producer surplus occur in the Great Plains because that region becomes dramatically more productive during climate change.

The largest gains in consumer surplus occur for the more dramatic climate change scenarios ((1), (2) and (3) in Tables 4.2 and 4.3). Recall that the ecological scenarios capture spatial variation in the underlying climate changes, so that climate change in any particular region may vary dramatically from the US average. Thus, while scenario 2 (5°C, +7 per cent precipitation), with the OSU climate model, indicates drying in the United States in general, much of this drying occurs in the Southwest. There is little timber effect in this region because it is not a major producer to begin with. The rest of the country does not experience such dramatic effects, causing fairly large, positive consumer effects for that scenario.

Producer effects capture much of the variation in climate change and the resulting ecological effects. Considering the OSU climate model in scenario (2), the Southwest gets warmer and dries out. Alternatively, the Northern Plains experience less warming and gain more precipitation than average. Thus, producers in the Southwest lose welfare in this scenario, while producers in the Northern Plains gain surplus. All of the climate scenarios show a regional 'hotspot' in the Southeast, where some areas get relatively more warming and relatively less precipitation than the country on average. These hotspots are part of the reason for the losses in producer surplus in the Southeast under this set of scenarios.

One difference between these results and the earlier Sohngen and Mendelsohn (1999) results is that in some cases in the Southeast and Midwest the regeneration scenarios do not produce larger gains than the dieback scenarios. During early periods, the dieback scenarios tend to have higher prices relative to the regeneration scenarios. Even though dieback reduces stock, these higher prices help reduce losses in regions that experience less dieback than the national average. For example, the South loses few trees from dieback in the 2.5°C, +15 per cent precipitation scenario. The higher prices associated with dieback in other regions actually help Southern producers.

Most of the gains in producer surplus in the Great Plains occur in the southern part of that region because southern species move west of their current range into parts of eastern Texas and Oklahoma where they currently do not thrive. Although these regions experience some losses in early periods because of planting costs, the overall effects are positive. Some of the gain does occur in the Northern Plains; these gains, however, occur far in the future because the Northern Plains become more productive for traditional western conifer species that take long periods of time to mature.

Tables 4.2 and 4.3 also present the range of effects that occur across the different ecological scenarios. These ranges reveal considerable uncertainty about the magnitude of effects in each region and sometimes even the sign changes. The Northeast and Midwest have the largest range of effects across models because the ecological models have widely divergent predictions about the extent of the movement of Southern pines northward, both across models and across climate predictions. The Southeast also has a large range of potential effects. This is driven by different ecological predictions of the impact of drying on the range of existing Southern pine forests, as well as changes in productivity in other parts of the South.

Annual effects in 2060

Annual effects for 2060 are also investigated to assess the scale of potential climate change effects on the future economy. To get a sense for the scale of the US economy in 2060, baseline consumer, producer and net surplus are presented in Table 4.4. Annual welfare effects are then shown in Tables 4.5 and 4.6. Appendices C and D present the full set of results for net surplus and producer surplus.

Table 4.4   Annual net surplus in 2060 for baseline case (billions 1998 USD)

Region	Consumer surplus	Producer surplus	Net surplus
Northeast	5.77	0.34	6.11
Midwest	4.99	0.34	5.33
Great Plains	2.58	0.07	2.64
Northwest	0.89	1.96	2.84
Southeast	5.10	4.24	9.33
Southwest	4.24	0.33	4.58
Total US	23.56	7.27	30.83

Note: Baseline case is 2060 without climate change.

For the most part, the signs of the welfare effects for 2060 are similar to the net present value of welfare effects shown above. However, some interesting differences occur. For instance, producers in the Midwest region tend to gain in 2060. In the present value analysis performed above, producers in the Midwest region lost welfare in a number of scenarios. These losses in net present value were caused by losses in early periods, while the long-term outlook for producers in the Midwest is generally positive.

The scale of the percentage change calculation is larger for 2060 than for the present value of the time path of change. As Figures 4.1 through 4.4 show, the largest changes tend to occur fairly far in the future. Discounting these gains reduces their overall effect for the present value calculations. The gains or losses are amplified in the future in part because of productivity effects on forests. Although climate affects tree growth rates only up to 2060, for some of the longer-lived species the effect of this change may not have its full impact for many more years.

The 2060 effects should be interpreted with some caution because they represent only one year out of many future years, and the effects vary from decade to decade. Figures 4.1 through 4.4 present the time path of annual effects for different regions and two ecological model combinations under dieback and regeneration. The central climate scenario (2.5°C, +7 per cent precipitation) is used for the comparison. The Dynamic Global Phytogeography (DOLY) and Terrestrial Ecosystem Model (TEM) scenario is used because it generates the largest gain in welfare overall, while the Mapped Atmospheric Plant Soil System (MAPSS) and BIOME–Biogeochemistry Cycle model (BIOME–BGC) combination is chosen because it generates the smallest gains in welfare overall.

As the figures show, 2060 actually may be a relatively good year for the Northeast (NE), Midwest (MW) and Great Plains (GP). However, the figures

Table 4.5 Dieback scenario: Annual value in 2060 of surplus changes averaged across ecosystem changes (billions 1998 USD)

Region	Surplus	(1) 5°C, 15% (UKMO × 1.0)		(2) 5°C, 7% (OSU × 1.0)		(3) 2.5°C, 15% (GFDL × 0.65)		(4) 2.5°C, 7% (UKMO × 0.5)		(5) 1.5°C, 7% (GFDL × 0.33)	
		$	Percent	$	Percent	$	Percent	$	Percent	$	Percent
Northeast	CS	1.89	33	2.17	38	1.56	27	0.93	16	0.85	15
	PS	1.55	457	0.20	59	0.02	7	0.91	268	0.14	42
		1.04–8.46		*(0.01)–0.39*		*(0.20)–0.17*		*0.21–3.09*		*0.00–0.28*	
	NS	3.43	56	2.37	39	1.58	26	1.84	30	0.99	16
		0.08–4.77		*1.57–3.78*		*0.92–2.45*		*0.38–2.95*		*0.74–1.32*	
Midwest	CS	1.63	33	1.88	38	1.35	27	0.80	16	0.73	15
	PS	1.27	377	0.99	293	(0.01)	-3	0.53	157	0.02	9
		(1.66)–2.22		*0.41–1.58*		*(1.29)–0.52*		*(1.44)–1.11*		*(0.21)–0.45*	
	NS	2.90	55	2.88	54	1.33	25	1.33	25	0.77	14
		0.17–4.08		*1.92–4.38*		*(0.08)–2.12*		*(0.77)–2.45*		*0.37–1.20*	
Great Plains	CS	0.84	33	0.97	38	0.70	27	0.41	16	0.38	15
	PS	0.59	881	1.23	1839	0.52	785	0.41	626	0.66	994
		(0.02)–1.24		*0.55–1.97*		*(3.79)–2.77*		*(0.01)–1.48*		*(0.04)–1.32*	
	NS	1.43	54	2.19	83	1.22	46	0.84	32	1.04	39
		0.12–2.78		*1.25–3.00*		*(3.16)–3.73*		*0.07–2.17*		*0.44–1.69*	
Northwest	CS	0.28	33	0.33	38	0.24	27	0.14	16	0.13	15
	PS	(0.50)	-25	(0.47)	-24	(0.22)	-12	(0.26)	-14	(0.22)	-11
		(0.77)–0.01		*(0.59)–0.32*		*(0.81)–0.97*		*(0.65)–0.02*		*(0.57)–0.01*	
	NS	(0.21)	-7	(0.14)	-5	0.01	0	(0.12)	-4	(0.09)	-3
		(0.50)–1.53		*(0.25)–(0.04)*		*(0.48)–1.18*		*(0.41)–0.58*		*(0.47)–0.14*	

Southeast	CS	1.66	33	1.92	38	1.37	27	0.83	16	0.74	15
	PS	(2.87)	-68	(1.91)	-45	(0.09)	-2	(1.39)	-33	(0.41)	-10
		(3.80)–1.05		*(2.57)–(1.37)*		*(1.91)–4.20*		*(3.15)–1.13*		*(1.57)–0.09*	
	NS	1.20	-13	0.01	0	1.27	14	0.57	-6	0.34	4
		(2.94)–3.13		*(1.42)–1.26*		*(0.02)–5.43*		*(1.77)–1.90*		*(0.85)–0.90*	
Southwest	CS	1.39	33	1.59	38	1.14	27	0.68	16	0.63	15
	PS	0.02	8	(0.09)	-27	0.05	15	0.05	13	0.02	6
		(0.08)–0.39		*(0.14)–(0.04)*		*(0.08)–0.19*		*(0.04)–0.35*		*(0.07)–0.12*	
	NS	1.42	31	1.51	33	1.19	26	0.73	16	0.65	14
		0.18–2.64		*0.87–2.42*		*0.57–1.81*		*0.19–1.33*		*0.32–0.92*	
US	CS	7.71	33	8.87	38	6.35	27	3.80	16	3.46	15
	PS	0.07	1	(0.06)	-1	0.26	4	0.25	3	0.22	3
	NS	7.78	25	8.83	29	6.61	21	4.05	13	3.68	12

Note: Real interest rates of 5%; ranges in italics; CS = consumer surplus; PS = producer surplus; NS = net surplus.

Table 4.6   Regeneration scenario: Annual value in 2060 of surplus changes averaged across ecosystem changes (billions 1998 USD)

Region	Surplus	(1) 5°C, 15% (UKMO × 1.0) $	Percent	(2) 5°C, 7% (OSU × 1.0) $	Percent	(3) 2.5°C, 15% (GFDL × 0.65) $	Percent	(4) 2.5°C, 7% (UKMO × 0.5) $	Percent	(5) 1.5°C, 7% (GFDL × 0.33) $	Percent
Northeast	CS	1.90	33	2.30	40	1.77	31	1.03	18	0.92	16
	PS	1.17	345	0.34	101	0.25	72	1.52	450	0.37	108
		0.72–2.03		0.13–0.55		0.05–0.53		(0.15)–7.29		0.09–0.67	
	NS	3.07	50	2.64	43	2.02	33	2.55	42	1.29	21
		1.72–4.22		1.84–3.88		0.99–3.26		0.76–8.44		0.80–1.83	
Midwest	CS	1.65	33	1.99	40	1.53	31	0.89	18	0.80	16
	PS	0.48	144	0.86	255	0.08	26	0.28	83	0.05	16
		0.22–1.23		0.27–1.81		(0.26)–0.83		(0.08)–1.27		(0.30)–0.45	
	NS	2.14	40	2.86	54	1.62	30	1.17	22	0.85	16
		1.11–3.33		1.88–4.34		0.87–3.19		0.47–2.23		0.35–1.60	
Great Plains	CS	0.85	33	1.03	40	0.79	31	0.46	18	0.41	16
	PS	0.45	673	1.03	1547	0.93	1396	0.84	1264	0.84	1263
		(0.01)–1.65		0.60–1.92		0.08–2.45		0.00–4.77		0.12–1.53	
	NS	1.30	49	2.07	78	1.72	65	1.30	49	1.25	47
		0.51–2.67		1.55–2.77		0.39–3.67		0.09–5.27		0.44–2.18	
Northwest	CS	0.30	33	0.35	40	0.27	31	0.15	18	0.14	16
	PS	(0.39)	-20	(0.51)	-26	(0.32)	-17	(0.70)	-35	(0.22)	-11
		(1.23)–0.02		(0.67)–(0.28)		(0.57)–(0.02)		(4.43)–0.05		(0.39)–(0.01)	
	NS	(0.11)	-4	(0.15)	-6	(0.05)	-2	(0.53)	-19	(0.08)	-3
		(0.87)–0.54		(0.39)–0.06		(0.30)–0.27		(4.25)–0.22		(0.25)–0.13	

		(1)		(2)		(3)		(4)		(5)	
		value	%	value	%	value	%	value	%	value	%
Southeast	CS	1.68	33	2.03	40	1.56	31	0.91	18	0.81	16
	PS	(1.82)	-43	(1.76)	-42	(1.06)	-25	(2.24)	-53	(0.92)	-22
	range	*(3.92)–(1.22)*		*(2.42)–(1.17)*		*(3.65)–0.05*		*(11.42)–0.17*		*(2.55)–0.12*	
	NS	(0.14)	-2	0.27	3	0.50	5	(1.33)	-14	(0.11)	-1
	range	*(1.92)–1.69*		*(0.91)–1.76*		*(1.24)–1.48*		*(10.41)–1.22*		*(1.36)–1.22*	
Southwest	CS	1.40	33	1.70	40	1.30	31	0.76	18	0.67	16
	PS	0.13	40	(0.07)	-21	0.06	19	0.40	121	0.04	10
	range	*(0.07)–0.51*		*(0.12)–0.00*		*(0.11)–0.25*		*(0.01)–2.50*		*(0.06)–0.15*	
	NS	1.53	34	1.63	36	1.36	30	1.16	25	0.71	16
	range	*0.81–2.80*		*1.03–2.47*		*0.77–1.96*		*0.15–3.34*		*0.41–0.96*	
US	CS	7.78	33	9.40	40	7.23	31	4.20	18	3.76	16
	PS	0.02	0	(0.11)	-1	(0.07)	-1	0.12	2	0.15	2
	NS	7.79	25	9.31	30	7.16	23	4.32	14	3.92	13

Note: Real interest rates of 5%; ranges in italics; CS = consumer surplus; PS = producer surplus; NS = net surplus.

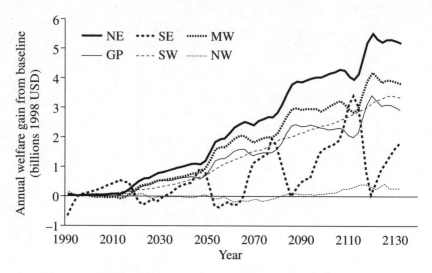

Figure 4.1   Annual change in net surplus from the baseline for the DOLY–
TEM dieback scenario and the central climate scenario (2.5°C,
+7% precipitation)

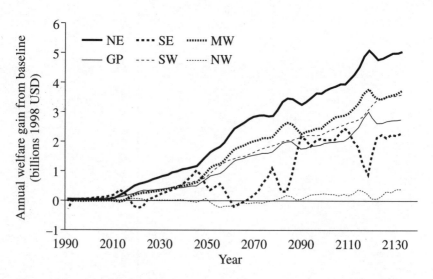

Figure 4.2   Annual change in net surplus from the baseline for the DOLY–
TEM regeneration scenario and the central climate scenario
(2.5°C, +7% precipitation)

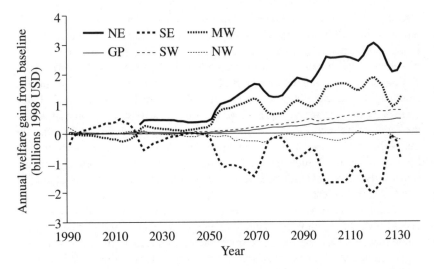

Figure 4.3   Annual change in net surplus from the baseline for the MAPSS–
              BGC dieback scenario and the central climate scenario (2.5°C,
              +7% precipitation)

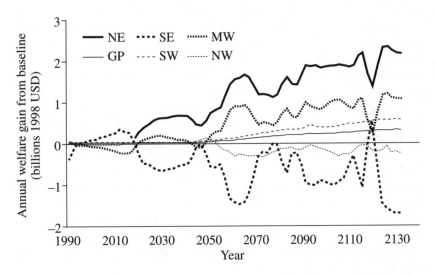

Figure 4.4   Annual change in net surplus from the baseline for the MAPSS–
              BGC regeneration scenario and the central climate scenario
              (2.5°C, +7% precipitation)

also show that the Southeast (SE) impacts fluctuate from decade to decade. It happens that 2060 is a relatively bad year for the Southeast. The large swings in net surplus result from changes in producer surplus caused by the age class distribution of timber. For instance, under the MAPSS and BIOME–BGC ecological models, landowners start planting southern pines in the Northeast, Midwest and Great Plains in early periods of climate change, while landowners in the Southeast must manage existing, mature stocks, some of which are undergoing dieback. As the new southern pine stands become mature in the Northeast, Midwest and Great Plains in 2015–30, these regions harvest heavily while the Southeast holds on to its now younger stock. The cycle repeats itself, so that the Southeast contains relatively immature stands in 2060, and its harvests are low.

The figures also provide more background on why the Northwest experiences losses during climate change on average. The DOLY and TEM ecological combination under the central climate scenario suggests mild forest losses. Approximately 2.5 per cent of the productive western region of Washington and Oregon is lost, but the models predict gains of about 12 per cent of these productive species in Idaho. Tree growth increases by 17 per cent. Despite these positive ecological effects, the Northwest experiences some early losses in climate change because of lower prices. Table 4.6 shows that losses to producers from lower prices outweigh gains to consumers in that region. Although long-term effects beyond 2060 are positive for the Northwest, the early losses due to early low prices suggest an overall welfare loss for the region. The MAPSS and BIOME–BGC model presents an even more negative picture for the region, with losses of 28 per cent of the existing western forests, no gains of these types of forests to the east and an overall 1.5 per cent loss in tree growth. These negative effects, while evident in early periods in Figures 4.3 and 4.4, are greatest in later periods.

Approximately 75 per cent of the gain in welfare in the Great Plains region in 2060 occurs in the southern part of that region (Texas and Oklahoma). This results from the conversion of less productive grasslands to southern pine forests. The northern part of the Great Plains experiences gains as well because of conversion of additional lands to western conifers and in some cases pacific northwestern conifers. These gains occur mostly in future periods, however, because the species entering the northern area of the Great Plains have longer rotation ages than the southern pines entering the southern area of the Great Plains. The model explicitly considers the lost agriculture (grazing land) associated with these changes as part of the cost of these changes.

Varying regional climate scenarios

The study then analyzes the impact of regional climate variation. The average and range of climate effects for the VEMAP models are presented in the first part of Table 4.7. We then examine what would happen if we change the regional forecast of climate for each region, holding the rest of the country with the central climate scenario. The purpose of this exercise is to try to understand the importance of varying regional climate predictions. Note that

Table 4.7   *Average ecological change predictions for nine VEMAP scenarios under three climate scenarios (central, mild, harsh)*

Region	Dieback	Relative size	Productivity
	(Percentage change)		
Central climate scenario (UKMO × 0.5), 2.5°C, +7% precipitation			
Northeast	45	118	3
Midwest	45	121	3
Great Plains	34	460	5
Northwest	24	97	7
Southeast	12	103	3
Southwest	34	100	13
US average	24	114	5
Mild climate scenario (GFDL × 0.33), 1.5°C, +7% precipitation			
Northeast	30	104	1
Midwest	30	108	1
Great Plains	17	323	3
Northwest	11	111	3
Southeast	2	106	2
Southwest	17	118	5
US average	11	113	3
Harsh climate scenario (UKMO full), 5°C, +15% precipitation			
Northeast	90	136	0
Midwest	90	139	0
Great Plains	67	896	6
Northwest	48	88	15
Southeast	23	106	−1
Southwest	67	80	22
US average	48	125	4

because all of the scenarios come from GCMs, one is actually comparing one GCM scenario with another. Some of the effects across regions are due to the differences in the regional climate forecasts of each GCM, making some of the results difficult to interpret.

The first column of Table 4.8 is the net present value of producer surplus in the national central scenario. Similarly, the first column in Table 4.9 presents the annual producer surplus in 2060 with the central scenario. Note that although these studies compare scenarios, none of the climate scenarios in the timber study is uniform. All the scenarios come from GCMs and comparisons are made across GCM scenarios. Some of the effects across regions are due to the different estimates of regional climate variation by the GCMs. Differences in estimates may not just be the result of moving from a mild to a

Table 4.8   Varying regional climate scenarios: present value of producer impacts

Region	Regional producer surplus	Change from central scenario
Northeast (central scenario PS = $7.32)		
Mild	6.89	(0.41)
Harsh	7.04	(0.27)
Midwest (central scenario PS = $7.32)		
Mild	6.89	(0.41)
Harsh	7.06	(0.26)
Great Plains (central scenario PS = $2.66)		
Mild	2.16	(0.48)
Harsh	3.12	0.47
Northwest (central scenario PS = $28.40)		
Mild	28.60	0.20
Harsh	27.97	(0.45)
Southeast (central scenario PS = $59.35)		
Mild	62.19	2.83
Harsh	55.76	(3.61)
Southwest (central scenario PS = $6.89)		
Mild	6.90	0.01
Harsh	6.95	0.06

Note: These results are for the dieback scenario only. Values represent the present value of the time path of changes over 150 years (r = 0.05). The values are contrasted with climate scenario where tested region experiences the central scenario along with the rest of the country.

Table 4.9   *Varying regional climate scenarios: 2060 producer impacts (billions 1998 USD).*

Region	Regional producer surplus	Change from central scenario
Northeast (central scenario PS = $1.03)		
Mild	0.47	(0.56)
Harsh	1.13	0.10
Midwest (central scenario PS = $1.03)		
Mild	0.47	(0.56)
Harsh	1.13	0.10
Great Plains (central scenario PS = $1.05)		
Mild	0.61	(0.43)
Harsh	1.44	0.39
Northwest (central scenario PS = $1.23)		
Mild	1.27	0.04
Harsh	0.98	(0.25)
Southeast (central scenario PS = $1.66)		
Mild	2.50	0.85
Harsh	1.94	0.28
Southwest (central scenario PS = $0.38)		
Mild	0.34	(0.04)
Harsh	0.60	0.22

Note: These results are for the dieback scenario only. Values represent the effect in 2060. The values are contrasted with climate scenario where tested region experiences the central scenario along with the rest of the country.

harsh climate but also the result of a relative change in the regional climate predicted by the different GCMs.

The second column in Tables 4.8 and 4.9 represents the producer surplus associated with a milder and a harsher regional climate. The third column is the change in producer surplus from the uniform scenario. Consumer effects are ignored here because prices are not affected by changes in regional climates. Without price effects, consumer surplus remains the same. The regional climate scenarios lead to only producer surplus effects in the regions that are being affected.

The results in Table 4.8 reveal the net present value results for each region. The scenarios used to capture mild and harsh climates are not uniform across regions. Consequently, there is much variation across regions between these scenarios. For example, the central climate scenario has a higher net present value for the Northeast and the Midwest than either the mild or harsh scenario. The results do suggest, however, that the losses with milder climate change are slightly more severe than the losses with harsher climate change. The annual results in 2060 are similar, although more climate change appears to be optimal for these regions in the long run. The net present value estimates highlight early effects of climate change, while the 2060 results highlight the longer-term consequences. Thus, while more climate change leads to more dieback in these regions, which has negative consequences in early periods, it also leads to larger expansions of southern forests in the Northeast and Midwest in future periods, which has positive effects. In the harsh climate scenario, more dieback in early periods has negative consequences that are overcome in the long run by a larger increase in the area of productive southern forests in the region. From today's perspective, however, enduring additional dieback now for future gains is a large hurdle to cross.

Alternatively, the Southeast and the Northwest are better off with milder climate change and worse off with harsher changes. The ecological effects in those regions are milder for less climate change and therefore have less of an effect on the economic results. Dieback losses are smaller and the gain in forest area is the same or larger for the mild climate scenario. While the Northwest experiences larger productivity gains for the harsh climate scenario, these effects are overwhelmed by the dieback and lost forest areas. The 2060 results indicate positive effects for the Southeast in the harsh climate scenario, but these effects occur because 2060 is a relatively good year while most future years are negative for that region.

The Great Plains do worse with milder climate change and better with harsher climate changes. These effects are concentrated heavily in the southern states of Texas and Oklahoma. More climate change means greater gains in southern forests at the expense of former grasslands. The Southwest, on the other hand, does better in both the harsh and mild climate cases for the net present value results, but slightly worse for mild climate change in 2060. Even though more climate change suggests more dieback and fewer acres of new forests for the Southwest, the region gains much more productive forests in the harsh climate scenario than in the mild climate scenario. Despite the fact that the region uses less land for forestry, each hectare that is used for forestry is much more productive than those used in the central climate scenario.

CONCLUSION

The national climate scenarios in the first analysis identify the Southeast and Northwest as the two regions with the largest producer surplus effects. This makes sense because these two regions comprise the largest share of US production before climate change impacts, and the effects of species redistribution and altered timber growth rates shift productive forestry away from these regions. In contrast, northern regions tend to gain the most producer surplus from climate change because they gain more valuable species as a result of climate change. The model suggests, however, that the largest welfare effects are likely to be consumer surplus changes. These impacts are distributed in proportion to economic activity. Consequently, the Midwest and Northeast have the largest timber welfare impacts from climate change even though these regions are not the primary timber growing regions of the country.

These results suggest the importance of dynamic analysis such as this, which captures potential changes in both timber growth and species range. While most timber studies have explored changes in timber growth (Joyce *et al.* 1995, Perez-Garcia *et al.* 1997, Burton *et al.* 1998, McCarl *et al.* 2000), no other studies have explored changes in species distribution. Consequently, Perez-Garcia *et al.* (1997) find that higher timber growth leads to losses for US producers and landowners. Similarly, McCarl *et al.* (2000) find that higher growth for any particular region reduces both regional and national producer surplus, both in the short run and in 2040. In contrast, this study finds that the aggregate effects on US producers are likely to be positive for smaller climate changes, but negative for larger climate changes. In particular regions, this study finds that northern regions may benefit even when timber growth increases because those regions can substitute faster growing species for slower growing species. The effects become even larger in future years (2060). Looking at the effects on growth rates alone may bias the results for particular regions that have the capacity to adapt by choosing alternative species.

A limitation with these results is that they do not consider global climate impacts. Global impacts are particularly important for measuring welfare implications because studies suggest that future prices are likely to be heavily influenced by offshore timber production (see Sohngen *et al.* 2000). Understanding how climate change affects timber species across the globe will be important for predicting future prices, and future adaptation in the United States. For instance, Sohngen *et al.* (2000) suggest that North American producers may be particularly vulnerable to climate change because they experience species redistribution in the short run, while other regions benefit from rapid enhanced growth, thus driving down global prices in the next 50 years. In some scenarios they explore, global climate effects drive down early prices enough to reduce aggregate North American welfare.

The regional climate variation analyses reveal that regions are vulnerable to local climate change that is harsher or lighter than the climate change that occurs in other regions. Getting precise climate change predictions for each region is important. However, the regional climate impacts are not that different from the results found using the national scenarios. The results of the national climate scenarios provide a reasonable picture of the sensitivity of each region to climate change.

NOTES

1. The original model looked at the Northeast, Southeast, Rocky Mountains and the western portion of the Pacific Northwest, but did not differentiate effects by region.
2. This analysis was unable to divide the Great Plains into Northern and Southern Plains. Where possible, effects in the Northern and Southern Plains are discussed qualitatively.
3. The regional UKMO estimates were 'scaled' (for example, Mitchell *et al.* 1999) by dividing all of the relevant regional estimates by 2. This assumes that the changes in regional climate remain proportional.

REFERENCES

Burton, D.M., B.A. McCarl, N.M. de Sousa, D.M. Adams, R.A. Alig and S.M. Winnett (1998), 'Economic dimensions of climate change impacts on southern forests', in S. Fox and R. Mickler (eds), *The Productivity and Sustainability of Southern Forest Ecosystems in a Changing Environment*, New York: Springer-Verlag.

Joyce, L.A., J.R. Mills, L.S. Heath, A.D. McGuire, R.W. Haynes and R.A. Birdsey (1995), 'Forest sector impacts from changes in forest productivity under climate change', *Journal of Biogeography*, 22, 703–13.

McCarl, B.A., D.M. Adams, R.D. Alig and C. Chen (2000), 'Effects of global climate change on the US forest sector: Response functions derived from a dynamic resource and market simulator, *Climate Research*, 5(3): 195–205.

Mendelsohn, R. and J.E. Neumann (eds) (1999), *The Impact of Climate Change on the United States Economy*, Cambridge, UK: Cambridge University Press.

Mitchell, J.F.B., T.C. Johns, M. Eagles, W.J. Ingram and R.A. Davis (1999), 'Towards the construction of climate change scenarios', *Climate*, 41, 547–81.

Perez-Garcia, J., L.A. Joyce, A.D. McGuire and C.S. Binkley (1997), 'Economic impact of climatic change on the global forest sector', in R.A. Sedjo, R.N. Sampson and J. Wisniewski (eds), *Economics of Carbon Sequestration in Forestry*, Boca Raton, FL: Lewis Publishers.

Sohngen, B. and R. Mendelsohn (1998), 'Valuing the market impact of large-scale ecological change: The effect of climate change on US timber', *American Economic Review*, 88, 686–710.

Sohngen, B. and R. Mendelsohn (1999), 'The impacts of climate change on the US timber market', R. Mendelsohn and J. E. Neumann (eds), *The Impact of Climate Change on the United States Economy*, Cambridge, UK: Cambridge University Press, pp. 94–132.

Sohngen, B., R. Mendelsohn and R. Sedjo (2000), A Global Model of Climate

Change Impacts on Timber Markets. Working Paper. Department of Agricultural Economics, Ohio State University.

VEMAP (1995), 'Vegetation/Ecosystem Modeling and Analysis Project: Comparing biogeography and biogeochemistry models in a continental scale study of terrestrial ecosystem responses to climate change and CO_2 doubling', *Global Biogeochemical Cycles*, 9(4), 407–37.

Appendix A

NET SURPLUS

Regional present values from alternative ecological scenarios (billions 1998 USD).

Table A4.1   MAPPS and TEM ecological change, dieback scenario (billions 1998 USD)

Climate scenario	NE	SE	MW	GP	SW	NW	Total
(1) 5°C, 15% (UKMO × 1.0)	9.49	0.59	7.23	3.12	4.98	0.70	26.10
(2) 5°C, 7% (OSU × 1.0)	11.82	4.81	11.48	5.97	8.19	1.14	43.41
(3) 2.5°C, 15% (GFDL × 0.65)	7.60	3.59	6.81	5.29	5.69	0.55	29.52
(4) 2.5°C, 7% (UKMO × 0.5)	6.21	1.44	4.47	3.15	3.69	(0.64)	18.33
(5) 1.5°C, 7% (GFDL × 0.33)	7.09	2.83	3.35	3.21	3.73	0.64	20.85

Table A4.2   MAPPS and TEM ecological change, regeneration scenario (billions 1998 USD)

Climate scenario	NE	SE	MW	GP	SW	NW	Total
(1) 5°C, 15% (UKMO × 1.0)	11.91	1.39	6.73	3.72	6.01	1.16	30.90
(2) 5°C, 7% (OSU × 1.0)	13.15	4.97	12.40	6.35	9.36	1.97	48.18
(3) 2.5°C, 15% (GFDL × 0.65)	13.25	3.79	7.86	5.78	7.81	(0.47)	38.02
(4) 2.5°C, 7% (UKMO × 0.5)	11.40	(0.61)	4.26	3.02	4.71	(0.06)	22.72
(5) 1.5°C, 7% (GFDL × 0.33)	10.28	2.17	3.85	4.08	5.30	0.46	26.13

Table A4.3   MAPPS and BIOME–BGC ecological change, dieback scenario (billions 1998 USD)

Climate scenario	NE	SE	MW	GP	SW	NW	Total
(1) 5°C, 15% (UKMO × 1.0)	2.60	(1.59)	1.50	0.17	0.34	0.60	3.60
(2) 5°C, 7% (OSU × 1.0)	5.19	1.81	5.46	2.91	3.59	0.89	19.85
(3) 2.5°C, 15% (GFDL × 0.65)	6.14	1.64	3.88	3.48	3.22	(0.19)	18.16
(4) 2.5°C, 7% (UKMO × 0.5)	2.43	(0.13)	0.17	0.17	0.32	0.07	3.03
(5) 1.5°C, 7% (GFDL × 0.33)	5.31	1.46	1.56	2.45	2.34	0.37	13.49

Table A4.4   MAPPS and BIOME–BGC ecological change, regeneration scenario (billions 1998 USD)

Climate scenario	NE	SE	MW	GP	SW	NW	Total
(1) 5°C, 15% (UKMO × 1.0)*	–	–	–	–	–	–	–
(2) 5°C, 7% (OSU × 1.0)	6.76	0.76	6.93	3.42	4.51	0.48	22.84
(3) 2.5°C, 15% (GFDL × 0.65)	8.91	1.04	3.59	3.87	4.39	(1.24)	20.56
(4) 2.5°C, 7% (UKMO × 0.5)	8.48	(3.76)	0.01	1.01	1.55	(0.60)	6.69
(5) 1.5°C, 7% (GFDL × 0.33)	7.78	0.83	1.11	2.87	3.28	0.20	16.06

Note: *The file for this scenario was corrupted, and therefore not used in this analysis.

Table A4.5   MAPPS and CENTURY ecological change, dieback scenario (billions 1998 USD)

Climate scenario	NE	SE	MW	GP	SW	NW	Total
(1) 5°C, 15% (UKMO × 1.0)	6.04	(1.75)	4.28	1.53	2.47	0.35	12.93
(2) 5°C, 7% (OSU × 1.0)	6.79	1.57	7.13	3.74	4.60	0.50	24.32
(3) 2.5°C, 15% (GFDL × 0.65)	6.82	1.73	4.55	4.15	3.79	(0.72)	20.34
(4) 2.5°C, 7% (UKMO × 0.5)	8.37	0.15	3.09	1.57	2.55	(0.39)	15.34
(5) 1.5°C, 7% (GFDL × 0.33)	6.63	4.46	1.94	2.82	2.97	0.21	19.03

Table A4.6   MAPPS and CENTURY ecological change, regeneration scenario (billions 1998 USD)

Climate scenario	NE	SE	MW	GP	SW	NW	Total
(1) 5°C, 15% (UKMO × 1.0)	7.49	(1.30)	3.27	1.69	2.87	1.05	15.07
(2) 5°C, 7% (OSU × 1.0)	8.21	3.39	8.18	4.07	5.57	0.54	29.96
(3) 2.5°C, 15% (GFDL × 0.65)	10.44	0.94	4.78	4.77	5.48	(1.75)	24.65
(4) 2.5°C, 7% (UKMO × 0.5)	13.76	(3.10)	2.36	2.83	4.39	(1.27)	18.96
(5) 1.5°C, 7% (GFDL × 0.33)	9.64	0.67	1.95	3.65	4.39	(0.67)	19.62

Table A4.7   BIOME2 and TEM ecological change, dieback scenario (billions 1998 USD)

Climate scenario	NE	SE	MW	GP	SW	NW	Total
(1) 5°C, 15% (UKMO × 1.0)	11.81	5.16	8.27	4.81	6.93	0.61	37.61
(2) 5°C, 7% (OSU × 1.0)	11.12	4.79	9.57	6.91	7.84	0.99	41.22
(3) 2.5°C, 15% (GFDL × 0.65)	7.73	4.65	4.68	4.46	5.04	0.34	26.89
(4) 2.5°C, 7% (UKMO × 0.5)	7.73	2.99	3.54	2.63	3.71	0.39	20.99
(5) 1.5°C, 7% (GFDL × 0.33)	5.31	3.04	1.58	2.69	2.83	0.28	15.73

Table A4.8   BIOME2 and TEM ecological change, regeneration scenario (billions 1998 USD)

Climate scenario	NE	SE	MW	GP	SW	NW	Total
(1) 5°C, 15% (UKMO × 1.0)	15.30	5.61	8.47	5.38	7.93	1.83	44.52
(2) 5°C, 7% (OSU × 1.0)	12.93	5.58	10.11	6.56	8.66	1.45	45.31
(3) 2.5°C, 15% (GFDL × 0.65)	10.07	4.73	4.99	4.84	5.90	1.09	31.60
(4) 2.5°C, 7% (UKMO × 0.5)	9.46	2.62	3.58	2.96	4.38	1.58	24.57
(5) 1.5°C, 7% (GFDL × 0.33)	6.58	3.89	1.84	2.67	3.39	0.42	18.80

Table A4.9   BIOME2 and BIOME–BGC ecological change, dieback scenario (billions 1998 USD)

Climate scenario	NE	SE	MW	GP	SW	NW	Total
(1) 5°C, 15% (UKMO × 1.0)	5.99	0.34	3.04	2.07	2.22	0.41	14.09
(2) 5°C, 7% (OSU × 1.0)	4.74	2.14	3.99	3.80	3.39	0.70	18.75
(3) 2.5°C, 15% (GFDL × 0.65)	4.41	2.36	1.92	3.42	2.71	(0.11)	14.74
(4) 2.5°C, 7% (UKMO × 0.5)	4.19	1.85	0.74	1.17	1.46	0.61	10.02
(5) 1.5°C, 7% (GFDL × 0.33)	3.73	2.18	0.31	2.03	1.76	0.12	10.12

Table A4.10 *BIOME2 and BIOME–BGC ecological change, regeneration scenario (billions 1998 USD)*

Climate scenario	NE	SE	MW	GP	SW	NW	Total
(1) 5°C, 15% (UKMO × 1.0)	9.04	1.46	2.83	2.54	3.22	1.38	20.47
(2) 5°C, 7% (OSU × 1.0)	6.77	3.10	5.04	4.55	4.34	0.80	24.61
(3) 2.5°C, 15% (GFDL × 0.65)	6.79	3.07	2.21	3.35	3.61	0.80	19.82
(4) 2.5°C, 7% (UKMO × 0.5)	6.24	1.86	0.84	1.57	2.27	1.11	13.89
(5) 1.5°C, 7% (GFDL × 0.33)	5.07	2.91	0.57	2.37	2.35	0.32	13.59

Table A4.11 *BIOME2 and CENTURY ecological change, dieback scenario (billions 1998 USD)*

Climate scenario	NE	SE	MW	GP	SW	NW	Total
(1) 5°C, 15% (UKMO × 1.0)	8.87	1.99	5.52	3.37	4.39	0.28	24.45
(2) 5°C, 7% (OSU × 1.0)	5.84	2.77	4.93	4.33	4.15	0.78	22.81
(3) 2.5°C, 15% (GFDL × 0.65)	5.06	3.22	2.38	3.30	3.19	(0.02)	17.13
(4) 2.5°C, 7% (UKMO × 0.5)	5.56	2.57	1.86	1.76	2.40	0.73	14.88
(5) 1.5°C, 7% (GFDL × 0.33)	3.99	2.29	0.51	2.12	1.91	0.12	10.95

Table A4.12 *BIOME2 and CENTURY ecological change, regeneration scenario (billions 1998 USD)*

Climate scenario	NE	SE	MW	GP	SW	NW	Total
(1) 5°C, 15% (UKMO × 1.0)	12.05	3.28	5.50	3.86	5.37	1.37	31.41
(2) 5°C, 7% (OSU × 1.0)	7.79	3.39	5.91	4.92	5.06	0.72	27.79
(3) 2.5°C, 15% (GFDL × 0.65)	7.40	3.09	2.69	3.79	4.04	0.81	21.82
(4) 2.5°C, 7% (UKMO × 0.5)	8.05	2.40	2.23	2.29	3.33	1.17	19.46
(5) 1.5°C, 7% (GFDL × 0.33)	5.33	3.25	0.81	2.12	2.55	0.31	14.37

Table A4.13 *DOLY and TEM ecological change, dieback scenario (billions 1998 USD)*

Climate scenario	NE	SE	MW	GP	SW	NW	Total
(1) 5°C, 15% (UKMO × 1.0)	12.20	4.80	9.64	6.08	7.92	0.42	41.06
(2) 5°C, 7% (OSU × 1.0)	11.54	4.09	9.76	6.36	7.68	0.11	39.54
(3) 2.5°C, 15% (GFDL × 0.65)	10.53	3.52	8.68	5.95	7.06	(0.04)	35.71
(4) 2.5°C, 7% (UKMO × 0.5)	7.65	2.04	4.59	3.58	4.24	0.02	22.11
(5) 1.5°C, 7% (GFDL × 0.33)	6.55	2.38	4.72	3.80	4.14	0.14	21.74

*Table A4.14   DOLY and TEM ecological change, regeneration scenario
(billions 1998 USD)*

Climate scenario	NE	SE	MW	GP	SW	NW	Total
(1) 5°C, 15% (UKMO × 1.0)	13.18	5.26	8.80	5.72	8.12	1.55	42.63
(2) 5°C, 7% (OSU × 1.0)	13.00	4.76	9.83	6.20	8.44	1.42	43.64
(3) 2.5°C, 15% (GFDL × 0.65)	11.86	2.73	9.20	6.45	7.73	0.54	38.52
(4) 2.5°C, 7% (UKMO × 0.5)	8.84	1.77	4.40	3.50	4.89	0.25	23.62
(5) 1.5°C, 7% (GFDL × 0.33)	7.50	0.94	5.02	4.06	4.55	0.31	22.38

*Table A4.15   DOLY and BIOME–BGC ecological change, dieback scenario
(billions 1998 USD)*

Climate scenario	NE	SE	MW	GP	SW	NW	Total
(1) 5°C, 15% (UKMO × 1.0)	4.06	1.19	2.74	2.38	2.14	0.27	12.78
(2) 5°C, 7% (OSU × 1.0)	4.77	2.07	3.63	2.96	2.97	(0.20)	16.20
(3) 2.5°C, 15% (GFDL × 0.65)	6.97	1.43	5.62	4.58	4.46	(0.02)	23.03
(4) 2.5°C, 7% (UKMO × 0.5)	6.90	0.02	2.61	3.07	2.91	(0.02)	15.51
(5) 1.5°C, 7% (GFDL × 0.33)	5.31	1.99	3.45	3.30	3.15	0.46	17.66

*Table A4.16   DOLY and BIOME–BGC ecological change, regeneration
scenario (billions 1998 USD)*

Climate scenario	NE	SE	MW	GP	SW	NW	Total
(1) 5°C, 15% (UKMO × 1.0)	5.77	0.02	2.58	2.61	2.63	0.54	14.17
(2) 5°C, 7% (OSU × 1.0)	6.68	1.50	4.35	3.42	3.91	0.72	20.58
(3) 2.5°C, 15% (GFDL × 0.65)	9.53	1.13	7.03	5.77	5.83	(0.41)	28.87
(4) 2.5°C, 7% (UKMO × 0.5)	8.90	0.66	2.35	3.34	3.73	0.25	19.22
(5) 1.5°C, 7% (GFDL × 0.33)	7.30	1.44	4.24	3.91	4.15	0.68	21.72

*Table A4.17   DOLY and CENTURY ecological change, dieback scenario
(billions 1998 USD)*

Climate scenario	NE	SE	MW	GP	SW	NW	Total
(1) 5°C, 15% (UKMO × 1.0)	8.19	1.96	6.28	4.38	4.89	0.12	25.78
(2) 5°C, 7% (OSU × 1.0)	5.81	1.49	4.81	3.78	3.63	(0.06)	19.45
(3) 2.5°C, 15% (GFDL × 0.65)	7.80	0.87	6.57	5.38	5.02	(0.15)	25.50
(4) 2.5°C, 7% (UKMO × 0.5)	7.38	0.51	3.93	3.37	3.69	(0.31)	18.56
(5) 1.5°C, 7% (GFDL × 0.33)	6.10	2.57	3.86	3.33	3.66	(0.12)	19.39

*Table A4.18   DOLY and CENTURY ecological change, regeneration
scenario (billions 1998 USD)*

Climate scenario	NE	SE	MW	GP	SW	NW	Total
(1) 5°C, 15% (UKMO × 1.0)	9.39	2.40	5.66	4.15	5.30	1.09	27.98
(2) 5°C, 7% (OSU × 1.0)	7.20	2.01	4.97	3.69	4.31	1.22	23.38
(3) 2.5°C, 15% (GFDL × 0.65)	9.11	1.48	6.73	5.17	5.72	0.39	28.58
(4) 2.5°C, 7% (UKMO × 0.5)	9.03	0.55	3.65	3.49	4.44	0.37	21.54
(5) 1.5°C, 7% (GFDL × 0.33)	7.46	0.48	4.60	4.14	4.27	0.07	21.03

Appendix B

PRODUCER SURPLUS

Regional present values of producer surplus from alternative ecological scenarios (billions 1998 USD).

*Table B4.1   MAPPS and TEM ecological change, dieback scenario
              (billions 1998 USD)*

Climate scenario	NE	SE	MW	GP	SW	NW	Total
(1) 5°C, 15% (UKMO × 1.0)	2.25	(5.81)	0.97	(0.13)	(0.34)	(0.41)	(3.47)
(2) 5°C, 7% (OSU × 1.0)	(0.38)	(5.96)	0.92	0.51	(0.78)	(0.72)	(6.41)
(3) 2.5°C, 15% (GFDL × 0.65)	(0.07)	(3.19)	0.18	1.86	0.06	(0.63)	(1.78)
(4) 2.5°C, 7% (UKMO × 0.5)	2.49	(1.84)	1.26	1.49	0.97	(1.20)	3.16
(5) 1.5°C, 7% (GFDL × 0.33)	2.95	(0.83)	(0.24)	1.36	0.68	0.00	3.94

*Table B4.2   MAPPS and TEM ecological change, regeneration scenario
              (billions 1998 USD)*

Climate scenario	NE	SE	MW	GP	SW	NW	Total
(1) 5°C, 15% (UKMO × 1.0)	3.78	(5.78)	(0.31)	0.08	0.02	(0.08)	(2.29)
(2) 5°C, 7% (OSU × 1.0)	(0.59)	(7.17)	0.52	0.20	(0.74)	(0.14)	(7.94)
(3) 2.5°C, 15% (GFDL × 0.65)	4.60	(3.86)	0.37	1.91	1.45	(1.79)	2.67
(4) 2.5°C, 7% (UKMO × 0.5)	6.76	(4.71)	0.25	0.94	1.30	(0.77)	3.78
(5) 1.5°C, 7% (GFDL × 0.33)	5.81	(1.78)	(0.02)	2.09	2.01	(0.22)	7.86

Table B4.3   MAPPS and BIOME–BGC ecological change, dieback scenario (billions 1998 USD)

Climate scenario	NE	SE	MW	GP	SW	NW	Total
(1) 5°C, 15% (UKMO × 1.0)	2.30	(1.86)	1.24	0.02	0.12	0.55	2.38
(2) 5°C, 7% (OSU × 1.0)	(0.48)	(3.21)	0.55	0.38	(0.59)	0.01	(3.34)
(3) 2.5°C, 15% (GFDL × 0.65)	1.84	(2.16)	0.17	1.56	0.06	(0.84)	0.60
(4) 2.5°C, 7% (UKMO × 0.5)	1.99	(0.52)	(0.22)	(0.04)	0.00	0.00	1.22
(5) 1.5°C, 7% (GFDL × 0.33)	2.97	(0.60)	(0.46)	1.42	0.63	0.01	3.96

Table B4.4   MAPPS and BIOME–BGC ecological change, regeneration scenario (billions 1998 USD)

Climate scenario	NE	SE	MW	GP	SW	NW	Total
(1) 5°C, 15% (UKMO × 1.0)*	–	–	–	–	–	–	–
(2) 5°C, 7% (OSU × 1.0)	0.00	(5.22)	1.09	0.40	(0.46)	(0.54)	(4.76)
(3) 2.5°C, 15% (GFDL × 0.65)	4.44	(2.90)	(0.27)	1.86	1.10	(1.92)	2.30
(4) 2.5°C, 7% (UKMO × 0.5)	7.23	(4.86)	(1.06)	0.46	0.64	(0.79)	1.60
(5) 1.5°C, 7% (GFDL × 0.33)	5.31	(1.35)	(1.03)	1.77	1.46	(0.19)	5.97

Note: *The file for this scenario was corrupted, and therefore not used in this analysis.

Table B4.5   MAPPS and CENTURY ecological change, dieback scenario (billions 1998 USD)

Climate scenario	NE	SE	MW	GP	SW	NW	Total
(1) 5°C, 15% (UKMO × 1.0)	2.42	(4.94)	1.16	(0.09)	(0.20)	(0.20)	(1.85)
(2) 5°C, 7% (OSU × 1.0)	(0.39)	(4.78)	0.91	0.53	(0.67)	(0.60)	(5.02)
(3) 2.5°C, 15% (GFDL × 0.65)	2.43	(2.15)	0.76	2.18	0.57	(1.39)	2.41
(4) 2.5°C, 7% (UKMO × 0.5)	6.23	(1.75)	1.24	0.61	0.98	(0.72)	6.60
(5) 1.5°C, 7% (GFDL × 0.33)	4.06	2.19	(0.28)	1.68	1.09	(0.18)	8.56

Table B4.6	*MAPPS and CENTURY ecological change, regeneration scenario (billions 1998 USD)*

Climate scenario	NE	SE	MW	GP	SW	NW	Total
(1) 5°C, 15% (UKMO × 1.0)	3.17	(5.12)	(0.47)	(0.25)	(0.31)	0.39	(2.58)
(2) 5°C, 7% (OSU × 1.0)	(0.40)	(4.22)	0.72	0.21	(0.76)	(0.78)	(5.23)
(3) 2.5°C, 15% (GFDL × 0.65)	5.10	(3.79)	0.14	2.37	1.53	(2.57)	2.80
(4) 2.5°C, 7% (UKMO × 0.5)	11.08	(5.48)	0.04	1.63	2.42	(1.69)	8.01
(5) 1.5°C, 7% (GFDL × 0.33)	6.71	(1.91)	(0.58)	2.35	2.24	(1.12)	7.68

Table B4.7	*BIOME2 and TEM ecological change, dieback scenario (billions 1998 USD)*

Climate scenario	NE	SE	MW	GP	SW	NW	Total
(1) 5°C, 15% (UKMO × 1.0)	1.72	(3.75)	(0.45)	0.31	(0.48)	(0.93)	(3.58)
(2) 5°C, 7% (OSU × 1.0)	(0.37)	(5.35)	(0.35)	1.77	(0.59)	(0.77)	(5.64)
(3) 2.5°C, 15% (GFDL × 0.65)	0.24	(1.97)	(1.81)	1.11	(0.47)	(0.81)	(3.72)
(4) 2.5°C, 7% (UKMO × 0.5)	2.68	(1.48)	(0.83)	0.38	(0.01)	(0.39)	0.35
(5) 1.5°C, 7% (GFDL × 0.33)	1.35	(0.46)	(1.85)	0.91	(0.07)	(0.32)	(0.44)

Table B4.8	*BIOME2 and TEM ecological change, regeneration scenario (billions 1998 USD)*

Climate scenario	NE	SE	MW	GP	SW	NW	Total
(1) 5°C, 15% (UKMO × 1.0)	4.40	(4.02)	(0.96)	0.51	(0.07)	0.15	0.00
(2) 5°C, 7% (OSU × 1.0)	0.52	(5.39)	(0.64)	1.00	(0.46)	(0.45)	(5.42)
(3) 2.5°C, 15% (GFDL × 0.65)	1.58	(2.76)	(2.34)	1.04	(0.33)	(0.21)	(3.02)
(4) 2.5°C, 7% (UKMO × 0.5)	3.65	(2.51)	(1.45)	0.37	0.12	0.68	0.85
(5) 1.5°C, 7% (GFDL × 0.33)	1.78	(0.35)	(2.31)	0.51	(0.15)	(0.31)	(0.84)

Table B4.9	*BIOME2 and BIOME–BGC ecological change, dieback scenario (billions 1998 USD)*

Climate scenario	NE	SE	MW	GP	SW	NW	Total
(1) 5°C, 15% (UKMO × 1.0)	2.83	(2.45)	0.31	0.65	(0.12)	(0.07)	1.13
(2) 5°C, 7% (OSU × 1.0)	(0.35)	(2.37)	(0.42)	1.52	(0.37)	(0.08)	(2.09)
(3) 2.5°C, 15% (GFDL × 0.65)	0.28	(1.29)	(1.64)	1.58	(0.32)	(0.73)	(2.10)
(4) 2.5°C, 7% (UKMO × 0.5)	2.25	0.13	(0.94)	0.30	0.04	0.32	2.08
(5) 1.5°C, 7% (GFDL × 0.33)	1.35	0.08	(1.76)	0.97	0.00	(0.25)	0.38

Table B4.10   BIOME2 and BIOME–BGC ecological change, regeneration scenario (billions 1998 USD)

Climate scenario	NE	SE	MW	GP	SW	NW	Total
(1) 5°C, 15% (UKMO × 1.0)	4.93	(2.16)	(0.71)	0.70	0.21	0.74	3.72
(2) 5°C, 7% (OSU × 1.0)	0.52	(2.42)	(0.37)	1.76	(0.26)	(0.17)	(0.93)
(3) 2.5°C, 15% (GFDL × 0.65)	1.66	(1.45)	(2.22)	1.06	(0.14)	0.02	(1.05)
(4) 2.5°C, 7% (UKMO × 0.5)	3.49	(0.57)	(1.53)	0.33	0.24	0.68	2.66
(5) 1.5°C, 7% (GFDL × 0.33)	1.85	0.06	(2.23)	0.93	(0.02)	(0.18)	0.42

Table B4.11   BIOME2 and CENTURY ecological change, dieback scenario (billions 1998 USD)

Climate scenario	NE	SE	MW	GP	SW	NW	Total
(1) 5°C, 15% (UKMO × 1.0)	2.48	(3.66)	(0.01)	0.51	(0.32)	(0.70)	(1.70)
(2) 5°C, 7% (OSU × 1.0)	(0.30)	(2.64)	(0.37)	1.58	(0.37)	(0.15)	(2.25)
(3) 2.5°C, 15% (GFDL × 0.65)	0.52	(0.80)	(1.55)	1.26	(0.17)	(0.72)	(1.45)
(4) 2.5°C, 7% (UKMO × 0.5)	2.23	(0.35)	(1.01)	0.27	(0.04)	0.22	1.32
(5) 1.5°C, 7% (GFDL × 0.33)	1.35	(0.04)	(1.77)	0.94	(0.02)	(0.28)	0.18

Table B4.12   BIOME2 and CENTURY ecological change, regeneration scenario (billions 1998 USD)

Climate scenario	NE	SE	MW	GP	SW	NW	Total
(1) 5°C, 15% (UKMO × 1.0)	4.83	(3.09)	(0.76)	0.63	0.06	0.27	1.92
(2) 5°C, 7% (OSU × 1.0)	0.55	(3.00)	(0.35)	1.69	(0.26)	(0.39)	(1.76)
(3) 2.5°C, 15% (GFDL × 0.65)	1.71	(1.94)	(2.23)	1.24	(0.15)	(0.06)	(1.42)
(4) 2.5°C, 7% (UKMO × 0.5)	3.71	(1.45)	(1.53)	0.34	0.13	0.51	1.70
(5) 1.5°C, 7% (GFDL × 0.33)	1.82	0.14	(2.23)	0.55	(0.04)	(0.22)	0.02

Table B4.13   DOLY and TEM ecological change, dieback scenario (billions 1998 USD)

Climate scenario	NE	SE	MW	GP	SW	NW	Total
(1) 5°C, 15% (UKMO × 1.0)	0.34	(5.66)	(0.61)	0.77	(0.80)	(1.39)	(7.34)
(2) 5°C, 7% (OSU × 1.0)	0.14	(5.97)	(0.09)	1.26	(0.70)	(1.64)	(7.00)
(3) 2.5°C, 15% (GFDL × 0.65)	1.38	(4.57)	0.77	1.85	0.34	(1.44)	(1.66)
(4) 2.5°C, 7% (UKMO × 0.5)	1.58	(3.32)	(0.66)	0.86	(0.21)	(0.91)	(2.66)
(5) 1.5°C, 7% (GFDL × 0.33)	1.58	(2.01)	0.41	1.58	0.50	(0.63)	1.45

Table B4.14   DOLY and TEM ecological change, regeneration scenario (billions 1998 USD)

Climate scenario	NE	SE	MW	GP	SW	NW	Total
(1) 5°C, 15% (UKMO × 1.0)	0.78	(5.71)	(1.94)	0.17	(1.00)	(0.35)	(8.06)
(2) 5°C, 7% (OSU × 1.0)	0.33	(6.44)	(1.14)	0.52	(0.87)	(0.53)	(8.14)
(3) 2.5°C, 15% (GFDL × 0.65)	1.52	(6.41)	0.26	1.83	0.13	(1.04)	(3.71)
(4) 2.5°C, 7% (UKMO × 0.5)	2.29	(4.01)	(1.26)	0.58	0.08	(0.76)	(3.09)
(5) 1.5°C, 7% (GFDL × 0.33)	1.97	(3.94)	0.24	1.59	0.48	(0.54)	(0.20)

Table B4.15   DOLY and BIOME–BGC ecological change, dieback scenario (billions 1998 USD)

Climate scenario	NE	SE	MW	GP	SW	NW	Total
(1) 5°C, 15% (UKMO × 1.0)	0.71	(1.78)	(0.18)	0.87	(0.33)	(0.24)	(0.94)
(2) 5°C, 7% (OSU × 1.0)	0.18	(1.98)	(0.33)	0.91	(0.40)	(0.91)	(2.53)
(3) 2.5°C, 15% (GFDL × 0.65)	1.68	(3.26)	1.03	2.21	0.57	(0.84)	1.39
(4) 2.5°C, 7% (UKMO × 0.5)	4.66	(1.96)	0.66	2.07	1.26	(0.37)	6.32
(5) 1.5°C, 7% (GFDL × 0.33)	2.23	(0.73)	0.77	1.92	0.87	(0.01)	5.05

Table B4.16   DOLY and BIOME–BGC ecological change, regeneration scenario (billions 1998 USD)

Climate scenario	NE	SE	MW	GP	SW	NW	Total
(1) 5°C, 15% (UKMO × 1.0)	5.77	0.02	2.58	2.61	2.63	0.54	14.17
(2) 5°C, 7% (OSU × 1.0)	6.68	1.50	4.35	3.42	3.91	0.72	20.58
(3) 2.5°C, 15% (GFDL × 0.65)	9.53	1.13	7.03	5.77	5.83	(0.41)	28.87
(4) 2.5°C, 7% (UKMO × 0.5)	8.90	0.66	2.35	3.34	3.73	0.25	19.22
(5) 1.5°C, 7% (GFDL × 0.33)	7.30	1.44	4.24	3.91	4.15	0.68	21.72

Table B4.17   DOLY and CENTURY ecological change, dieback scenario (billions 1998 USD)

Climate scenario	NE	SE	MW	GP	SW	NW	Total
(1) 5°C, 15% (UKMO × 1.0)	8.19	1.96	6.28	4.38	4.89	0.12	25.78
(2) 5°C, 7% (OSU × 1.0)	5.81	1.49	4.81	3.78	3.63	(0.06)	19.45
(3) 2.5°C, 15% (GFDL × 0.65)	7.80	0.87	6.57	5.38	5.02	(0.15)	25.50
(4) 2.5°C, 7% (UKMO × 0.5)	7.38	0.51	3.93	3.37	3.69	(0.31)	18.56
(5) 1.5°C, 7% (GFDL × 0.33)	6.10	2.57	3.86	3.33	3.66	(0.12)	19.39

*Table B4.18   DOLY and CENTURY ecological change, regeneration
scenario (billions 1998 USD)*

Climate scenario	NE	SE	MW	GP	SW	NW	Total
(1) 5°C, 15% (UKMO × 1.0)	9.39	2.40	5.66	4.15	5.30	1.09	27.98
(2) 5°C, 7% (OSU × 1.0)	7.20	2.01	4.97	3.69	4.31	1.22	23.38
(3) 2.5°C, 15% (GFDL × 0.65)	9.11	1.48	6.73	5.17	5.72	0.39	28.58
(4) 2.5°C, 7% (UKMO × 0.5)	9.03	0.55	3.65	3.49	4.44	0.37	21.54
(5) 1.5°C, 7% (GFDL × 0.33)	7.46	0.48	4.60	4.14	4.27	0.07	21.03

Appendix C: *2060*

NET SURPLUS

Regional annual 2060 net impacts from alternative ecological scenarios (billions 1998 USD).

Table C4.1   MAPPS and TEM ecological change, dieback scenario
            (billions 1998 USD)

Climate scenario	NE	SE	MW	GP	SW	NW	Total
(1) 5°C, 15% (UKMO × 1.0)	4.00	(1.26)	3.71	0.94	1.49	(0.34)	8.52
(2) 5°C, 7% (OSU × 1.0)	3.78	1.26	4.38	2.24	2.42	(0.06)	14.02
(3) 2.5°C, 15% (GFDL × 0.65)	1.96	0.85	1.97	1.62	1.30	(0.05)	7.63
(4) 2.5°C, 7% (UKMO × 0.5)	2.12	(0.37)	1.73	0.47	0.76	(0.11)	4.61
(5) 1.5°C, 7% (GFDL × 0.33)	1.04	0.90	0.90	0.44	0.77	0.14	4.18

Table C4.2   MAPPS and TEM ecological change, regeneration scenario
            (billions 1998 USD)

Climate scenario	NE	SE	MW	GP	SW	NW	Total
(1) 5°C, 15% (UKMO × 1.0)	3.42	0.61	2.57	0.99	1.59	(0.24)	8.97
(2) 5°C, 7% (OSU × 1.0)	3.88	1.33	4.34	2.18	2.47	(0.14)	14.07
(3) 2.5°C, 15% (GFDL × 0.65)	2.47	1.14	1.94	1.53	1.48	(0.11)	8.45
(4) 2.5°C, 7% (UKMO × 0.5)	1.03	1.22	0.94	0.53	0.87	0.22	4.81
(5) 1.5°C, 7% (GFDL × 0.33)	1.51	0.31	1.06	1.06	0.79	(0.06)	4.67

Table C4.3   MAPPS and BIOME–BGC ecological change, dieback scenario (billions 1998 USD)

Climate scenario	NE	SE	MW	GP	SW	NW	Total
(1) 5°C, 15% (UKMO × 1.0)	2.25	(2.94)	2.18	0.12	0.18	(0.41)	1.40
(2) 5°C, 7% (OSU × 1.0)	1.79	0.01	2.44	1.25	1.06	(0.18)	6.38
(3) 2.5°C, 15% (GFDL × 0.65)	0.92	0.94	1.06	1.12	0.57	(0.11)	4.51
(4) 2.5°C, 7% (UKMO × 0.5)	1.24	(1.12)	0.96	0.07	0.12	(0.21)	1.05
(5) 1.5°C, 7% (GFDL × 0.33)	0.74	(0.40)	0.65	1.03	0.32	(0.17)	2.16

Table C4.4   MAPPS and BIOME–BGC ecological change, regeneration scenario (billions 1998 USD)

Climate scenario	NE	SE	MW	GP	SW	NW	Total
(1) 5°C, 15% (UKMO × 1.0)*	–	–	–	–	–	–	–
(2) 5°C, 7% (OSU × 1.0)	2.28	(0.91)	3.29	1.58	1.16	(0.39)	7.01
(3) 2.5°C, 15% (GFDL × 0.65)	0.99	0.97	0.87	0.39	0.77	0.14	4.12
(4) 2.5°C, 7% (UKMO × 0.5)	0.76	(0.44)	0.47	0.09	0.15	(0.07)	0.98
(5) 1.5°C, 7% (GFDL × 0.33)	1.27	(0.72)	0.72	1.25	0.41	(0.25)	2.69

Note: *The file for this scenario was corrupted, and therefore not used in this analysis.

Table C4.5   MAPPS and CENTURY ecological change, dieback scenario (billions 1998 USD)

Climate scenario	NE	SE	MW	GP	SW	NW	Total
(1) 5°C, 15% (UKMO × 1.0)	3.39	(2.78)	3.21	0.50	0.79	(0.50)	4.61
(2) 5°C, 7% (OSU × 1.0)	2.38	(0.40)	3.30	1.66	1.37	(0.25)	8.08
(3) 2.5°C, 15% (GFDL × 0.65)	1.23	0.86	1.44	1.48	0.73	(0.28)	5.45
(4) 2.5°C, 7% (UKMO × 0.5)	0.74	0.24	0.61	0.24	0.39	0.00	2.21
(5) 1.5°C, 7% (GFDL × 0.33)	0.83	0.65	0.60	0.93	0.39	(0.47)	2.91

Table C4.6   MAPPS and CENTURY ecological change, regeneration scenario (billions 1998 USD)

Climate scenario	NE	SE	MW	GP	SW	NW	Total
(1) 5°C, 15% (UKMO × 1.0)	3.20	(1.60)	2.23	0.51	0.81	(0.57)	4.57
(2) 5°C, 7% (OSU × 1.0)	2.58	(0.52)	3.47	1.69	1.43	(0.31)	8.33
(3) 2.5°C, 15% (GFDL × 0.65)	1.51	0.60	1.30	0.97	0.93	(0.04)	5.26
(4) 2.5°C, 7% (UKMO × 0.5)	0.86	0.39	0.64	0.28	0.47	0.00	2.66
(5) 1.5°C, 7% (GFDL × 0.33)	0.80	0.51	0.63	0.44	0.51	0.02	2.90

Table C4.7   BIOME2 and TEM ecological change, dieback scenario (billions 1998 USD)

Climate scenario	NE	SE	MW	GP	SW	NW	Total
(1) 5°C, 15% (UKMO × 1.0)	4.77	0.14	3.49	2.01	2.31	0.21	12.93
(2) 5°C, 7% (OSU × 1.0)	3.19	1.14	3.26	3.00	2.27	(0.04)	12.83
(3) 2.5°C, 15% (GFDL × 0.65)	2.11	(0.02)	1.63	3.73	1.76	(0.48)	8.72
(4) 2.5°C, 7% (UKMO × 0.5)	2.68	0.17	1.71	1.06	1.16	(0.21)	6.55
(5) 1.5°C, 7% (GFDL × 0.33)	1.24	0.61	0.73	1.38	0.92	(0.18)	4.72

Table C4.8   BIOME2 and TEM ecological change, regeneration scenario (billions 1998 USD)

Climate scenario	NE	SE	MW	GP	SW	NW	Total
(1) 5°C,15% (UKMO × 1.0)	4.20	1.69	3.15	1.76	2.51	0.54	13.84
(2) 5°C, 7% (OSU × 1.0)	3.45	1.76	3.15	2.57	2.38	(0.01)	13.31
(3) 2.5°C, 15% (GFDL × 0.65)	2.57	1.36	1.75	2.08	1.92	(0.15)	9.52
(4) 2.5°C, 7% (UKMO × 0.5)	2.90	(0.05)	1.64	1.11	1.29	0.08	6.97
(5) 1.5°C, 7% (GFDL × 0.33)	1.43	0.77	0.70	1.10	0.96	(0.07)	4.89

Table C4.9   BIOME2 and BIOME–BGC ecological change, dieback scenario (billions 1998 USD)

Climate scenario	NE	SE	MW	GP	SW	NW	Total
(1) 5°C, 15% (UKMO × 1.0)	3.34	(2.10)	2.12	1.24	0.97	0.00	5.58
(2) 5°C, 7% (OSU × 1.0)	1.57	(0.96)	1.98	2.64	1.06	(0.09)	6.21
(3) 2.5°C, 15% (GFDL × 0.65)	1.19	0.47	0.92	1.81	1.07	(0.35)	5.11
(4) 2.5°C, 7% (UKMO × 0.5)	0.38	1.90	(0.77)	1.03	0.70	0.58	0.05
(5) 1.5°C, 7% (GFDL × 0.33)	0.84	0.30	0.37	1.18	0.59	(0.19)	3.09

Table C4.10   BIOME2 and BIOME–BGC ecological change, regeneration scenario (billions 1998 USD)

Climate scenario	NE	SE	MW	GP	SW	NW	Total
(1) 5°C, 15% (UKMO × 1.0)	3.00	(0.94)	1.59	1.10	1.10	0.14	5.99
(2) 5°C, 7% (OSU × 1.0)	1.84	(0.33)	1.88	2.16	1.19	(0.07)	6.68
(3) 2.5°C, 15% (GFDL × 0.65)	1.69	0.19	0.94	1.98	1.25	(0.30)	5.75
(4) 2.5°C, 7% (UKMO × 0.5)	1.89	(0.40)	0.78	0.68	0.70	0.11	3.74
(5) 1.5°C, 7% (GFDL × 0.33)	1.07	0.11	0.35	1.20	0.70	(0.18)	3.26

Table C4.11   BIOME2 and CENTURY ecological change, dieback scenario (billions 1998 USD)

Climate scenario	NE	SE	MW	GP	SW	NW	Total
(1) 5°C, 15% (UKMO × 1.0)	0.08	3.13	0.17	2.29	1.32	1.53	0.11
(2) 5°C, 7% (OSU × 1.0)	1.73	0.18	1.92	2.16	1.23	(0.15)	7.08
(3) 2.5°C, 15% (GFDL × 0.65)	1.39	0.77	1.12	1.58	1.18	(0.31)	5.73
(4) 2.5°C, 7% (UKMO × 0.5)	2.29	(0.54)	1.36	0.90	0.87	0.04	4.92
(5) 1.5°C, 7% (GFDL × 0.33)	0.90	0.34	0.42	1.22	0.64	(0.17)	3.34

Table C4.12   BIOME2 and CENTURY ecological change, regeneration scenario (billions 1998 USD)

Climate scenario	NE	SE	MW	GP	SW	NW	Total
(1) 5°C, 15% (UKMO × 1.0)	3.68	0.07	2.28	1.45	1.73	0.30	9.52
(2) 5°C, 7% (OSU × 1.0)	2.15	(0.55)	2.24	2.77	1.36	(0.32)	7.63
(3) 2.5°C, 15% (GFDL × 0.65)	1.82	0.40	1.07	1.92	1.36	(0.26)	6.31
(4) 2.5°C, 7% (UKMO × 0.5)	2.18	(0.19)	1.07	0.83	0.94	0.18	5.02
(5) 1.5°C, 7% (GFDL × 0.33)	1.10	0.48	0.38	0.98	0.72	(0.19)	3.47

Table C4.13   DOLY and TEM ecological change, dieback scenario (billions 1998 USD)

Climate scenario	NE	SE	MW	GP	SW	NW	Total
(1) 5°C, 15% (UKMO × 1.0)	4.52	0.14	4.08	2.78	2.64	(0.15)	14.03
(2) 5°C, 7% (OSU × 1.0)	3.41	0.72	3.79	2.73	2.19	(0.11)	12.73
(3) 2.5°C, 15% (GFDL × 0.65)	2.45	2.14	2.12	1.11	1.81	0.37	10.01
(4) 2.5°C, 7% (UKMO × 0.5)	2.95	(1.77)	2.45	2.17	1.33	(0.41)	6.73
(5) 1.5°C, 7% (GFDL × 0.33)	1.32	0.76	1.20	0.96	0.92	0.05	5.20

Table C4.14   DOLY and TEM ecological change, regeneration scenario
(billions 1998 USD)

Climate scenario	NE	SE	MW	GP	SW	NW	Total
(1) 5°C, 15% (UKMO × 1.0)	4.22	1.18	3.33	2.22	2.80	(0.05)	13.71
(2) 5°C, 7% (OSU × 1.0)	3.61	1.72	3.36	2.28	2.35	0.06	13.38
(3) 2.5°C, 15% (GFDL × 0.65)	3.26	(1.24)	3.19	3.67	1.96	(0.14)	10.68
(4) 2.5°C, 7% (UKMO × 0.5)	1.75	1.06	1.45	0.84	1.23	0.19	6.53
(5) 1.5°C, 7% (GFDL × 0.33)	1.83	(1.36)	1.59	2.18	0.93	0.13	5.30

Table C4.15   DOLY and BIOME–BGC ecological change, dieback scenario
(billions 1998 USD)

Climate scenario	NE	SE	MW	GP	SW	NW	Total
(1) 5°C, 15% (UKMO × 1.0)	2.12	(1.60)	2.01	1.69	0.98	(0.35)	4.84
(2) 5°C, 7% (OSU × 1.0)	1.66	(1.42)	2.44	2.15	0.87	(0.21)	5.51
(3) 2.5°C, 15% (GFDL × 0.65)	1.19	5.43	(0.08)	(3.16)	1.12	1.18	5.69
(4) 2.5°C, 7% (UKMO × 0.5)	1.31	(1.23)	1.03	1.11	0.55	(0.25)	2.54
(5) 1.5°C, 7% (GFDL × 0.33)	1.04	(0.85)	1.16	1.69	0.59	0.04	3.67

Table C4.16   DOLY and BIOME–BGC ecological change, regeneration
scenario (billions 1998 USD)

Climate scenario	NE	SE	MW	GP	SW	NW	Total
(1) 5°C, 15% (UKMO × 1.0)	1.72	(0.34)	1.11	0.99	1.06	(0.17)	4.37
(2) 5°C, 7% (OSU × 1.0)	1.95	(0.33)	1.92	1.77	1.03	(0.22)	6.11
(3) 2.5°C, 15% (GFDL × 0.65)	1.92	(0.39)	1.83	1.98	1.23	0.12	6.69
(4) 2.5°C, 7% (UKMO × 0.5)	3.17	(3.17)	1.26	2.08	1.44	(1.29)	3.49
(5) 1.5°C, 7% (GFDL × 0.33)	1.11	0.14	0.94	1.00	0.68	0.13	4.00

Table C4.17   DOLY and CENTURY ecological change, dieback scenario
(billions 1998 USD)

Climate scenario	NE	SE	MW	GP	SW	NW	Total
(1) 5°C, 15% (UKMO × 1.0)	3.36	(0.57)	3.08	2.27	1.82	(0.41)	9.55
(2) 5°C, 7% (OSU × 1.0)	1.84	(0.44)	2.35	1.92	1.07	(0.21)	6.55
(3) 2.5°C, 15% (GFDL × 0.65)	1.75	0.04	1.84	1.70	1.18	0.12	6.62
(4) 2.5°C, 7% (UKMO × 0.5)	1.32	0.31	1.13	0.78	0.81	0.02	4.38
(5) 1.5°C, 7% (GFDL × 0.33)	0.93	0.73	0.83	0.55	0.66	0.11	3.81

Table C4.18   DOLY and CENTURY ecological change, regeneration scenario (billions 1998 USD)

Climate scenario	NE	SE	MW	GP	SW	NW	Total
(1) 5°C, 15% (UKMO × 1.0)	4.19	(1.92)	2.94	2.67	2.17	(0.87)	9.16
(2) 5°C, 7% (OSU × 1.0)	2.08	0.32	2.05	1.55	1.26	(0.01)	7.23
(3) 2.5°C, 15% (GFDL × 0.65)	1.91	1.48	1.68	0.97	1.38	0.27	7.67
(4) 2.5°C, 7% (UKMO × 0.5)	8.44	(10.41)	2.27	5.27	3.34	(4.25)	4.67
(5) 1.5°C, 7% (GFDL × 0.33)	1.46	(1.14)	1.26	2.07	0.70	(0.24)	4.11

Appendix D: *2060*

PRODUCER SURPLUS

Regional annual 2060 producer surplus from alternative ecological scenarios (billions 1998 USD).

Table D4.1   MAPPS and TEM ecological change, dieback scenario (billions 1998 USD)

Climate scenario	NE	SE	MW	GP	SW	NW	Total
(1) 5°C, 15% (UKMO × 1.0)	1.86	(3.16)	1.84	(0.02)	(0.08)	(0.67)	(0.24)
(2) 5°C, 7% (OSU × 1.0)	0.31	(1.79)	1.38	0.68	(0.13)	(0.59)	(0.14)
(3) 2.5°C, 15% (GFDL × 0.65)	0.08	(0.81)	0.34	0.78	(0.08)	(0.34)	(0.04)
(4) 2.5°C, 7% (UKMO × 0.5)	1.04	(1.31)	0.80	(0.01)	(0.04)	(0.27)	0.20
(5) 1.5°C, 7% (GFDL × 0.33)	0.00	(0.02)	(0.01)	(0.04)	0.00	(0.01)	(0.08)

Table D4.2   MAPPS and TEM ecological change, regeneration scenario (billions 1998 USD)

Climate scenario	NE	SE	MW	GP	SW	NW	Total
(1) 5°C, 15% (UKMO × 1.0)	1.16	(1.38)	0.61	(0.01)	(0.07)	(0.58)	(0.27)
(2) 5°C, 7% (OSU × 1.0)	0.35	(1.78)	1.30	0.60	(0.12)	(0.67)	(0.32)
(3) 2.5°C, 15% (GFDL × 0.65)	0.32	(0.76)	0.08	0.57	(0.11)	(0.44)	(0.32)
(4) 2.5°C, 7% (UKMO × 0.5)	(0.15)	0.17	(0.08)	0.00	0.01	0.05	(0.02)
(5) 1.5°C, 7% (GFDL × 0.33)	0.38	(0.70)	0.08	0.55	(0.05)	(0.22)	0.05

Table D4.3   MAPPS and BIOME–BGC ecological change, dieback
scenario (billions 1998 USD)

Climate scenario	NE	SE	MW	GP	SW	NW	Total
(1) 5°C, 15% (UKMO × 1.0)	1.97	(3.19)	1.94	(0.01)	(0.02)	(0.45)	0.22
(2) 5°C, 7% (OSU × 1.0)	0.22	(1.38)	1.09	0.55	(0.09)	(0.41)	(0.01)
(3) 2.5°C, 15% (GFDL × 0.65)	0.09	0.21	0.34	0.76	(0.05)	(0.24)	1.12
(4) 2.5°C, 7% (UKMO × 0.5)	1.07	(1.27)	0.80	0.00	(0.01)	(0.25)	0.35
(5) 1.5°C, 7% (GFDL × 0.33)	0.28	(0.81)	0.25	0.81	(0.02)	(0.24)	0.26

Table D4.4   MAPPS and BIOME–BGC ecological change, regeneration
scenario (billions 1998 USD)

Climate scenario	NE	SE	MW	GP	SW	NW	Total
(1) 5°C, 15% (UKMO × 1.0)*	–	–	–	–	–	–	–
(2) 5°C, 7% (OSU × 1.0)	0.55	(2.42)	1.81	0.80	(0.11)	(0.65)	(0.01)
(3) 2.5°C, 15% (GFDL × 0.65)	(0.05)	0.05	(0.02)	(0.08)	0.00	(0.02)	(0.12)
(4) 2.5°C, 7% (UKMO × 0.5)	0.53	(0.63)	0.28	0.00	0.00	(0.11)	0.08
(5) 1.5°C, 7% (GFDL × 0.33)	0.67	(1.26)	0.20	0.98	(0.04)	(0.33)	0.21

Note: *The file for this regeneration scenario was corrupted, and therefore not used in this analysis.

Table D4.5   MAPPS and CENTURY ecological change, dieback scenario
(billions 1998 USD)

Climate scenario	NE	SE	MW	GP	SW	NW	Total
(1) 5°C, 15% (UKMO × 1.0)	2.24	(3.80)	2.22	(0.01)	(0.06)	(0.67)	(0.07)
(2) 5°C, 7% (OSU × 1.0)	0.39	(2.16)	1.58	0.78	(0.09)	(0.55)	(0.08)
(3) 2.5°C, 15% (GFDL × 0.65)	0.17	(0.08)	0.52	0.99	(0.05)	(0.45)	1.10
(4) 2.5°C, 7% (UKMO × 0.5)	0.21	(0.24)	0.15	0.00	(0.01)	(0.08)	0.04
(5) 1.5°C, 7% (GFDL × 0.33)	0.20	0.09	0.06	0.65	(0.07)	(0.57)	0.35

Table D4.6 MAPPS and CENTURY ecological change, regeneration scenario (billions 1998 USD)

Climate scenario	NE	SE	MW	GP	SW	NW	Total
(1) 5°C, 15% (UKMO × 1.0)	2.03	(2.64)	1.23	(0.01)	(0.05)	(0.74)	(0.19)
(2) 5°C, 7% (OSU × 1.0)	0.50	(2.37)	1.65	0.76	(0.11)	(0.63)	(0.20)
(3) 2.5°C, 15% (GFDL × 0.65)	0.20	(0.55)	0.17	0.38	(0.02)	(0.24)	(0.08)
(4) 2.5°C, 7% (UKMO × 0.5)	0.21	(0.19)	0.08	0.00	(0.01)	(0.09)	0.00
(5) 1.5°C, 7% (GFDL × 0.33)	0.09	(0.12)	0.02	0.12	0.00	(0.08)	0.02

Table D4.7 BIOME2 and TEM ecological change, dieback scenario (billions 1998 USD)

Climate scenario	NE	SE	MW	GP	SW	NW	Total
(1) 5°C, 15% (UKMO × 1.0)	1.60	(2.64)	0.76	0.59	(0.01)	(0.27)	0.04
(2) 5°C, 7% (OSU × 1.0)	(0.01)	(1.68)	0.47	1.56	(0.08)	(0.52)	(0.27)
(3) 2.5°C, 15% (GFDL × 0.65)	(0.02)	(1.91)	(0.21)	2.77	0.19	(0.81)	0.00
(4) 2.5°C, 7% (UKMO × 0.5)	1.13	(1.20)	0.37	0.37	0.01	(0.45)	0.24
(5) 1.5°C, 7% (GFDL × 0.33)	0.14	(0.34)	(0.21)	0.90	0.12	(0.34)	0.26

Table D4.8 BIOME2 and TEM ecological change, regeneration scenario (billions 1998 USD)

Climate scenario	NE	SE	MW	GP	SW	NW	Total
(1) 5°C, 15% (UKMO × 1.0)	0.81	(1.31)	0.22	0.25	0.02	0.02	0.01
(2) 5°C, 7% (OSU × 1.0)	0.13	(1.17)	0.27	1.09	(0.05)	(0.52)	(0.26)
(3) 2.5°C, 15% (GFDL × 0.65)	0.25	(0.70)	(0.26)	1.04	0.21	(0.51)	0.05
(4) 2.5°C, 7% (UKMO × 0.5)	1.24	(1.51)	0.20	0.35	0.06	(0.18)	0.17
(5) 1.5°C, 7% (GFDL × 0.33)	0.28	(0.25)	(0.30)	0.59	0.11	(0.25)	0.18

Table D4.9 BIOME2 and BIOME–BGC ecological change, dieback scenario (billions 1998 USD)

Climate scenario	NE	SE	MW	GP	SW	NW	Total
(1) 5°C, 15% (UKMO × 1.0)	2.07	(3.22)	1.03	0.66	0.04	(0.20)	0.37
(2) 5°C, 7% (OSU × 1.0)	0.07	(2.28)	0.68	1.97	(0.04)	(0.32)	0.08
(3) 2.5°C, 15% (GFDL × 0.65)	(0.01)	(0.59)	(0.12)	1.27	0.19	(0.53)	0.21
(4) 2.5°C, 7% (UKMO × 0.5)	3.09	1.13	(1.44)	0.38	0.35	0.02	(0.07)
(5) 1.5°C, 7% (GFDL × 0.33)	0.18	(0.30)	(0.21)	0.89	0.11	(0.28)	0.37

Table D4.10   BIOME2 and BIOME–BGC ecological change, regeneration scenario (billions 1998 USD)

Climate scenario	NE	SE	MW	GP	SW	NW	Total
(1) 5°C, 15% (UKMO × 1.0)	1.63	(2.16)	0.40	0.48	0.09	(0.07)	0.37
(2) 5°C, 7% (OSU × 1.0)	0.22	(1.77)	0.47	1.44	0.00	(0.32)	0.05
(3) 2.5°C, 15% (GFDL × 0.65)	0.32	(1.01)	(0.24)	1.37	0.25	(0.50)	0.19
(4) 2.5°C, 7% (UKMO × 0.5)	1.06	(1.13)	0.06	0.31	0.08	(0.02)	0.37
(5) 1.5°C, 7% (GFDL × 0.33)	0.34	(0.54)	(0.28)	0.87	0.15	(0.30)	0.25

Table D4.11   BIOME2 and CENTURY ecological change, dieback scenario (billions 1998 USD)

Climate scenario	NE	SE	MW	GP	SW	NW	Total
(1) 5°C, 15% (UKMO × 1.0)	8.46	1.05	(1.66)	0.50	0.39	0.01	(0.21)
(2) 5°C, 7% (OSU × 1.0)	(0.01)	(1.37)	0.41	1.38	(0.05)	(0.41)	(0.04)
(3) 2.5°C, 15% (GFDL × 0.65)	(0.01)	(0.47)	(0.09)	0.96	0.14	(0.52)	(0.01)
(4) 2.5°C, 7% (UKMO × 0.5)	1.16	(1.55)	0.38	0.39	0.04	(0.13)	0.30
(5) 1.5°C, 7% (GFDL × 0.33)	0.17	(0.31)	(0.21)	0.89	0.09	(0.28)	0.35

Table D4.12   BIOME2 and CENTURY ecological change, regeneration scenario (billions 1998 USD)

Climate scenario	NE	SE	MW	GP	SW	NW	Total
(1) 5°C, 15% (UKMO × 1.0)	1.40	(1.95)	0.30	0.44	0.06	(0.06)	0.20
(2) 5°C, 7% (OSU × 1.0)	0.27	(2.22)	0.61	1.92	(0.02)	(0.60)	(0.04)
(3) 2.5°C, 15% (GFDL × 0.65)	0.31	(0.93)	(0.24)	1.25	0.24	(0.48)	0.13
(4) 2.5°C, 7% (UKMO × 0.5)	1.00	(1.23)	0.06	0.30	0.07	0.00	0.20
(5) 1.5°C, 7% (GFDL × 0.33)	0.31	(0.21)	(0.30)	0.63	0.14	(0.31)	0.26

Table D4.13   DOLY and TEM ecological change, dieback scenario (billions 1998 USD)

Climate scenario	NE	SE	MW	GP	SW	NW	Total
(1) 5°C, 15% (UKMO × 1.0)	1.05	(2.93)	1.07	1.24	0.09	(0.68)	(0.15)
(2) 5°C, 7% (OSU × 1.0)	0.24	(2.08)	1.04	1.30	(0.14)	(0.59)	(0.25)
(3) 2.5°C, 15% (GFDL × 0.65)	(0.01)	(0.04)	(0.01)	0.01	0.00	(0.01)	(0.06)
(4) 2.5°C, 7% (UKMO × 0.5)	1.39	(3.15)	1.11	1.48	0.18	(0.65)	0.35
(5) 1.5°C, 7% (GFDL × 0.33)	0.06	(0.35)	0.11	0.39	(0.01)	(0.15)	0.04

*Table D4.14　DOLY and TEM ecological change, regeneration scenario
(billions 1998 USD)*

Climate scenario	NE	SE	MW	GP	SW	NW	Total
(1) 5°C, 15% (UKMO × 1.0)	0.83	(1.83)	0.39	0.70	0.30	(0.57)	(0.19)
(2) 5°C, 7% (OSU × 1.0)	0.28	(1.23)	0.48	0.79	(0.09)	(0.46)	(0.22)
(3) 2.5°C, 15% (GFDL × 0.65)	0.53	(3.65)	0.83	2.45	(0.04)	(0.57)	(0.42)
(4) 2.5°C, 7% (UKMO × 0.5)	0.12	(0.38)	0.04	0.09	0.02	(0.06)	(0.15)
(5) 1.5°C, 7% (GFDL × 0.33)	0.50	(2.55)	0.44	1.58	(0.06)	(0.08)	(0.17)

*Table D4.15　DOLY and BIOME–BGC ecological change, dieback scenario
(billions 1998 USD)*

Climate scenario	NE	SE	MW	GP	SW	NW	Total
(1) 5°C, 15% (UKMO × 1.0)	1.04	(2.57)	1.06	1.20	0.18	(0.52)	0.38
(2) 5°C, 7% (OSU × 1.0)	0.35	(2.57)	1.31	1.56	(0.08)	(0.41)	0.15
(3) 2.5°C, 15% (GFDL × 0.65)	(0.20)	4.20	(1.29)	(3.79)	0.11	0.97	0.00
(4) 2.5°C, 7% (UKMO × 0.5)	0.76	(1.71)	0.55	0.86	0.15	(0.34)	0.26
(5) 1.5°C, 7% (GFDL × 0.33)	0.21	(1.57)	0.45	1.32	(0.01)	(0.09)	0.31

*Table D4.16　DOLY and BIOME–BGC ecological change, regeneration
scenario (billions 1998 USD)*

Climate scenario	NE	SE	MW	GP	SW	NW	Total
(1) 5°C, 15% (UKMO × 1.0)	0.72	(1.22)	0.25	0.54	0.33	(0.32)	0.32
(2) 5°C, 7% (OSU × 1.0)	0.47	(1.64)	0.65	1.11	(0.06)	(0.45)	0.08
(3) 2.5°C, 15% (GFDL × 0.65)	0.27	(1.84)	0.40	1.25	0.01	(0.14)	(0.04)
(4) 2.5°C, 7% (UKMO × 0.5)	2.42	(3.84)	0.60	1.73	0.89	(1.40)	0.41
(5) 1.5°C, 7% (GFDL × 0.33)	0.21	(0.66)	0.17	0.60	0.02	(0.01)	0.32

*Table D4.17　DOLY and CENTURY ecological change, dieback scenario
(billions 1998 USD)*

Climate scenario	NE	SE	MW	GP	SW	NW	Total
(1) 5°C, 15% (UKMO × 1.0)	1.04	(2.62)	1.06	1.23	0.11	(0.77)	0.05
(2) 5°C, 7% (OSU × 1.0)	0.26	(1.84)	0.98	1.22	(0.09)	(0.45)	0.06
(3) 2.5°C, 15% (GFDL × 0.65)	0.13	(1.40)	0.42	0.98	(0.02)	(0.14)	(0.04)
(4) 2.5°C, 7% (UKMO × 0.5)	0.28	(0.61)	0.24	0.32	0.05	(0.14)	0.12
(5) 1.5°C, 7% (GFDL × 0.33)	0.04	(0.06)	0.05	0.14	0.00	(0.04)	0.12

Table D4.18   DOLY and CENTURY ecological change, regeneration scenario (billions 1998 USD)

Climate scenario	NE	SE	MW	GP	SW	NW	Total
(1) 5°C, 15% (UKMO × 1.0)	1.94	(3.92)	0.98	1.65	0.51	(1.23)	(0.07)
(2) 5°C, 7% (OSU × 1.0)	0.31	(1.24)	0.52	0.76	(0.04)	(0.28)	0.02
(3) 2.5°C, 15% (GFDL × 0.65)	0.04	(0.18)	0.06	0.13	0.00	(0.02)	0.01
(4) 2.5°C, 7% (UKMO × 0.5)	7.29	(11.42)	1.27	4.77	2.50	(4.43)	(0.01)
(5) 1.5°C, 7% (GFDL × 0.33)	0.52	(1.98)	0.45	1.64	0.00	(0.39)	0.22

5. Water resources: Economic analysis

Brian Hurd and Megan Harrod

INTRODUCTION

Water systems may be economically vulnerable to changes in global climate. The indicators of climate change – including higher temperatures, new patterns of precipitation, changes in evaporation rates and changes in the frequency and intensity of droughts and storms – can have important consequences for water users and the institutions that regulate water supply and demand. Analyses of climate change impacts on water supply and use have evolved from projections of runoff changes to methods that link physical and water management models. Early studies used statistical models to relate climate (temperature and precipitation) to runoff at the river basin scale level (for example, Stockton and Boggess 1979, Revelle and Waggoner 1983). Nemec and Schaake (1982) improved on these approaches by calibrating a physical runoff model and projecting the effects of climate changes on runoff. Other researchers (for example, Gleick 1987, Lettenmaier *et al.* 1993) helped advance the state of the art in hydrologic modeling and raised interesting issues about how climate change might influence competition for water. These studies, however, did not grapple directly with allocation issues in a quantitative fashion. This assessment aims to provide researchers and policy makers with a more in-depth analysis of specific regional impacts from climate change.

Our assessment is based on four watershed optimization models that simulate major regional economic and physical attributes of water resource supply and use. The four US watersheds simulated are the Colorado, Missouri, Delaware and Apalachicola–Flint–Chattahoochee. These were selected on the basis of regional and national significance, diversity of climate, geography and water use patterns. They are broadly representative of the diverse range of water resources and climates across the United States. Results from these four models are extrapolated to remaining US watersheds. Hydrologic changes were estimated only for the four modeled watersheds. The regional results are extrapolations from these four watersheds and should be viewed as only a rough gauge of the sensitivity of regional water resources to climate change.

Ideally, one would want to examine a representative set of watersheds in each region, but limited resources prevented this more thorough approach.

MODEL OVERVIEW

The watershed models simulate economic factors in relation to the physical characteristics of water use and supply within the watershed. The models view the watershed from the perspective of an overall manager who can distribute and manage water supplies to generate the greatest economic value. These models treat water as a commodity and assume that water can be traded across both space and time, to the extent allowed by physical conditions such as reservoirs and water delivery systems. The models do not consider changing water infrastructure, building or removing dams and canals; they do consider how climate might change both runoff and the demand for water. By weighing the economic tradeoffs between alternative water uses, the models determine the most efficient allocation and storage of water given the watershed's economic and physical characteristics, and a given sequence and spatial pattern of runoff. A seasonal time-step simulates the inflow and movement of water throughout the watershed.

The models embody efficient adaptation. As runoff changes in each scenario, it is assumed that water is reallocated to its highest use. Current water distribution systems are not this efficient, so it is reasonable to question whether this adaptation will take place. Encouraging public institutions to manage water more efficiently is an important adaptation to climate change.

A sequence of simulated runoff data is the primary input to the water allocation models. These data characterize changes in mean climatic conditions, primarily changes in average temperature and average precipitation rates. The runoff sequence is calibrated off a 38-year historical record (1949–87) and simulates changes in average water use and allocations. The models assume that the water administrator is aware of not only this year's runoff but also all future runoff as well (that is, the model has perfect foresight). In this assessment, we hold the current water infrastructure fixed. For example, the models do not consider removing or adding dams or canals. They do, however, allow agricultural irrigation demand to change.

Thus, our analysis examines how known changes in long-term levels and timing of water resources affect efficient water allocations. The models do not take into account uncertainty surrounding existing or future runoff. We assume that the water manager can look forward with perfect foresight and make the best possible decisions given what is coming. The impact estimates may be underestimated because they do not include uncertainty. Nonetheless, the models are well suited to investigate large-scale and long-term effects of prescribed changes in the water system. The models, however, are not suitable for simulating day-to-day management or short-run system needs, both of which must be responsive to the current state of the system and expectations of short-run changes in demand and supply.

Two additional climate change scenarios not included in the previous study are reported here, +1.5°C, 0 per cent change in precipitation and +2.5°C, 0 per cent precipitation. Furthermore, the analysis drops the scenarios hypothesizing a 10 per cent decrease in precipitation under each of the temperature changes. Readers with interest in the details of the analytic methods and models should see Hurd *et al.* (1999a).

REGIONAL SCOPE

Our current focus is on the potential impacts to each of seven regions. Table 5.1 lists the regions, the associated US water resource regions and the modeled

Table 5.1   Regional definitions and pairing of modeled river basins to US water resource regions

Region	Approximate US water resource region	Model proxy
Northeast	New England	Delaware River
	Mid-Atlantic	
Midwest	Upper Mississippi	Missouri River
	Great Lakes	Delaware River
	Ohio	
Northern Plains	Missouri	Missouri River
	Souris–Red–Rainy	
Northwest	Pacific Northwest	Missouri River
Southeast	South Atlantic	Appalachicola–Flint–
	Tennessee	Chattahoochee Rivers
	Lower Mississippi	
Southern Plains	Arkansas–White–Red	Missouri River
	Texas–Gulf	
Southwest	Rio Grande	Colorado River
	Upper Colorado	
	Lower Colorado	
	Great Basin	
	California	

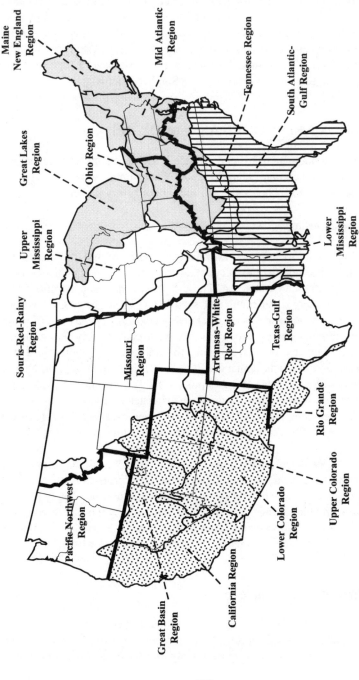

Figure 5.1   Spacial association and aggregations for the regional water assessment. Shading indicates which watersheds are associated with each one of the four watershed models (see Table 5.1).

watersheds assumed to approximate for each of the extrapolated regions. Figure 5.1 also illustrates the regions and model associations. We emphasize that characterizing regional water resources by using a proxy model from another region is an important limitation of this analysis. Caution should be used in interpreting the results for those regions where no rivers were explicitly modeled (Northwest, Midwest and Southern Plains).

SCENARIOS AND MODEL ASSUMPTIONS

The watershed models are based on scenarios of socioeconomic change through 2060 (baseline) and climate change in 2060. Water supply and demand conditions are estimated for 2060, both with and without climate change.

Baseline assumptions

The baseline scenario assumes no change in climate and projects water demands in 2060, taking into account factors such as historical trends in population, income and water use. These historical data suggest that water demand in the energy and municipal sectors has been growing over time, whereas irrigation demand has been relatively constant. The growth of water demand by thermal energy producers has been considerably less than the growth of demand by municipal users. In addition, we hypothesized that future growth in electricity demand will be increasingly met by technologies that are less water intensive (for example, solar, gas turbines, dry cooling). Based on these historical trends, demand for water in 2060 is estimated to increase 23 per cent and 10.2 per cent (0.3 per cent and 0.14 per cent annually) from 1990 levels for the municipal and thermal energy sectors, respectively.

Irrigation demand has been relatively constant over the last 20 years, partly because there have been few new federal irrigation projects. Projections of irrigation demand assume that no significant new federal water supply projects will be built, and that changes in irrigation technology will offset increases in the demand for irrigation water. That is, the overall demand for irrigation water is assumed to remain constant at current levels under baseline climate conditions.

Water demand under climate change

Demand for water may be sensitive to climate change. Greater rates of evaporation and evapotranspiration in plants will increase the irrigation requirements of a variety of uses, most notably for agriculture but also for some municipal uses such as lawns, gardens, parks and golf courses. In estimating climate-induced changes in water demand, we focus on the agriculture sector because of its overall scale and critical linkage to climate and water resources. Changes in the water demands of other sectors such as municipal and industrial are plausible, but lacking clear empirical measures on the sensitivity of water demand to temperature changes in these sectors, we conservatively assumed no climate sensitivity in these sectors.

In assessing the effect of climate change on agricultural water demand, we used the research results reported by Peterson and Keller (1990) to estimate changes in regional irrigation demand. These estimates do not take into account the potential water savings from increased water use efficiency of some plants in response to increased CO_2, so therefore we may overstate the impacts to agriculture.

DATA AND METHODS

The watershed models are used to measure changes in economic welfare that are driven by changes in hydrologic conditions and water demand caused by climate change. Hydrologic runoff data were developed for this study by Dr. Dennis Lettenmaier (University of Washington) and Dr. Eric Wood (Princeton University). These data describe how the level and timing of runoff are estimated to change as a result of climate change. The baseline is calibrated to historical runoff between 1949 and 1987, and runoff changes under each climate change scenario are estimated by adjusting the historical sequence to account for changes in average annual temperature and percentage changes in precipitation. These data are the principal driving force affecting water supply within the watershed models.

The watershed models are dynamic, nonlinear optimization models sometimes referred to as spatial equilibrium models. The model objective is to allocate available water supplies to competing economic uses across space and time to maximize the total value of water within the watershed within physical, economic and institutional constraints. The models also assume 'perfect foresight', which means that the optimization occurs with full knowledge and anticipation of future runoff and system changes. This assumption is common to long-run optimization models, and implies that adjustments and responses in water use to climate changes are made more efficiently and more certainly than they might otherwise be (that is, the estimated welfare effects are likely to be understated). Economic welfare for consumptive uses is defined by consumer and producer surplus, and is measured by the underlying demand and supply relationships (the benefits and costs). Valuation of nonconsumptive uses such as hydropower is based on reservoir and river flows and is measured by the market value of electricity produced. The models are constrained by runoff, physical and institutional features governing water flow, distribution, storage and water exports. Parameters for the models' objective and constraint functions are based on available data on water use, prices and other information from a variety of both primary and secondary sources, including the US Geological Survey (USGS), local water utilities and agricultural extension agents. Details on the models can be found in Hurd *et al.* (1999a).

To extend our analysis beyond the four modeled watersheds, data on water supply and use were developed for each of the 18 USGS water resource regions in the coterminous United States. Baseline data on water use were obtained from the USGS (Solley *et al.* 1993) by region and by sector. These data identified current water allocations in each of the regions, which are aggregated to form the baseline data for the seven regions of this study according to Table 5.1.

To assess how climate change might affect water use and welfare in each of these regions, we developed a spreadsheet model to analyze potential changes in regional water use using the allocation response and welfare changes estimated in the four modeled watersheds. Changes in sector water use, for example, are estimated by scaling the baseline regional water use for that sector (based on Solley *et al.* 1993) by the estimated change in sector allocation from the modeled result from the reference watershed model. This scaling procedure is described further in the discussion of the welfare changes in the next section. Note that in developing these regional estimates, the regional water use data from Solley *et al.* were not adjusted for changes in baseline use and allocation. Since this analysis focuses on relative climate change impacts, not the impacts of baseline changes, and since we account for baseline changes within each watershed model, it is more important to account for the relative changes in water use and the economic consequences of these changes rather than absolute levels of regional water use.

Brown (1999) underscores the key critical issues in estimating baseline changes in water use. He estimates baseline changes in regional water use by sector out to 2040 based on estimated changes in population, income and recent trends. Such an analysis requires assumptions regarding future water supplies such that if water use in one sector grows, reductions may be needed in other sectors, particularly in dry regions. His analysis shows that the greatest changes are estimated for domestic and public use, which, he expects, will closely follow population growth trends. He estimated the increase in national domestic water use between 1995 and 2040 to be about 42 per cent; the estimated municipal and industrial demand increase used in the watershed models (not the extrapolated regions) over this time period is about 15 per cent. He also estimated slight increases for thermoelectric and industrial use over this period of 9 per cent and 6 per cent, respectively, and a decrease in irrigation of 3 per cent. Following Brown (1999), we assume that domestic and public sector use is highly price inelastic and, therefore, unresponsive to changes in price. Our watershed model results, as shown in Hurd *et al.* (1999a) and here, suggest that there are likely to be only very small changes in domestic water use as a result of runoff and climate change, although there could be significant changes in water costs.

Economic welfare in this study measures the net value associated with the provision and use of water. Like other commodities, water can be used in a variety of ways to generate economic value: in producing goods and services that are exchanged in markets, by direct consumption of domestic water users, and in producing nonmarket services such as water pollution control, flood control and ecosystem support. Through market exchanges and allocation changes, water supplies can be directed toward those uses with the greatest economic potential. Thus, the economic damages from climate change could be reduced by lessening consumption in sectors where the marginal economic contribution is least. Institutional changes that facilitate such transfers, such as water banks, can contribute significantly during times of intense water supply stress.

Regional welfare estimates are derived by assessing the market value of changes for each sector and region as a result of runoff and demand changes. Conceptually for consumptive sectors, the net change in economic welfare (consumer and producer surplus) is measured by the change in the area below the water demand curve net of marginal water supply costs.

In this model, we assume linear demands in each sector. Figure 5.2 illustrates this by showing the net demand for water, or the willingness to pay for water in excess of its marginal supply costs (net demand equals demand price minus marginal supply cost). Another way to interpret this is to view the premium above the marginal supply cost as the market opportunity cost of the water in serving other users elsewhere in the system or in delaying use to the future. In the figure, baseline equilibrium is given by point *E*, at which the price and water use are given by points *A* and *G*, respectively. If, under climate change, water scarcity increases, a new equilibrium emerges at point *C*, where price moves up from *A* to *B* and water use declines from *G* to *F*. As a result of this change, net economic welfare falls by the change in area under the net demand curve, shown by the area *CEGF*. In notation, the economic welfare measure for each sector in each region is defined as:

$$\Delta R_{ij} = (P_{ij_0} \cdot \Delta W_{ij}) + \frac{1}{2}(P_{ij_0} \cdot \Delta W_{ij})$$

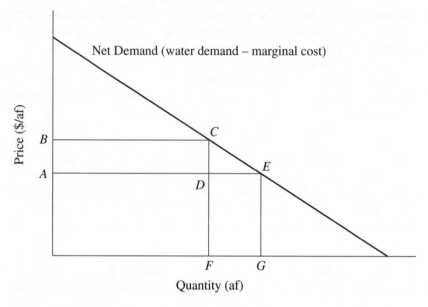

Figure 5.2   Demand for water consumption

where ΔR_{ij} is the change in welfare in sector i and region j. The variable P_{ij_0} is the baseline net marginal value of water estimated in the proxy regional model j_0 (point A in Figure 5.2), and W_{ij} is the baseline water use for sector i and region j (based on estimates from Solley *et al.* 1993). The variable ΔW_{ij} is the change in water withdrawal by sector i in region j (the change in quantity, G minus F), and is estimated by the baseline water use patterns in region $j(W_{ij})$, the simulated changes in sector water use in the modeled region j_0, and relative runoff changes between paired region j and modeled region j_0, given as:

$$\Delta W_{ij} = W_{ij}(1 + \%\Delta W_{ij_0}),$$

where W_{ij_0} is the efficient water withdrawal to sector i determined in basin model j_0. This term, therefore, assumes that changes in water use patterns are proportional across paired regions and sectors. We also recognize the difference between withdrawals and consumptive use, and that efficient use depends on equalizing the marginal value across consumptive uses, after accounting for return flows. However, consistent data on consumptive use were not available. If average return flow rates are approximately the same within a given sector across regions, then no particular bias is introduced.

This analysis accounts for differences in river volumes across regions; however, it assumes that the response of water users to price and runoff changes (within each economic sector) is the same between the modeled regions and paired regions. It assumes, for example, that agricultural water use in the upper Mississippi region has the same demand elasticity as agricultural water use in the Missouri region.

This approach assumes that the value of water in a modeled region is largely similar to those in the extrapolated regions. This assumption may be more valid for estimating national level impacts, as in the previous study, and could produce some misleading results for some regional estimates. For example, water use in the Pacific Northwest, and in particular in the Columbia basin, is constrained in ways that are very different from those in the Missouri basin, which we use as a model proxy. Instream values associated with salmon are the most striking difference. The water needs of salmon require adjustments in the management of reservoirs and in the timing and volume of offstream withdrawals. These adjustments, therefore, could raise the instream value of water within the Columbia system in comparison to the Missouri, and thus underestimate the magnitude of economic impacts in this study. Therefore, extreme caution in interpreting these results is advised.

RESULTS

Estimated changes in water resource services are driven by shifts in both water supply and demand. As a primary indicator of the direction and magnitude of changes in service levels, modeled changes in annual average runoff (Lettenmaier and Wood 1995) are a useful measure to compare against the estimated changes in welfare and water use. As described earlier, runoff changes are an input into the watershed models and become a driver for redistributing water resources across time and space. The four runoff datasets are summarized in Table 5.2 for each modeled watershed and climate change scenario.

With only two small exceptions for the Apalachicola–Flint–Chattahoochee, the estimated hydrologic changes simulated by Lettenmaier and Wood (1995) for each modeled watershed show the same change in direction in annual runoff, either increases or decreases, in response to a given climate change scenario. Thus, the differences across the regions tend to be differences in the estimated magnitude of the response to climate change. With respect to the estimated magnitude, there also appears to be a tendency for the absolute magnitudes to be greater in the western watersheds than in the eastern watersheds, particularly in the drier scenarios.

These observed trends suggest that extrapolations of the direction and range of estimated hydrologic changes from the modeled watersheds to other

Table 5.2   Summary of estimated percentage changes in annual runoff for the modeled watersheds

Scenario	Appalachicola–Flint–Chattahoochee	Delaware	Missouri	Colorado
Baseline[a]	24,363 (kaf/yr)	13,660 (kaf/yr)	56,651 (kaf/yr)	17,058 (kaf/yr)
2.5°C, +7% precipitation	0.26	–4.08	–9.07	–4.17
5.0°C, +7% precipitation	–12.43	–22.27	–30.61	–22.38
1.5°C, +7% precipitation	5.07	2.72	1.04	3.97
2.5°C, +15% precipitation	13.70	9.87	9.13	14.13
5.0°C, +15% precipitation	0.51	–8.73	–15.52	–6.92
1.5°C, +15% precipitation	18.69	16.83	20.50	23.49
5.0°C, 0% precipitation	–23.53	–33.87	–42.39	–34.70
1.5°C, 0% precipitation	–6.68	–9.51	–14.79	–11.81
2.5°C, 0% precipitation	–11.32	–16.19	–23.77	–18.89

Note: a Baseline figures in this row are reported as absolute annual runoff.

Source: Lettenmaier and Woods 1995.

'similar' regions may not be grossly inconsistent with the results that might have been generated by simulating hydrologic changes in each watershed specifically. Even for the Northwest, which is the most different from its hypothesized proxy, the Missouri, there is likely to be a similar change in the direction of runoff changes, although the magnitude is not well characterized.

Given these simulated changes in runoff and climate-shifted changes in agricultural water demand, we find a wide range of changes in water resource services and welfare across regions and scenarios. Figure 5.3 illustrates the range of total welfare changes across the regions and scenarios.

At the national level, the total estimated annual impacts range from –$10.6 billion to +$2.5 billion for the 5.0°C, +0 per cent precipitation and 1.5°C, +15 per cent precipitation scenarios, respectively. In contrast, Frederick and Schwarz (1999) recently estimated for the US National Assessment that the total cost to water resource under the relatively severe Canadian Climate

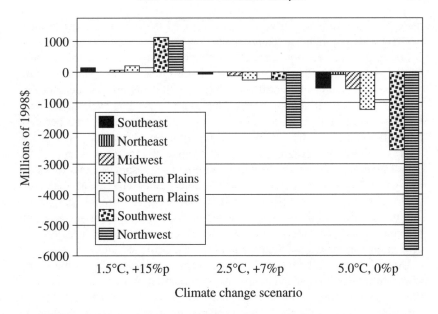

Figure 5.3   Summary of changes in the regional welfare of water resources for selected climate change scenarios

Model would range between $105 and $251 billion annually. Under that scenario, average temperature for the United States rises by 2.1°C and average precipitation declines by 4 per cent. Their analysis is based on the assumption that runoff in a number of basins in the southeastern and south-central United States will decline by up to 92 per cent (in the Texas–Gulf region), whereas our study estimates that it will decline by only 42 per cent in the Missouri watershed. In addition, their analysis includes several nonmarket effects that are not examined in this regional study, including the costs of increased conservation and the valuation of impacts to freshwater ecosystems as a result of diminished instream flows. This accounts for 53 per cent of their estimated impact under their efficient management scenario. Under this scenario, they estimate the costs of developing new supplies to meet projected demands at $45 billion annually. They also estimate the losses to agriculture at $3.2 billion, which is very close to the $3.0 billion we estimate as the impact to agriculture.

It is difficult to compare the results from these two studies because they differ significantly in their approaches and scope. The Frederick and Schwarz study includes nonmarket effects that are outside the scope of this study. We do not consider changes in infrastructure, neither the costs nor the benefits of building new dams or canals, whereas Frederick and Schwarz do allow for these activities (albeit at a very high cost of $1,000 per acre foot) to meet nonirrigated offstream use requirements.

Looking at the aggregated welfare changes across sectors, the western United States, including both regions of the Great Plains, is much more responsive to changes in runoff and climate, with the Northwest demonstrating the greatest variability. In the Northwest, estimated welfare changes range between –43 per cent and +7.5 per cent for the 5.0°C, +0 per cent precipitation and 1.5°C, +15 per cent precipitation scenarios, respectively. This is followed by the Southwest, with a range of –16 per cent and +7 per cent. In contrast, the eastern watersheds show little responsiveness to runoff changes. Of the eastern watersheds, the Southeast shows the greatest variability, ranging between –2.4 per cent and +0.7 per cent. We strongly emphasize that these estimates do not take changes in flood frequency or severity into account, which our watershed level analysis showed could be a major concern in the eastern United States, and in particular in the Southeast.

Underlying the differences in welfare changes across regions is the extent of agricultural irrigation and hydropower production. With respect to agriculture, it is interesting to contrast the relative share of water use to the share of value. As a share of the total value of water resource services, agriculture in the western United States accounts for 18 per cent in the Southern Plains, 37 per cent in the Northern Plains, 27 per cent in the Northwest and 34 per cent in the Southwest. However, in terms of water withdrawals, agriculture accounts for 49 per cent in the Southern Plains, 67 per cent in the Northern Plains, 89 per cent in the Northwest and 84 per cent in the Southwest. In the eastern United States, agriculture's share is only 6 per cent in the Southeast and less than 1 per cent in the Northeast and Midwest. The high agricultural water use in the western United States is a key feature of US water use. Because agriculture tends to place the lowest value on water of the major users, efficiency requires that agriculture be the first user to give up water when runoff declines. The model consequently requires agriculture to give up the biggest share of water when water gets scarce. If society did not permit other users to buy water from agriculture, the welfare impacts of reduced runoff would increase.

Hydropower makes a much larger contribution to water-derived welfare in the West than in the rest of the country. Hydropower's contribution to water derived welfare is 19 per cent in the Southwest and 52 per cent in the Northwest. In the rest of the country, hydropower accounts for only 7 to 8 per cent of welfare.

Even under the central scenario (2.5°C, +7 per cent precipitation), water users in the West experience relatively greater changes from existing water use patterns. Under this scenario they could experience higher water costs, resulting in 6 to 10 per cent reductions in agricultural use, and a consequent

1.3 to 3.9 per cent loss in agricultural welfare; however, total welfare losses range between only 0.6 per cent and 2.2 per cent under this scenario.

Under the scenarios where average runoff declines, water costs rise as competition between users increases. These higher costs generally cut across sectors and locations within a watershed, and result in the migration of water from lower valued economic uses into higher valued ones that can better absorb the higher costs. The general regional results underscore the scale and economic importance of agricultural irrigation and hydropower generation in western water use, and the high sensitivity of these sectors to runoff changes. The result is a strong east–west dichotomy of potential impacts (ignoring flooding and water quality issues).

REVIEW OF REGIONAL IMPACTS

Absent a detailed analysis of hydrologic changes in each of the regions, the regional results are best understood as a sensitivity analysis using hypothetical runoff changes.

Northeast

Water use in the heavily populated Northeast is dominated by municipal and industrial uses (M&I) and thermoelectric power, with 33 per cent and 65 per cent of total stream withdrawals, respectively, and agriculture accounts for 2 per cent (Solley *et al.* 1993). Most of the thermoelectric energy withdrawals are returned to the system; less than 10 per cent is consumed as evaporation in cooling processes. The impacts in the Northeast, which are based on the extrapolated hydrologic changes from the Delaware watershed, are summarized in Table A5.1. (All tabular results across regions and scenarios can be found in Tables A5.1–A5.7 at the end of the chapter.) The total welfare changes in the Northeast are relatively small, ranging between –0.7 per cent and +0.03 per cent. Agricultural users may be affected the most, on a percentage basis; their small share of total water use, however, does not contribute much to the overall regional welfare. Thermoelectric users may experience the greatest welfare changes, estimated to range between –$58 million and +$1.2 million (out of $3.6 billion in baseline welfare). The potential for changes in flood risk is highlighted in Hurd *et al.* (1999b): several watersheds throughout the region have large populations living within the 500-year floodplain. Source water protection and the maintenance of water quality for domestic users are other potential concerns.

Midwest

The assessment for the Midwest, summarized in Table A5.2, is based on results from both the Delaware and the Missouri watershed results. As with the eastern watersheds, the estimated total welfare changes are relatively small, between −1.7 per cent and +0.2 per cent. Irrigated agriculture is potentially the most sensitive to these changes, with withdrawal changes between −33 per cent and +9 per cent and welfare changes between −$21 million and +$3.9 million. However, as a share of regional economic loss, changes in hydropower production may have the greatest regional impact, with welfare changes between −$318 million and +$47 million. Thermoelectric generators may also be affected, with welfare changes between −14 per cent and +2 per cent, or −$189 million and +$3.9 million.

Northern Plains

In contrast to the previous regions, irrigation dominates water use in the Northern Plains, accounting for about 67 per cent of total withdrawals, followed by thermoelectric water use with about 27 per cent. Based on the estimates for the Missouri watershed, summarized in Table A5.3, total welfare changes may range from −16 per cent to +1 per cent. Changes in agricultural withdrawals range between −54 per cent and +14 per cent (a welfare change of between −$778 million and +$13.5 million annually). Hydropower welfare changes range between −$411 million and +$72 million (−67 per cent and +12 per cent). The Northern Plains may also be vulnerable to climate change as a result of relatively high rates of groundwater overdraft, high runoff variability and high levels of streamflow withdrawals relative to streamflow (Hurd *et al.* 1999b). Also, flooding, a significant concern for many communities in the region, is not reflected in these estimates.

Northwest

The Northwest region appears to be the most sensitive to changes in water use under climate change because of its intensive use of water. Irrigation is the dominant water use in the Northwest, accounting for over 85 to 90 per cent of withdrawals. Instream water uses are also vital to the region as a major source of electric power and in support of important recreation and ecosystem services (for example, salmon). This is the most difficult region to extrapolate to, because there are key differences between water use in this region and water use in the Missouri basin, which is the basis for the extrapolated results. The results, summarized in Table A5.4, indicate that total welfare changes range between −21 per cent and +14 per cent, and are primarily distributed between agriculture and hydropower. Losses to both sectors under the more extreme runoff changes are considerable, approaching –$995 million and –$4,655 million for agriculture and hydropower, respectively. Flooding in the western portion of the region could become a greater concern.

Southeast

The findings for the Southeast, summarized in Table A5.5, are based on extrapolating the analysis of changes in the Appalachicola–Flint–Chattahoochee watershed. Ignoring the effects of flooding and water quality changes, the impacts to total welfare in this region range between –2.4 per cent and +0.75 per cent. The relatively low share of runoff that is withdrawn for use accounts for this small range in estimated impacts. Hurd *et al.* (1999b) further underscore this point by examining the ratio of streamflow to withdrawals under current climate and conclude that this region is relatively less vulnerable to changes in runoff. Increased irrigation demand is likely to draw a greater share of available water under climate change. Much of the Southeast is relatively vulnerable to flooding under current climate (Hurd *et al.* 1999b), and changes that bring greater precipitation and runoff, and possibly greater storm intensity, could exacerbate the negative impacts of climate change.

Southern Plains

The Southern Plains span the Texas–Gulf region and the Arkansas–White–Red region. The dominant water use is agricultural irrigation, followed by thermoelectric and M&I uses. Based on the Missouri watershed results, total welfare is estimated to range between –10 per cent and +2 per cent, and total withdrawals to range between –27 per cent and +7 per cent. Key findings are summarized in Table A5.6. Agriculture is potentially the most affected sector, with estimated withdrawal changes ranging between –54 per cent and +14 per cent. The welfare effects for agriculture are significant, with a loss of $428 million (–28 per cent) estimated for a +5°C increase and no change in precipitation. Under this scenario, hydropower losses are estimated at –$450 million (–68 per cent).

Southwest

This region comprises a variety of climatic zones, from water-rich areas in Northern California to extreme deserts in the Lower Colorado, Great Basin and Rio Grande areas. Agricultural irrigation dominates water use, exceeding 80 per cent. The results, summarized in Table A5.7, are based on those from the Colorado watershed model and indicate that total welfare changes range between −16 per cent and +7 per cent, suggesting that this region is very sensitive to changes in runoff, with hydropower and agriculture the most affected sectors. Welfare changes in agricultural range from −$986 million (−18 per cent) to +$321 million (+6 per cent). Hydropower value is estimated to change between −$1,217 million and +$783 million.

SUMMARY AND CONCLUSIONS

By extending the previous analysis to focus on regional changes, this research highlights the importance of considering regional differences in assessing water resource impacts and adaptation potential. Comparisons can be drawn between these results and those of previous regional assessments such as Gleick (1990) and Hurd *et al.* (1999b). Consistent with the results from these studies, which indicate the relative vulnerability of the western United States under current climate conditions, this assessment further underscores the potential impacts as climate changes in these regions.

The study finds especially that western watersheds have a high probability of experiencing runoff reductions from climate change. These reductions would cause significant impacts to agriculture in the West. The important hydropower resources of the West would also be sensitive to these runoff reductions. To adapt to these adverse circumstances, regional economic forces must use water more efficiently by maintaining supplies to high valued users and taking the water away from low valued users. Agriculture will tend to lose the largest share of water because many of the lowest valued uses for water are in agriculture. Although this study makes some reasonable predictions about water impacts across regions in the United States, the extrapolated regional estimates remain highly uncertain. Additional watershed studies need to be conducted in each region to reduce this uncertainty. Flooding remains a large uncertainty that is not well accounted for by examining changes in mean climate conditions and regional extrapolations. Flooding may be a more widespread concern than runoff reductions, because every region needs to be wary of increases in flood conditions.

It needs to be restated here that the regional assessments presented in this chapter concern only market effects. Many important nonmarket impacts to water resources, such as impacts on water quality and other instream uses, are not measured here. In a national analysis, Hurd *et al.* (1999b) point to a number of indicators of vulnerability related to consumptive and instream water use, including flooding, and a more comprehensive regional approach might incorporate some of these indicators in estimating the effects of climate change and regional adaptation. For example, water quality measures such as dissolved oxygen can indicate how well a water body can support aquatic ecosystems suitable for providing valued habitat and recreation. It is important to remember that climate change could have adverse and significant impacts on the quality of life and recreation in sensitive regions. For example, the Southeast may be very sensitive to increases in precipitation rates, which could exacerbate flooding; and semi-arid regions may find altered streamflows are insufficient to meet both consumptive uses and minimum flow requirements for ecosystems.

REFERENCES

Brown, T.C. (1999), Past and Future Freshwater Use in the United States: A Technical Document Supporting the 2000 USDA Forest Service RPA Assessment, Gen. Tech. Rep. RMRS-GTR-39, Fort Collins, CO: US Department of Agriculture, Forest Service, Rocky Mountain Research Station.

Frederick, K.D. and G.E. Schwarz (1999), 'Socioeconomic impacts of climate change on US water supplies', *Journal of the American Water Resources Association*, 35(6), 1563–83.

Gleick, P.H. (1987), 'The development and testing of a water balance model for climate impacts assessment: Modeling the Sacramento Basin', *Water Resources Research*, 23, 1049–61.

Gleick, P.H. (1990), 'Vulnerability of water systems', in P.E. Waggoner (ed.), *Climate Change and U.S. Water Resources*, New York: John Wiley and Sons, pp. 223–40.

Hurd, B.H., J.M. Callaway, J.B. Smith and P. Kirshen (1999a), 'Economic effects of climate change on U.S. water resources', in R. Mendelsohn and J.E. Neumann (eds), *The Impact of Climate Change on the United States Economy*, Cambridge, UK: Cambridge University Press, pp. 133–77.

Hurd, B.H., N. Leary, R. Jones and J.B. Smith (1999b), 'Relative regional vulnerability of water resources to climate change', *Journal of the American Water Resources Association*, December, 35(6), 1399–410.

Lettenmaier, D. and E. Wood (1995), Implementation of the VIC-2L Land and Surface Scheme to Model the Hydrology of Large Continental Rivers, report prepared for Electric Power Research Institute, Palo Alto, CA.

Lettenmaier, D.P., K.L. Brettmann, L.W. Vail, S.B. Yabusaki and M.J. Scott (1993), 'Sensitivity of Pacific Northwest water resources to global warming', *Water Resources Research*, 26, 69–86.

Nemec, J. and J. Schaake (1982), 'Sensitivity of water resource systems to climate variation', *Hydrological Sciences Journal*, 27, 327–48.

Peterson, D.F. and A.A. Keller (1990), 'Effects of climate change on U.S. irrigation', *Journal of Irrigation and Drainage Engineering*, 116(2), 194–210.

Revelle, R.R. and P.E. Waggoner (1983), 'Effects of a carbon dioxide induced climatic change on water supplies in the western United States', in *Changing Climate: Report of the Carbon Dioxide Assessment Committee*, Washington, DC: National Academy Press, pp. 419–32.

Solley, W.B., R.R. Pierce, and H.A. Perlman (1993), Estimated Use of Water in the United States in 1990, USGS Circular 1081, Washington, DC: US Government Printing Office.

Stockton, C.W. and W.R. Boggess (1979), Geohydrological Implications of Climate Change on Water Resource Development, Fort Belvoir, VA: US Army Coastal Engineering Research Center.

Table A5.1 Simulated effect of climate change on the welfare of water users in the Northeast (millions 1998 USD)

Climate change scenario	% change in runoff	Total welfare			Agriculture			M&I			Thermoelectric			Hydropower	
		% change in with-drawals	Change in welfare ($) Absolute	Percent	% change in with-drawals	Change in welfare ($) Absolute	Percent	% change in with-drawals	Change in welfare ($) Absolute	Percent	% change in with-drawals	Change in welfare ($) Total	Percent	Change in welfare ($) Total	Percent
Baseline[a]	216,763 (kaf/yr)	28,966 (kaf/yr)	12,941		484 (kaf/yr)	44		12,128 (kaf/yr)	8,147		16,354 (kaf/yr)	3,738		1,012	
1.5°C, 0%P[b]	−9.51	−0.64	−3.7	−0.028	−3.00	−0.3	−0.592	−0.20	−0.3	−0.004	−0.90	−3.1	−0.08	0.0	0.00
2.5°C, 0%P	−16.19	−1.41	−9.5	−0.073	−7.50	−0.7	−1.590	−0.50	−0.7	−0.009	−1.90	−8.0	−0.21	0.0	0.00
5.0°C, 0%P	−33.87	−5.12	−89.5	−0.691	−8.16	−1.0	−2.309	−1.96	−3.2	−0.039	−7.38	−60.0	−1.60	−5.0	−2.50
1.5°C, 7%P	2.72	0.00	−0.0	0.000	0.00	0.0	0.000	0.01	0.0	0.000	−0.01	−0.0	−0.00	0.0	0.00
2.5°C, 7%P	−4.08	−0.42	−2.5	−0.019	−2.72	−0.2	−0.521	−0.14	−0.4	−0.005	−0.57	−1.8	−0.05	0.0	0.00
5.0°C, 7%P	−22.27	−2.59	−21.8	−0.169	−12.93	−1.4	−3.108	−0.89	−1.4	−0.017	−3.54	−19.1	−0.51	0.0	0.00
1.5°C, 15%P	16.83	0.42	1.7	0.013	3.40	0.2	0.569	0.18	0.3	0.003	0.52	1.2	0.03	0.0	0.00
2.5°C, 15%P	9.87	0.17	0.7	0.006	1.36	0.1	0.237	0.08	0.1	0.001	0.19	0.5	0.01	0.0	0.00
5.0°C, 15%P	−8.73	−1.03	−6.4	−0.050	−5.44	−0.5	−1.091	−0.33	−0.5	−0.006	−1.42	−5.5	−0.15	0.0	0.00

Notes:
Negative values indicate baseline damages.
a. Figures in this row are baseline estimates presented in absolute unit terms.
b. P = precipitation.

Table A5.2   Simulated effect of climate change on the welfare of water users in the Midwest (millions 1998 USD)

Climate change scenario	% change in runoff West[b]	% change in runoff East[b]	Total welfare % change in withdrawals	Total welfare Change in welfare ($) Absolute	Percent	Agriculture % change in withdrawals	Agriculture Change in welfare ($) Absolute	Percent	M&I % change in withdrawals	M&I Change in welfare ($) Absolute	Percent	Thermoelectric % change in withdrawals	Thermoelectric Change in welfare ($) Total	Percent	Hydropower Change in welfare ($) Total	Percent
Baseline[a]	378,255 (kaf/yr)		93,649 (kaf/yr)	32,826		1,392 (kaf/yr)	134		21,463 (kaf/yr)	14,397		70,793 (kaf/yr)	16,043		2,251	
1.5°C, 0%P[c]	−14.79	−9.51	−0.67	−119.9	−0.365	−7.25	−3.9	−2.923	−0.18	−0.4	−0.003	−0.0069	−10.0	−0.063	−105.5	−4.69
2.5°C, 0%P	−23.77	−16.19	−1.44	−201.0	−0.6	−16.1	−9.1	−6.9	−0.44	−1.1	−0.01	−1.46	−25.1	−0.2	−166.0	−7.6
5.0°C, 0%P	−42.39	−33.87	−5.36	−548.8	−1.672	−32.52	−22.2	−16.53	−1.77	−4.9	−0.034	−0.0591	−194.9	−1.215	−326.7	−14.51
1.5°C, 7%P	1.04	2.72	−0.01	−29.5	−0.090	0.62	0.4	0.257	0.00	0.0	0.000	−0.0002	−0.2	−0.001	−29.7	−1.32
2.5°C, 7%P	−9.07	−4.08	−0.46	−108.0	−0.329	−6.10	−3.2	−2.405	−0.13	−0.7	−0.005	−0.0045	−5.9	−0.037	−98.2	−4.36
5.0°C, 7%P	−30.61	−22.27	−2.92	−342.7	−1.044	−31.52	−19.9	−14.81	−0.86	−2.2	−0.015	−0.0299	−63.3	−0.395	−257.3	−11.43
1.5°C, 15%P	20.50	16.83	0.46	57.2	0.174	9.18	4.0	2.938	0.15	0.4	0.003	0.0039	4.0	0.025	48.9	2.17
2.5°C, 15%P	9.13	9.87	0.16	−8.8	−0.027	2.62	1.2	0.900	0.06	0.2	0.001	0.0014	1.6	0.010	−11.8	−0.52
5.0°C, 15%P	−15.52	−8.73	−1.19	−210.3	−0.641	−17.20	−10.5	−7.782	−0.32	−0.8	−0.005	−0.0114	−17.7	−0.110	−181.4	−8.06

Notes:
Negative values indicate baseline damages.
a. Figures in this row are baseline estimates presented in absolute unit terms.
b. Runoff for two halves of the Great Lakes region reported separately because the region is modeled by two different watershed models, Delaware and Missouri. Land in the East (Delaware) basin comprises 61% (779,770 km²) of the region's total area; land in the West (Missouri) basin comprises 39% (489,827 km²) of the region's total area.
c. P = precipitation.

Table A5.3 Simulated effect of climate change on the welfare of water users in the Northern Plains (millions 1998 USD)

Climate change scenario	% change in runoff	Total welfare			Agriculture			M&I			Thermoelectric			Hydropower	
		% change in withdrawals	Change in welfare ($) Absolute	Percent	% change in withdrawals	Change in welfare ($) Absolute	Percent	% change in withdrawals	Change in welfare ($) Absolute	Percent	% change in withdrawals	Change in welfare ($) Total	Percent	Change in welfare ($) Total	Percent
Baseline[a]	167,219 (kaf/yr)	42,297 (kaf/yr)	7,781		28,378 (kaf/yr)	2,884		2,689 (kaf/yr)	1,793		11,231 (kaf/yr)	2,482		622	
1.5°C, 0%P[b]	-14.79	-7.41	-295.8	-3.802	-11.00	-137.2	-4.756	-0.10	0.0	-0.001	-0.10	-0.0	-0.001	-158.6	-25.501
2.5°C, 0%P	-23.77	-15.90	-561.0	-7.40	-23.6	-311.0	-11.10	-0.20	-0.0	-0.000	-0.20	-0.1	-0.000	-249.0	-41.20
5.0°C, 0%P	-42.39	-36.74	-1223.6	-15.725	-53.97	-799.4	-27.715	-0.94	-0.2	-0.011	-1.77	-1.9	-0.076	-422.1	-67.87
1.5°C, 7%P	1.04	0.77	-31.4	-0.403	1.17	13.3	0.459	-0.04	0.0	0.000	-0.05	-0.0	-0.001	-44.6	-7.17
2.5°C, 7%P	-9.07	-6.13	-259.8	-3.338	-9.08	-112.1	-3.887	-0.10	0.0	-0.002	-0.10	-0.0	-0.001	-147.6	-23.72
5.0°C, 7%P	-30.61	-32.55	-1081.1	-13.893	-47.88	-692.8	-24.020	-0.75	-0.2	-0.009	-1.40	-1.3	-0.051	-386.8	-62.20
1.5°C, 15%P	20.50	9.58	212.0	2.724	14.27	138.5	4.802	0.04	0.0	0.000	0.02	0.0	0.000	73.5	11.81
2.5°C, 15%P	9.13	2.49	23.3	0.299	3.72	41.0	1.421	-0.01	0.0	0.000	-0.03	-0.0	0.000	-17.7	-2.84
5.0°C, 15%P	-15.52	-18.60	-649.1	-8.342	-27.55	-376.2	-13.044	-0.27	-0.1	-0.003	-0.37	-0.2	-0.006	-272.7	-43.84

Notes:
Negative values indicate baseline damages.
a.   Figures in this row are baseline estimates presented in absolute unit terms.
b.   P = precipitation

Table A5.4 Simulated effect of climate change on the welfare of water users in the Northwest (millions 1998 USD)

Climate change scenario	% change in runoff	Total welfare			Agriculture			M&I			Thermoelectric			Hydropower	
		% change in with-drawals	Change in welfare ($) Absolute	Percent	% change in with-drawals	Change in welfare ($) Absolute	Percent	% change in with-drawals	Change in welfare ($) Absolute	Percent	% change in with-drawals	Change in welfare ($) Total	Percent	Change in welfare ($) Total	Percent
Baseline[a]	238,800 (kaf/yr)	40,704 (kaf/yr)	13,493		36,315 (kaf/yr)	3,691		3,991 (kaf/yr)	2,661		398 (kaf/yr)	88		7,054	
1.5°C, 0%P[b]	-14.79	-9.82	-1974.3	-14.63	-11.00	-175.5	-4.75	-0.10	0.0	-0.001	-0.10	-0.0	-0.001	-1798.8	-25.50
2.5°C, 0%P	-23.77	-21.08	-3221.0	-24.50	-23.60	-398.0	-11.10	-0.20	-0.1	-0.002	-0.20	-0.0	-0.00	-2823.0	-41.10
5.0°C, 0%P	-42.39	-48.26	-5811.2	-43.06	-53.97	-1023.0	-27.715	-0.94	-0.3	-0.011	-1.77	-0.1	-0.076	-4787.9	-67.87
1.5°C, 7%P	1.04	1.04	-489.2	-3.62	1.17	17.0	0.45	-0.04	0.0	0.000	-0.05	0.0	-0.001	-506.2	-7.17
2.5°C, 7%P	-9.07	-8.11	-1817.3	-13.46	-9.08	-143.5	-3.88	-0.10	-0.1	-0.002	-0.10	-0.0	-0.001	-1673.8	-23.72
5.0°C, 7%P	-30.61	-42.81	-5274.6	-39.09	-47.88	-886.6	-24.02	-0.75	-0.2	-0.009	-1.40	-0.0	-0.051	-4387.7	-62.20
1.5°C, 15%P	20.50	12.73	1010.4	7.48	14.27	177.2	4.80	0.04	0.0	0.000	0.02	0.0	0.000	833.1	11.81
2.5°C, 15%P	9.13	3.32	-148.3	-1.09	3.72	52.4	1.42	-0.01	0.0	0.000	-0.03	0.0	0.000	-200.7	-2.84
5.0°C, 15%P	-15.52	-24.61	-3574.2	-26.48	-27.55	-481.5	-13.04	-0.27	-0.1	-0.003	-0.37	-0.0	-0.006	-3092.6	-43.84

Notes:
Negative values indicate baseline damages.
a. Figures in this row are baseline estimates presented in absolute unit terms.
b. P = precipitation.

Table A5.5   Simulated effect of climate change on the welfare of water users in the Southeast (millions 1998 USD)

Climate change scenario	% change in runoff	Total welfare			Agriculture			M&I			Thermoelectric			Hydropower	
		% change in withdrawals	Change in welfare ($) Absolute	Percent	% change in withdrawals	Change in welfare ($) Absolute	Percent	% change in withdrawals	Change in welfare ($) Absolute	Percent	% change in withdrawals	Change in welfare ($) Total	Percent	Change in welfare ($) Total	Percent
Baseline[a]	634,165 (kaf/yr)	67,842 (kaf/yr)	21,766		15,097 (kaf/yr)	1,254		16,440 (kaf/yr)	10,875		36,304 (kaf/yr)	8,057		1,581	
1.5°C, 0%P[b]	-14.79	-0.33	-141.1	-0.64	-0.90	-0.2	-0.016	-0.10	0.0	0.000	-0.20	-0.4	-0.004	-140.5	-8.88
2.5°C, 0%P	-23.77	-0.60	-202.9	-0.93	-1.40	-0.4	-0.029	-0.10	0.0	0.000	-0.50	-1.1	-0.014	-201.4	-12.74
5.0°C, 0%P	-42.39	2.78	-529.2	-2.43	16.73	7.8	0.620	-0.30	-0.2	-0.002	-1.63	-7.0	-0.087	-529.8	-33.51
1.5°C, 7%P	1.04	-0.02	3.4	0.01	-0.12	0.0	-0.002	0.00	0.0	0.000	0.01	0.0	0.000	3.4	0.21
2.5°C, 7%P	-9.07	-0.27	-46.1	-0.21	-0.82	-0.2	-0.013	-0.03	0.0	0.000	-0.15	-0.3	-0.003	-45.7	-2.89
5.0°C, 7%P	-30.61	-0.82	-337.8	-1.55	-1.65	-0.5	-0.036	-0.12	0.0	0.000	-0.79	-2.2	-0.027	-335.1	-21.19
1.5°C, 15%P	20.50	0.14	154.2	0.70	0.12	0.0	0.001	0.03	0.0	0.000	0.19	0.2	0.003	154.0	9.74
2.5°C, 15%P	9.13	0.06	106.8	0.49	0.00	0.0	0.000	0.01	0.0	0.000	0.11	0.1	0.002	106.6	6.74
5.0°C, 15%P	-15.52	-0.60	-140.1	-0.64	-1.65	-0.4	-0.034	-0.08	0.0	0.000	-0.41	-0.9	-0.011	-138.8	-8.77

Notes:
Negative values indicate baseline damages.
a.   Figures in this row are baseline estimates presented in absolute unit terms.
b.   P = precipitation.

Table A5.6 Simulated effect of climate change on the welfare of water users in the Southern Plains (millions 1998 USD)

Climate change scenario	% change in runoff	Total welfare			Agriculture			M&I			Thermoelectric			Hydropower	
		% change in with-drawals	Change in welfare Absolute	Percent.	% change in with-drawals	Change in welfare Absolute	Percent.	% change in with-drawals	Change in welfare Absolute	Percent.	% change in with-drawals	Change in welfare Total	Percent.	Change in welfare Total	Percent.
Baseline[a]	239,833 (kaf/yr)	32,369 (kaf/yr)	8,786		15,688 (kaf/yr)	1,594		6,331 (kaf/yr)	4,221		10,350 (kaf/yr)	2,288		683	
1.5°C, 0%P	−14.79	−5.38	−250.1	−2.84	−11.00	−75.8	−4.756	−0.10	0.0	−0.001	−0.10	−0.0	−0.001	−174.2	−25.50
2.5°C, 0%P	−23.77	−11.54	−458.2	−5.21	−23.60	−177.0	−11.098	−0.20	−0.1	−0.002	−0.20	−0.1	−0.003	−281.1	−41.14
5.0°C, 0%P	−42.39	−26.90	−907.9	−10.33	−53.97	−441.9	−27.715	−0.94	−0.5	−0.011	−1.77	−1.7	−0.076	−463.7	−67.87
1.5°C, 7% P	1.04	0.54	−41.7	−0.47	1.17	7.3	0.459	−0.04	0.0	0.000	−0.05	−0.0	−0.001	−49.0	−7.17
2.5°C, 7% P	−9.07	−4.45	−224.2	−2.55	−9.08	−62.0	−3.887	−0.10	−0.1	−0.002	−0.10	−0.0	−0.001	−162.1	−23.72
5.0°C, 7% P	−30.61	−23.80	−809.5	−9.21	−47.88	−383.0	−24.020	−0.75	−0.4	−0.009	−1.40	−1.2	−0.051	−425.0	−62.20
1.5°C, 15% P	20.50	6.93	157.3	1.79	14.27	76.6	4.802	0.04	0.0	0.000	0.02	0.0	0.000	80.7	11.81
2.5°C, 15% P	9.13	1.79	3.2	0.03	3.72	22.7	1.421	−0.01	0.0	0.000	−0.03	0.0	0.000	−19.4	−2.84
5.0°C, 15% P	−15.52	−13.52	−507.8	−5.77	−27.55	−208.0	−13.044	−0.27	−0.1	−0.003	−0.37	−0.1	−0.006	−299.5	−43.84

Note:
Negative values indicate baseline damages.
a.   Figures in this row are baseline estimates presented in absolute unit terms.
b.   P = precipitation.

130

Table A5.7   Simulated effect of climate change on the welfare of water users in the Southwest (millions 1998 USD)

Climate change scenario	% change in runoff	Total welfare			Agriculture			M&I			Thermoelectric			Hydropower	
		% change in with-drawals	Change in welfare ($)		% change in with-drawals	Change in welfare ($)		% change in with-drawals	Change in welfare ($)		% change in with-drawals	Change in welfare ($)		Change in welfare ($)	
			Absolute	Percent.		Absolute	Percent.		Absolute	Percent.		Total	Percent.	Total	Percent.
Baseline[a]	152,988 (kaf/yr)	71,077 (kaf/yr)	15,949		59,625 (kaf/yr)	5,467		10,801 (kaf/yr)	7,339		651 (kaf/yr)	173		2,970	
1.5°C, 0%P	-14.79	11.12	134.7	0.84	13.20	133.7	2.44	0.30	0.6	0.009	0.60	0.351	0.20	* 0.0	0.00
2.5°C, 0%P	-23.77	5.89	-116.5	-0.73	7.00	75.1	1.37	0.10	0.2	0.003	0.20	0.118	0.06	-191.9	-6.46
5.0°C, 0%P	-42.39	-42.27	-2547.0	-15.96	-47.22	-1013.3	-18.53	-14.36	-33.8	-0.461	-52.29	-249.152	-144.20	-1250.7	-42.11
1.5°C, 7%P	1.04	4.97	177.8	1.11	5.92	63.7	1.16	0.07	0.1	0.002	0.15	0.086	0.05	113.9	3.83
2.5°C, 7%P	-9.07	-5.21	-264.0	-1.65	-6.16	-72.4	-1.32	-0.25	-1.1	-0.015	-0.59	-0.351	-0.20	-190.1	-6.40
5.0°C, 7%P	-30.61	-27.62	-1373.5	-8.61	-32.53	-505.2	-9.24	-1.81	-3.9	-0.053	-6.10	-4.086	-2.36	-860.4	-28.97
1.5°C, 15%P	20.50	29.40	1137.9	7.13	34.95	330.9	6.05	0.48	1.0	0.014	1.22	0.706	0.40	805.3	27.11
2.5°C, 15%P	9.13	17.69	669.3	4.19	21.02	210.7	3.85	0.30	0.6	0.009	0.78	0.456	0.26	457.4	15.40
5.0°C, 15%P	-15.52	-8.64	-446.2	-2.79	-10.21	-124.4	-2.27	-0.39	-0.8	-0.011	-0.93	-0.559	-0.32	-320.4	-10.78

Notes:
Negative values indicate baseline damages.
a.   Figures in this row are baseline estimates presented in absolute unit terms.
b.   P = precipitation.

6. Coastal structures: Dynamic economic modeling

James E. Neumann and Nicholas D. Livesay

INTRODUCTION

For at least the last two decades there has been concern over the potential for changes in climate to cause an increase in sea level (Hoffman *et al.* 1983, Warrick and Oerlemans 1990). Global warming increases thermal expansion and the melting of polar ice caps, resulting in sea level rise. Increases in sea level can present problems to individuals living in coastal and low-lying areas, and can damage structures and beachfront property along the coast. Consequently, sea level rise is likely to impose economic costs on the United States, including the cost of protecting coastal structures and the shoreline as well as the lost value associated with abandoning structures and property.

This chapter builds on previous work that has established the magnitude of these costs on a national level (Yohe *et al.* 1999) to develop regional estimates of the impacts of climate change. We generate economic impact estimates for five coastal regions, consistent with the regional designations established in Chapter 1. We examine four sea level rise scenarios: three examined in Yohe *et al.* (1999) (33, 67 and 100 cm by 2100) and a fourth that more closely approximates the expected rate of eustatic sea level rise (50 cm by 2100) established by the IPCC (Houghton *et al.* 1996).

The estimates presented here were generated using the national sea level rise impact estimation approach developed in Yohe *et al.* (1999). This model has three significant advantages over previous work on coastal inundation. First, it incorporates a careful, site-specific decision-making process to assess whether it is more efficient to protect or abandon specific parcels of land. The decision minimizes the cost to protect versus the lost value of coastal structures that would otherwise be inundated. Second, the model incorporates changes in property value over time, based on a representation of property value increases that relies on projections of GDP and population growth. Third, the model incorporates adaptive measures that could be taken by landowners to mitigate impacts in the coastal zone. Owners anticipating inundation could begin depreciating their buildings by reducing maintenance and avoiding improvements. This would reduce the lost value when the property is eventually abandoned. This final innovation has received criticism in the past because it appears to assume that owners have perfect foresight. Consequently, two alternative scenarios are explored, one where perfect foresight is assumed and one where owners have no foresight.

Despite the attention given to the owner's foresight, the critical innovation in this model is the timing and nature of the protection/abandonment decision. By postponing protection until the decade it is needed, and making only efficient responses in each decade, stakeholders can reduce the costs of coastal protection by roughly an order of magnitude. For more detail on the model and its characteristics, see Yohe *et al.* (1999), Yohe and Neumann (1997) and Yohe and Schlesinger (1997).

The damage estimates in this chapter come from a model of the effects of coastal property inundation. The model is deterministic and sea level is assumed to increase in a gradual consistent manner. However, in practice, much of the damage from sea level rise may actually come from storms. As the sea gradually rises, the severity of the impact of coastal storms increases because the storm surge is added to the higher sea level. In the long run, the expected effect of storms is captured by the deterministic model. However, in the short run, the storms come in random patterns, and the short-run damage is stochastic. If people and society have difficulty making efficient decisions in light of this uncertainty, the damages from sea level rise can increase. That is, the actual decision to protect the coast may either come too soon or too late, adding to the overall cost.

The damage estimates here are limited to effects on the economy. Sea level rise is likely to have nonmarket impacts as well. If seas rise, they will inundate undeveloped land. For example, coastal wetlands will be inundated, which will compromise important ecological service flows provided by these wetlands. These are important effects that should be included in the calculation of the overall damages from global warming, but they are also exceedingly difficult to quantify and monetize in any reliable way. For this reason, ecological damages and reductions in undeveloped land are not examined in this study. The National Assessment (National Assessment Synthesis Team 2000) provides qualitative characterizations of some of these nonmarket effects, as have some previous studies on either a national (Titus 1988) or regional level (Boesch *et al.* 1994; Reed 1995). The quantitative estimates of market effects on developed coastal land in this chapter provide a critical complement to the existing qualitative characterizations of nonmarket effects.

METHODS

The Yohe *et al.* (1999) coastal structure model estimates the cost of rising sea level over time. The study explicitly compares the cost of protecting the coastline from inundation and the benefits of this protection. The benefits of protection are the additional years of use of coastal property that would otherwise have been abandoned when inundated. The true opportunity cost of abandoning coastal property is the projected value of the property after inundation minus the costs of adaptive measures that would be taken to minimize property loss. The model therefore includes a representation of the future trajectory of property value for land and property threatened by inundation.

In addition, the model incorporates two types of adaptive measures. First, the value of land lost to inundation is represented by the value of land located inland from the ocean. At the point of inundation, any price gradient associated with closer proximity to the ocean simply migrates inland, so that in most cases the real loss is best represented by the value of inland property. Developed coastal barrier islands that are at risk of disappearing altogether are the exception. Second, if there is sufficient foresight, structure value should depreciate in the face of a growing risk of inundation. The depreciation serves to mitigate the losses associated with inundation. Full depreciation of structure value in anticipation of inundation is reflected in the perfect-foresight model runs. Alternatively, an efficient process of depreciation could be hampered by ineffective risk communication, faulty risk perception, or an incorrect expectation that land will be protected by public action. The no-foresight model runs reflect no depreciation of the structure value, effectively bounding the impact of this adaptive measure.

The cost of coastal protection is based on two protection alternatives: hard structure armoring through the construction of dikes, seawalls or bulkheads, and the placing of sand on the beach, often referred to as beach nourishment. A capital cost of hard structures of $885 per linear foot (1998 USD) was derived from a review of published studies; the value represents a central estimate from those studies. Maintenance costs are modeled as a percentage of construction costs, again based on estimates reported in published studies. A maintenance cost of 4 per cent per year was chosen as the central estimate, but 10 per cent was used for hard structures that might be built along coastline open directly to the ocean. The capital costs also reflect differences in cost of building structures of different heights. For example, because the base of the required protective structure expands with its height, the structure necessary to protect property from a 1 m rise costs more than twice as much to construct as that necessary to protect from a 0.5 m rise. Finally, costs to nourish beaches were modeled using estimates of the requisite volume to nourish the full beach profile at a rate that matched the relative sea level rise and regional estimates of the price of sand. Beach nourishment is assumed to be necessary starting immediately in 1990, and is assumed to be effective as long as the rise in sea level does not exceed 33 cm. Beyond that threshold, we assume that a hard structure constructed at the back of the beach is necessary to ensure protection of interior property.

The model simulates the protect/abandon decision as a dynamic cost and benefit comparison through time. Using a decadal time step, the model calculates the net benefits of protection at the point when inundation is imminent. If net benefits are positive, then the capital costs for a protective structure are incurred just before inundation, and maintenance costs are incurred for all subsequent years. If net benefits are negative, then the land is abandoned and the opportunity cost of losing both the land and structure value is incurred. In theory, the dynamic nature of the model allows for situations where it might be reasonable to protect for some period of time, but, as property values change over time, the benefit of protection could fall to a point where it is exceeded by the present value of the future stream of maintenance costs. In fact, the increasing trend in property values over time, associated mainly with increasing *per capita* income, ensures that once protection is calculated to be beneficial, continued protection remains the optimal course. The projected upward trend in development value reflects historical patterns of coastal development over the three decades before 1990, and is an important factor in accurately assessing future impacts in the coastal zone.

Along with the sea level rise scenarios (33, 50, 67 and 100 cm) and the assumption about foresight, a host of other factors influence the economic impact of sea level rise. Factors such as growth in GDP and population and the discount rate are model inputs. The model also takes as input site-specific economic parameters such as the value of land and structures and the re-quired length of protective structure necessary. For the model runs, this analysis applied the same input data used by Yohe *et al.* (1999). The results presented here were generated using a 3 per cent discount rate. Sensitivity tests suggest that the use of a higher discount rate would reduce impact estimates substantially, reducing the 100 cm national estimates by roughly 25 per cent for each 1 per cent increase in the discount rate.

The model does not directly estimate regional impacts of sea level rise. Rather, it generates site-specific cost estimates for a given set of inputs. We scale these site-specific model results to the regional level to estimate the impact of sea level rise in the Northeast, Southeast, Southern Plains (Texas), Southwest (California) and Northwest. These five regions, a subset of the US National Assessment regions, include the entire coastline of the 48 contiguous states.[1] Table 6.1 lists the coastal states belonging to each of these five regions.

Table 6.1   US national assessment of regions and coastal states

Region/state	Miles of coastline	Region/state	Miles of coastline
Northeast	789	Southern Plains	367
Maine	228	Texas	367
New Hampshire	13		
Massachusetts	192	Southwest	840
Rhode Island	40	California	840
New York	127		
New Jersey	130	Northwest	453
Delaware	28	Oregon	296
Maryland	31	Washington	157
Southeast	2,544		
Virginia	112		
North Carolina	301		
South Carolina	187		
Alabama	53		
Georgia	100		
Florida	1,350		
Mississippi	44		
Louisiana	397		

Under the four sea level rise scenarios and both foresight assumptions, we estimate the impact of sea level rise on 30 individual coastal sites. These 30 sites, listed in Table 6.2, were originally drawn from a larger set of sites chosen by Park *et al.* (1989),[2] to serve as a national sample for their assessment of the economic damage induced by sea level rise in the United States (see Yohe 1990). For modeling purposes, each site is divided into 500 m by 500 m grid cells. Then, based on the Park *et al.* estimates of the timing of the inundation for each grid cell, the model estimates the economic cost of sea level rise at each site.

Site-specific estimates from within a region are aggregated and adjusted upward using a scaling factor to generate regional impact estimates. The factor applied in this analysis is the ratio of the total number of US sites that have some coastline (identified by Park using US Geological Survey maps) to the number of sites analyzed in this assessment (980/30). This is the same factor that was used by Yohe *et al.* (1999) to estimate the national economic impact of sea level rise based on cost estimates for the same 30 coastal sites.

Table 6.2   Coastal assessment sites by region

Region	Site name	Northern latitude	Western longitude	Natural subsidence[a]
Northeast	Rockland, ME	44 07 30	69 07 30	1.0
	Westport, MA	41 37 30	71 07 30	1.5
	Watch Hill, RI	41 22 30	71 52 30	0.6
	Bridgeport, CT	41 15 00	73 15 00	0.9
	Long Beach Island, NJ	39 45 00	74 15 00	2.7
	Easton, MD	38 52 30	76 07 30	2.4
Southeast	Bloxom, VA	37 52 30	75 37 30	1.9
	Newport News, VA	37 07 30	76 30 00	3.1
	Long Bay, NC	35 00 00	76 30 00	0.6
	Charleston, SC	30 00 00	80 00 00	2.2
	Sea Island, GA	31 22 30	81 22 30	1.8
	St. Augustine, FL	30 07 30	81 30 00	1.8
	Miami, FL	25 52 30	80 15 00	1.1
	Key West, FL	24 37 30	81 52 30	1.0
	Port Richey, FL	28 30 00	83 45 00	0.7
	Apalachicola, FL	29 45 00	85 07 30	1.2
	St. Joseph, FL	29 52 30	85 30 00	0.7
	Pass Christian, MS	30 22 30	89 15 00	1.2
	Main Pass, LA	29 22 30	89 15 00	9.3
	Barataria, LA	29 45 00	90 22 30	9.3
	Grand Chenier, LA	29 52 30	93 00 00	8.5
Southern Plains	Palacios, TX	28 45 00	96 15 00	2.8
	Portland, TX	27 52 30	97 22 00	2.8
	Green Island, TX	26 30 00	97 22 00	3.9
Southwest	Albion, CA	39 15 00	123 52 30	0.0
	Point Sal, CA	35 00 00	120 45 00	0.0
	San Quentin, CA	38 00 00	122 30 00	0.1
Northwest	Yaquina, OR	44 45 00	124 07 30	−1.0
	Anacortes, WA	48 45 00	122 45 00	0.2
	Tacoma, WA	47 30 00	122 30 00	0.8

Note: a. Rate of shoreline subsidence in millimeters per year.

The suite of sites used in this assessment was originally selected by Yohe (1990) to be representative of the national impact of sea level rise. Yohe (1990) interprets the Park *et al.* (1989) sample to be 'roughly defined by selecting every tenth 30-minute cell provided by the US Geological Survey as one moves consecutively around the US coastline'. Yohe (1990) systematically selected 30 of the 93 Park sites. While the sample of 30 sites is dispersed relatively evenly throughout the United States and the five coastal regions, economic impact estimates for some regions may be influenced by the site distribution.[3] Generating regional estimates consistent with the regional definitions requires, in some cases, generating regional estimates from a relatively small number of sites. For example, the California coast is characterized by only three sites.

Small numbers of sample sites in some regions lead to two effects. First, small sample sizes lead to high standard errors on the regional estimates. Second, while the sample of 30 sites in aggregate provides a reasonable representation of the variability in national coastal conditions, a small number of sites in each region may not adequately represent the variability in that one region. The three California sites, for example, include no sites south of Santa Barbara, and only one site in an urbanized area (San Quentin). As a result, they reflect the coastal cliff topography that characterizes much of the northern two-thirds of the California coast, but do not capture impacts to the more gradual topography and more highly developed (and more economically valuable) land areas of the California coast that are more common in the Los Angeles and San Diego areas. We would expect that impacts in California would be concentrated in these areas south of Santa Barbara. As a result, impacts in California are most likely underestimated.[4] In addition, the three Texas sites do not include the most populous and developed portions of the Texas coast; the areas around Galveston and Corpus Christi Bay, for example, are omitted in the nationally oriented site selection process. The impacts in Texas are most likely also underestimated, although perhaps to a lesser degree than in California. In contrast, the urbanized areas in the national sample tend to be better reflected in the Northeast and Southeast regions. For example, the Southeast region includes Newport News, Charleston, and Miami, all relatively densely populated coastal cities with valuable land at risk of inundation (although New Orleans, the city perhaps most threatened by sea level rise, is not in the sample). To a modest extent, these two regions may over-represent coastal urban areas, but the bias is likely to be slight.

RESULTS AND DISCUSSION

Table 6.3 reports the economic cost of sea level rise under all four scenarios, with and without foresight, for the contiguous United States. The present value of the stream of costs is calculated using a 3 per cent discount rate. These calculations indicate that the total estimated economic impact of sea level rise in the United States ranges from $1.06 billion under the 33 cm perfect-foresight scenario to $7.56 billion under the 100 cm no-foresight scenario. Comparison across scenarios reveals that the estimates follow the expected pattern. The cost of sea level rise increases with steeper sea level rise trajectories. With no foresight, the present value of costs is $1.1 billion with 33 cm, $2.2 billion with 50 cm, $3.5 billion with 67 cm and $7.6 billion

Table 6.3   National impacts by sea level scenario (present value of damages in millions 1998 USD)

	Sea level scenario			
	33 cm	50 cm	67 cm	100 cm
Foresight	1,056	2,117	3,307	6,449
No foresight	1,098	2,231	3,527	7,561

Note: National estimates are calculated by applying a weight of 32.67 (98/30) to each site (Table 6.5). Present value calculated using 3% discount rate.

with 100 cm. The economic cost estimates assuming perfect foresight are lower, especially for the more severe scenarios, as people depreciate their structures prior to inundation. These predicted national impacts are much lower than earlier estimates by other researchers who did not examine the protection decision over time as carefully. For example, Fankhauser's (1994)

Table 6.4   Regional impacts by sea level scenario (present value of damages in millions 1998 USD)

	Sea level scenario			
Region 100 cm	33 cm	50 cm	67 cm
		Foresight		
Northeast	41	751	1,119	2,089
Northwest	26	93	165	371
Southeast	599	1,231	1,940	3,819
Southern Plains	1	2	4	4
Southwest	13	40	79	166
		No foresight		
Northeast	417	751	1,119	2,143
Northwest	26	93	168	435
Southeast	641	1,343	2,154	4,763
Southern Plains	1	4	7	15
Southwest	13	40	79	205

Note: Regional estimates are calculated by applying a weight of 32.67 (980/30) to each site (Table 6.5). Present value calculated using 3% discount rate.

Table 6.5 Local impacts by sea level scenario (present value of costs in millions 1998 USD)

Region Site name	33 cm 30 years foresight	33 cm 0 years foresight	50 cm 30 years foresight	50 cm 0 years foresight	67 cm 30 years foresight	67 cm 0 years foresight	100 cm 30 years foresight	100 cm 0 years foresight
Northeast								
Rockland, ME	0.14	0.14	0.352	0.352	0.563	0.563	1.278	1.278
Westport, MA	0.288	0.288	0.889	0.889	1.635	1.635	4.495	4.518
Watch Hill, RI	0.906	0.906	2.533	2.533	4.384	4.384	10.926	10.926
Bridgeport, CT	0.563	0.563	1.828	1.828	3.362	3.362	7.331	8.966
Long Beach Island, NJ[bc]	10.555	10.555	16.068	16.068	21.631	21.631	32.695	32.695
Easton, MD	0.312	0.312	1.306	1.306	2.670	2.670	7.2	7.2
Southeast								
Bloxom, VA	0.000	0.000	0.000	0.000	0.000	0.000	0.000	0.000
Newport News, VA[a]	2.801	2.801	8.216	8.216	14.971	14.971	38.499	38.724
-Suffolk	0.011	0.011	0.07	0.07	0.163	0.163	0.3	0.525
-Hampton	1.998	1.998	5.773	5.773	10.386	10.386	26.340	26.340
-Norfolk	0.417	0.417	1.407	1.407	2.779	2.779	7.643	7.643
-Portsmouth	0.376	0.376	0.968	0.968	1.643	1.643	4.216	4.216
Long Bay, NC	0.289	0.289	0.709	1.982	1.035	3.286	1.513	5.619
Charleston, SC[a]	1.123	1.455	2.576	3.254	4.101	4.974	10.586	21.41
-Charleston City	0.000	0.000	0.074	0.074	0.308	0.308	1.299	1.433
-Mt. Pleasant	0.588	0.588	1.717	1.717	2.844	3.009	4.787	7.419
-Avondale	0.000	0.000	0.000	0.000	0.000	0.000	0.208	0.218
-Dorchester	0.536	0.867	0.785	1.463	0.949	1.657	1.135	1.906
-Sullivan's Island[bc]	0.000	0.000	0.000	0.000	0.000	0.000	3.157	10.43

Location							
Sea Island, GA[bc]	2.562	2.562	3.958	3.958	5.403	5.403	8.475	8.475
St. Augustine, FL[bc]	0.950	1.864	1.501	2.301	2.006	2.740	2.638	3.305
Miami, FL[bc]	5.980	5.980	9.091	9.091	12.26	12.26	18.49	18.49
Key West, FL[c]	0.623	0.623	1.818	1.818	3.429	3.429	13.73	13.73
Port Richey, FL[c]	0.516	0.516	1.289	1.289	2.063	2.063	4.687	4.687
Apalachicola, FL	0.000	0.000	0.000	0.000	0.000	0.000	0.096	0.271
St. Joseph, FL	0.000	0.000	0.000	0.000	0.000	0.000	0.000	0.000
Pass Christian, MS	0.282	0.282	0.704	0.704	1.127	1.127	1.564	2.242
Main Pass, LA	0.000	0.000	0.000	0.000	0.000	0.000	0.000	0.000
Barataria, LA	2.412	2.412	6.029	2.489	10.745	9.645	13.466	19.615
Grand Chenier, LA	0.826	0.826	1.797	3.063	2.361	6.036	3.141	9.219
Southern Plains								
Palacios, TX	0.028	0.028	0.066	0.103	0.092	0.232	0.125	0.467
Portland, TX	0.000	0.000	0.000	0.000	0.000	0.000	0.000	0.000
Green Island, TX	0.000	0.000	0.000	0.000	0.000	0.000	0.000	0.000
Southwest								
Albion, CA	0.000	0.000	0.000	0.000	0.000	0.000	0.000	0.000
Point Sal, CA	0.000	0.000	0.000	0.000	0.000	0.000	0.000	0.000
San Quentin, CA	0.382	0.382	1.238	1.238	2.425	2.425	5.099	6.295
Northwest								
Yaquina, OR	0.089	0.089	0.33	0.33	0.708	0.708	2.246	2.246
Anacortes, WA	0.262	0.262	0.903	0.903	1.67	1.75	2.80	4.78
Tacoma, WA	0.459	0.459	1.61	1.61	2.68	2.68	6.28	2.77

Notes:
All values assume a rate of 4% was used for variable costs of protection, unless otherwise specified.
a.   Values are taken as a sum of all subsites analyzed at that site.
b.   A site involving a beach nourishment strategy.
c.   A site using 10% variable protection cost instead of 4%.

141

estimates imply a present value of national costs for a 100 cm rise of about $118 billion (1998 USD). Fankhauser's results are quite similar to the impacts predicted by the IPCC (Pearce *et al.* 1996).

This study, however, focuses on regional estimates. The regional costs of sea level rise in Table 6.4 indicate that the impact estimates are largest for the Northeast and Southeast, and considerably smaller for the remaining three regions. By itself the Southeast accounts for 55 to 65 per cent of the national impact of sea level rise; together with the Northeast these two regions account for more than 90 per cent of the total economic cost of sea level rise (Figure 6.1). The region with the third largest impact is the Northwest, followed by the Southwest and the Southern Plains, respectively. Table 6.5 presents the economic costs of sea level rise for the 30 sites within the five regions.

The vulnerability of a region to inundation is one of the primary factors that influence the magnitude of the impact of sea level rise. The Northeast and Southeast are both sections of the country with large low-lying coastal areas. This helps explain why the impact of sea level rise is so much larger in these two regions than in the rest of the United States. One measure of vulnerability is the rate of natural shoreline subsidence. Table 6.2 shows the baseline trends for natural shoreline subsidence at the 30 sites. Along the West Coast, relative sea level is expected to remain at a relatively constant height over time, with a few areas where the land is actually rising relative to

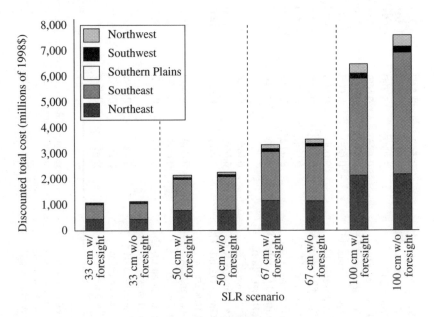

Figure 6.1   Regional economic cost of sea level rise

sea level. However, the land along the eastern seaboard and Gulf Coast is slowly sinking. The rate of subsidence is especially high in Mississippi and Louisiana, two states in the Southeast region.

In addition to vulnerability, the total coastal area of a region, along with the value of property and cost of protection, also contributes to the size of the regional economic impact of sea level rise. For example, the Texas coast is part of the low-lying, highly susceptible Gulf Coast. This region, however, contains only 367 miles of coastline. This is too small a portion of the total coastline of the 48 contiguous states to account for a significant fraction of the national impact of sea level rise, especially considering average property values are lower in this region than in other parts of the United States. The Southeast, on the other hand, accounts for approximately one-half of the US coastline. Average per site property values and protection costs tend to be higher in this region, and there is a comparatively high vulnerability to inundation. These two factors explain why the economic impact of sea level rise in the Southeast is so much larger than in other regions of the United States.

Examination of transient costs also provides insight into the regional economic impact of sea level rise. Figures 6.2 through 6.6 illustrate the transient costs of sea level rise under all four scenarios and both foresight assumptions for the Northeast, Southeast, Texas, Southern Plains, Southwest and North-

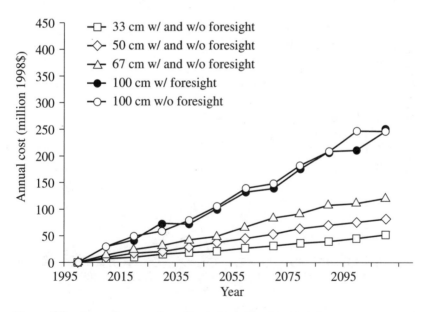

Figure 6.2   Annual costs of sea level rise – Northeast region

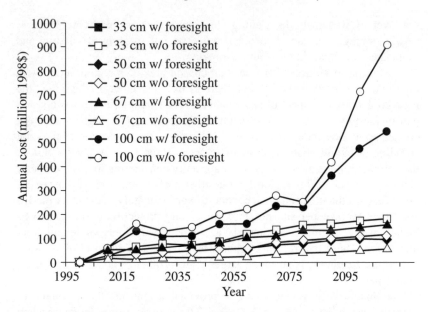

Figure 6.3   Annual costs of sea level rise – Southeast region

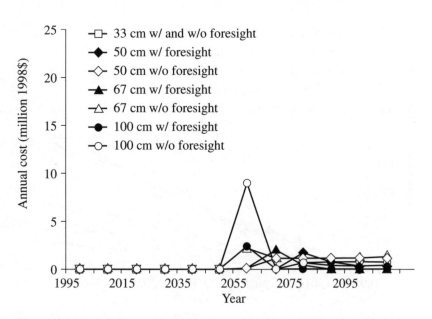

Figure 6.4   Annual costs of sea level rise – Southern Plains region

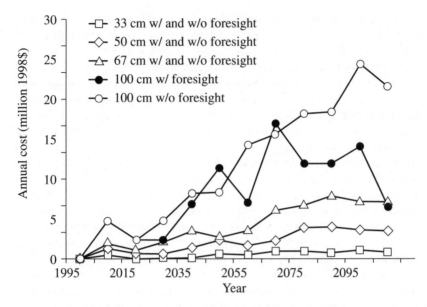

Figure 6.5   Annual costs of sea level rise – Southwest region

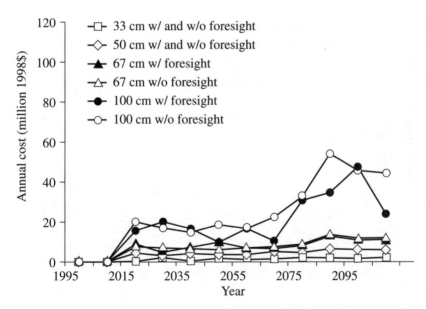

Figure 6.6   Annual costs of sea level rise – Northwest region

west, respectively. Not surprisingly, these figures show an increase in the cost of sea level rise over time across all scenarios. Given the small sample size in each region, the increase appears not to be steady. Capital investment in protection, for example, can trigger sizeable jumps in cost. These lump sum investments are then followed by smaller expenditures required for operation and maintenance. Large fluctuations in costs also frequently follow inundation when property is abandoned. The peaks in Figure 6.4 under both 100 cm scenarios and the 50 cm and 67 cm scenarios with foresight, for example, are the result of property being abandoned and allowed to flood. The peaks and troughs would tend to smooth out with larger samples, so the reader should not overinterpret these regional fluctuations. The remaining trend lines in this figure represent a protection strategy similar to the one described above, a one-time capital investment followed by smaller operating and maintenance costs. When examining transient costs for the Southern Plains region (Figure 6.4) and the Southwest tegion (Figure 6.5), it is important to remember that these estimates effectively reflect annual impact estimates for just a single site.[5] Regions with a smaller sample of sites tend to have more irregular transient cost trend lines; some of the fluctuation is smoothed in regions with larger samples of sites because an average of the site impact estimates is used to estimate transient costs. Even in the Southeast, however, a region with 15 sites, costs at a single site can dominate the trend line. The sharp increase in

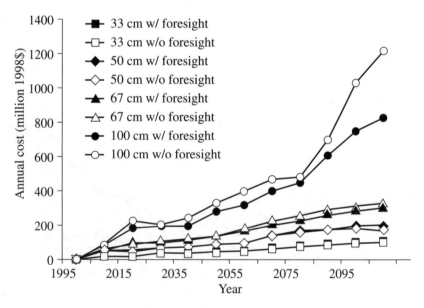

Figure 6.7   Annual costs of sea level rise – United States

the 100 cm scenario costs between 2075 and 2085 in Figure 6.3 is the result of a substantial cost increase at the Key West, Florida, site. Overall, the annual impact increases over time, growing slowly until the 2080s and then increasing more rapidly through 2100 for all coastal states (see Figure 6.7).

The regional effects of sea level rise are concentrated in the Southeast and Northeast. The Southeast is hit the hardest by sea level rise because it has a relatively large amount of flat coastline with a high economic value. With a 50 cm sea level trajectory by 2100, the Southeast is expected to endure damages of about $94 million per year by 2060. The Northeast will have damages of about $47 million per year. The remaining three coastal regions will have damages of less than $20 million per year.

In addition to providing a set of consistently developed regional esti-mates of the economic effects of sea level rise on coastal structures, this work offers the critical insight of the need for additional focus on potential 'hot spots' where impacts may be more severely experienced. Additional work is needed in two dimensions. First, the results for the Southwest region and, to a lesser extent, the Southern Plains clearly suggest that further site assessment is needed to reduce the high sampling error in these regions. Second, it is not clear whether governments will in fact make efficient decisions. It is possible that governments, for example, will be strongly influenced by the issue of who will benefit from coastal protection. One important improvement coastal studies could make is to track the winners and losers from different strategies. Analyses could then explore the consequences of alternative decision rules that protect certain groups or individuals even if such protection is not efficient.

NOTES

1. The regions defined in the National Assessment are different than the coastal regions reflected in Yohe *et al.* For example, in the Yohe *et al.* analysis, the Southeast region estimates reflect sites in North Carolina, South Carolina and Georgia, and on the Atlantic coast of Florida.
2. The Park *et al.* (1989) site selection is described as follows: 'Ninety-three sites were chosen, using an unbiased systematic sampling of US Geological Survey topographical maps at a scale of 1:24,000. Starting with the easternmost quadrangle in Maine and restricting the choice to those maps that included some part of the coast, every 15th quadrangle was picked as the center of a site consisting of one to four quadrangles.' As described in the text, Yohe (1990) interprets the results of the Park sampling to yield a roughly one-tenth sample of 30-minute cells, provided by the US Geological Survey. For the initial Yohe *et al.* (1990) work, and subsequent economic modeling, a subsample of 30 sites was chosen from the 93 Park sites.
3. For each region, the number of sites per meter of coastline is within an order of magnitude. The ratios for each of the five regions are Northeast 0.0076, Southeast 0.0059, Southern Plains 0.0082, Southwest 0.0036, and Northwest 0.0066. The average for the entire United States is 0.0060 sites per mile of coastline.

4. In subsequent work we hope to add additional sites in California to specifically address this
    concern, while nonetheless retaining an overall unbiased sample for that state.
5. In both the Southern Plains and Southwest regions the impact of sea level rise was modeled
    for three sites. In each region, even under the 100 cm scenario, the inundation mapping
    suggests only one of the three sites will experience any loss of developed land by 2100.

REFERENCES

Boesch, D.F., M.N. Josselyn, A.J. Mehta, J.T. Morris, W.K. Nuttle, C.A. Simenstad
and D.J.P. Swift (1994), 'Scientific assessment of coastal wetland loss, restoration
and management in Louisiana', *Journal of Coastal Research*, Special Issue No. 20.

Fankhauser, S. (1994), *Valuing Climate Change: The Economics of the Greenhouse
Effect*, London: Earthscan.

Hoffman J., D. Keyes and J. Titus (1983), *Projecting Future Sea Level Rise,* Washington, DC: US Environmental Protection Agency.

Houghton, J.T., L.G. Meira Filho, B.A. Callander, N. Harris, A. Kattenberg and K.
Maskell (1996), *Climate Change 1995, The Science of Climate Change,* Cambridge, UK: Cambridge University Press.

National Assessment Synthesis Team (2000), Climate Change Impacts on the United
States: The Potential Consequence of Climate Variability and Change, Report for
the US Global Change Research Program, Cambridge, UK: Cambridge University
Press.

Park, R., J. Trehan, P. Mausel and R. Howe (1989), 'The effects of sea level rise on
U.S. coastal wetlands', in *The Potential Effects of Global Climate Change on the
United States: Appendix B, Sea Level Rise*, Report to Congress, Washington, DC:
US Environmental Protection Agency.

Pearce, D.W., W.R. Cline, A.N. Achanta, S. Fankhauser, R.K. Pachauri, R.S.J. Tol
and P. Vellinga (1996), 'The social costs of climate change: Greenhouse damage
and the benefits of control', in J.P. Bruce, H. Lee, and E.F. Haites (eds), *Climate
Change 1995: Economic and Social Dimensions of Climate Change*, Cambridge,
UK: Cambridge University Press, pp.179–224.

Reed, D.J. (1995) 'The response of coastal marshes to sea-level rise: Survival or
submergence?', *Earth Surface Processes and Landforms*, 20, 39–48.

Titus, J.G. (ed.) (1988), *Greenhouse Effect, Sea Level Rise, and Coastal Wetlands*,
Washington, DC: US Environmental Protection Agency.

Warrick, R.A. and H. Oerlemans (1990), 'Sea-level rise', in J.T. Houghton, G.J.
Jenkins, and J.J. Ephraums (eds), *Climate Change: The IPCC Scientific Assessment*, Cambridge, UK: Cambridge University Press, pp. 257–81.

Yohe, G. (1990), 'The cost of not holding back the sea – toward a national sample of
economic vulnerability', *Coastal Management*, 18, 403–32.

Yohe, G. and J. Neumann (1997), 'Planning for sea level rise and shore protection
under climate uncertainty', *Climatic Change*, 37, 111–40.

Yohe, G. and M. Schlesinger (1997), 'Sea level change: The expected economic cost
of protection or abandonment in the United States,' *Climatic Change*, 38, 447–72.

Yohe, G., J.E. Neumann and P. Marshall (1999), 'The economic damage induced by
sea level rise in the United States', in R. Mendelsohn and J. Neumann (eds), *The
Impact of Climate Change on the United States Economy*, Cambridge, UK: Cambridge University Press, pp. 178–208.

7. Energy: Cross-sectional analysis

Robert Mendelsohn

INTRODUCTION

This study uses a cross-sectional analysis to estimate the climate sensitivity of regional energy demand (Morrison and Mendelsohn 1999, 2000). Energy expenditures of individual households and firms are regressed on a number of control variables and climate to estimate climate sensitivity. Because an approximately constant interior temperature is maintained in homes and buildings across all climates in the United States, the change in energy expenditures required to cope with a climate change provides an approximate measure of the welfare effects. Larger energy expenditures imply damages, or additional costs to maintain the same level of comfort, whereas lower energy expenditures would imply benefits, or savings in costs for energy.

Using energy expenditures to measure welfare is only an approximation because it may not take into account changes in building expenditures and comfort levels. Building expenditures can be important as firms and households change building characteristics such as insulation and cooling capacity in response to warming. To measure the importance of building characteristics, both a short-run measure that freezes building characteristics and a long-run measure that allows building characteristics to change are estimated. The difference between the two measures provides an indication of the importance of changing buildings to adjust to climate changes.

The energy expenditure measure is also approximate because households may respond to warming by changing their comfort levels. This may be especially important with respect to cooling, where many households currently do not purchase adequate cooling capacity to remain cool during hot summer days. This is currently an issue in cool northern regions. The hot summer days do not last long enough to encourage many households to install comprehensive cooling equipment. Households in these regions currently choose not to cool rather than adapt to the few hot days that they face. As temperatures warm, these households may choose to be more uncomfortable rather than spend more on cooling. The expenditure method will underestimate the damages from warming if it does not account for this lost

149

comfort. Because we forecast an increased penetration of air conditioning in the future, we expect the bias from omitting changes in comfort to be small.

The approach used in this study differs from the energy warming literature in several important ways. First, the study includes more adaptation than previous studies considered. Rosenthal *et al.* (1995) and Linder and Inglis (1989) examined the effect of climate change on existing structures; they did not consider whether structures might change in response to warming. Second, Linder and Inglis study energy demand in 1990, and Rosenthal *et al.* study energy demand in 2020. This study examines energy demand in 2060. Third, the Linder and Inglis study focused only on electricity, whereas the Rosenthal *et al.* and this study include all fuels. Finally, the Linder and Inglis and Rosenthal *et al.* studies estimated energy responses to climate through engineering models, not human behavior. This study uses cross-sectional evidence to measure energy impacts and thus includes human responses.

This study also differs from an earlier analysis by Morrison and Mendelsohn (1999) even though similar data and methods were used. In the earlier study, the authors use an annual description of climate, whereas in this study the analysis examines a seasonal model. The earlier study focused on national effects, and this study focuses on regional effects.

REGIONAL METHODOLOGY

The seven regions for this study are identified in Chapter 1. This study computed regional effects by examining households and firms that lie in each region. Unfortunately, the data set did not identify which state an observation came from. The most detailed geographic identifier was the US Census division. The Census divisions closely correspond to five of the regions of this study (Northeast, Midwest, Northern Plains, Southeast and Southern Plains). There is not exact correspondence for every state, however. The Rocky Mountain and far western states were difficult to fit into the study regions. The Census divides the West into a Pacific Coast region and an Intermountain region. This study divides the West into three regions: Southwest, Northwest and Northern Plains. It is not possible to get this exact division from the sample. To approximate these regions, the two Census divisions were divided on the basis of summer temperatures. The cooler half of the Pacific Coast division was assumed to be the Northwest. The cooler half of the Intermountain region was assumed to be in the Northern Plains. The warmer half of the Pacific Coast (California) and the warmer half of the intermountain region were combined into the Southwest region. Table 7.1 lists the states, the Census division, the desired region and the actual region.

Table 7.1   Regional definitions

State	Census division	Desired region	Actual region
Maine	Northeast	Northeast	Northeast
New Hampshire	Northeast	Northeast	Northeast
Vermont	Northeast	Northeast	Northeast
Massachusetts	Northeast	Northeast	Northeast
Rhode Island	Northeast	Northeast	Northeast
Connecticut	Northeast	Northeast	Northeast
New York	MidAtlantic	Northeast	Northeast
New Jersey	MidAtlantic	Northeast	Northeast
Pennsylvania	MidAtlantic	Northeast	Northeast
Delaware	Southeast	Northeast	Southeast
Maryland	Southeast	Northeast	Southeast
Virginia	Southeast	Northeast	Southeast
West Virginia	Southeast	Northeast	Southeast
Ohio	Midwest	Midwest	Midwest
Indiana	Midwest	Midwest	Midwest
Illinois	Midwest	Midwest	Midwest
Michigan	Midwest	Midwest	Midwest
Wisconsin	Midwest	Midwest	Midwest
Minnesota	Northern Plains	Midwest	Northern Plains
Iowa	Northern Plains	Midwest	Northern Plains
Missouri	Northern Plains	Midwest	Northern Plains
North Dakota	Northern Plains	Northern Plains	Northern Plains
South Dakota	Northern Plains	Northern Plains	Northern Plains
Nebraska	Northern Plains	Northern Plains	Northern Plains
Kansas	Northern Plains	Northern Plains	Northern Plains
Montana	Intermountain	Northern Plains	Northern Plains
Wyoming	Intermountain	Northern Plains	Northern Plains
North Carolina	Southeast	Southeast	Southeast
South Carolina	Southeast	Southeast	Southeast
Georgia	Southeast	Southeast	Southeast
Florida	Southeast	Southeast	Southeast
Kentucky	South Central	Southeast	Southeast
Tennessee	South Central	Southeast	Southeast
Alabama	Southeast	Southeast	Southeast
Mississippi	South Central	Southeast	Southeast
Louisiana	South Central	Southeast	South Plains
Arkansas	South Plains	South Plains	South Plains
Oklahoma	South Plains	South Plains	South Plains
Texas	South Plains	South Plains	South Plains
Idaho	Intermountain	Northwest	Northern Plains
Washington	Pacific West	Northwest	Northwest
Oregon	Pacific West	Northwest	Northwest
Colorado	Intermountain	Southwest	Northern Plains
Utah	Intermountain	Southwest	Northern Plains
California	Pacific West	Southwest	Southwest
Nevada	Intermountain	Southwest	Southwest
New Mexico	Intermountain	Southwest	Southwest
Arizona	Intermountain	Southwest	Southwest

National expenditure equations were estimated for both short-run and long-run energy expenditures. The residential equations are reported in Table 7.2 and the commercial results are reported in Table 7.3. Note that the functional form for both of these regressions is loglinear. Climate consequently has a proportional effect on energy expenditures, not an additive effect.

The regressions in this chapter are different from the regressions in Morrison and Mendelsohn (1999). In that earlier study, annual temperature was used and precipitation was dropped. In subsequent work, however, it was found that summer and winter temperature and precipitation variables provide a clearer explanation of the energy sector. This new winter–summer specification is used in this regional study. This change in specification is important for two reasons. First, the winter–summer specification clearly shows that winter warming would reduce energy expenditures because heating would go down, whereas summer warming would increase energy expenditures needed for cooling. Second, the new specification suggests that energy is more sensitive to warming than was previously thought. The aggregate national effects in this chapter are consequently about twice those reported in Morrison and Mendelsohn (1999). Further, the precipitation coefficients are now significant, although precipitation effects are small relative to temperature effects. Energy expenditures increase with precipitation, reflecting the increased cost of heating and cooling in higher humidity and the increased discomfort of cool and hot temperatures in high humidity.

Simulations were run to estimate the impacts of alternative climate scenarios to each household and firm. Nine climate change scenarios were run, as described in Chapter 1. The regional effects were calculated by summing effects across the households and firms in each region. The sum of all the regional effects equals the national impact. Because these effects were calculated using a cross-sectional empirical approach, one can calculate the 95 per cent confidence interval around each regional estimate. The scenarios emphasized in this chapter concern the energy sector as it is projected to be in 2060. These projections incorporate increases in population and economic growth. They also include expected modernization in both the residential and commercial sectors and changes in energy prices.

SIMULATION RESULTS

The results for the warming scenarios for the residential and commercial sectors are presented in Tables 7.4 and 7.5. Table 7.4 displays the welfare impacts for the residential sector along with the 95 per cent confidence interval. As expected, damages increase as temperatures rise in every case

Table 7.2   Regression of residential energy expenditures

Variable	Short run	Long run	Variable	Short run	Long run
Constant	39.81	18.70	log income	5.27e-2	0.10
	(7.58)	(3.86)		(7.35)	(14.17)
Jan. temp	−7.61e-3	−6.16e-3	log home area	0.18	0.28
	(−4.40)	(−3.41)		(12.28)	(26.34)
Jan. temp^2	−2.06e-4	−1.23e-4	log # floors	−0.10	−0.13
	(−1.73)	(−0.98)		(−7.86)	(−9.60)
Jan. precip	2.00e-2	2.23e-2	log year built	−4.61	−1.93
	(3.51)	(3.70)		(−6.66)	(−3.02)
Jan. precip^2	−1.68e-3	−1.13e-3	log family size	0.23	0.26
	(−2.44)	(−1.55)		(23.71)	(25.69)
July temp	1.34e-2	2.34e-2	log age of head	7.35e-2	0.11
	(4.13)	(7.00)		(4.22)	(5.89)
July temp^2	2.39e-3	1.50e-3	multiple units	−9.77e-2	−0.11
	(4.68)	(2.81)		(−5.84)	(−6.89)
July precip	1.75e-2	2.01e-2	tenant controls heat	0.18	0.23
	(3.93)	(4.31)		(4.39)	(5.39)
July precip^2	−4.56e-3	−5.29e-3	black/white	0.10	0.11
	(−2.81)	(−3.09)		(3.43)	(3.62)
Log electricity price	0.33	0.29	Hispanic	−4.76e-2	−6.75e-2
	(17.86)	(15.12)		(−2.54)	(−3.41)
Log natural gas price	0.17	0.19	over 65	−2.54e-2	−4.07e-2
	(8.43)	(9.24)		(−1.57)	(−2.40)
Log fuel oil price	−3.82e-2	−1.74e-2	cash aid	−0.19	−0.18
	(−1.26)	(−0.55)		(−3.86)	(−3.40)
Log lpg price	−8.29e-2	−6.57e-2	heat aid	7.13e-2	6.75e-2
	(−3.45)	(−2.61)		(2.76)	(2.48)
Log kerosene price	1.52e-2	−3.50e-2	wood burning	−5.20e-2	−4.27e-2
	(0.27)	(−0.60)		(−4.43)	(−3.49)
Metropolitan	2.00e-2	1.97e-2			
	(1.90)	(1.77)			
Log # rooms	0.12		dish/cloth wash/dry	0.10	
	(4.97)			(7.10)	
Log # doors/ windows	8.56e-2		central AC	0.16	
	(6.16)			(11.34)	
Basement	−9.21e-2		wall/window AC	4.47e-2	
	(−6.92)			(3.80)	
Poor insulation	3.96e-2		electric wall heat	9.15e-2	
	(3.36)			(6.87)	
Electricity discount	−6.71e-2		portable kerosene	0.20	
	(−2.44)			(3.05)	
Color TV	5.95e-2		natural gas available	−5.20e-2	
	(10.82)			(−4.54)	
Computer	3.71e-2				
	(2.81)				
Adjusted R^2	0.97	0.96			
Number of obs.	5,030	5,030			

Note: t-statistics in parentheses.

Table 7.3   Regression of commercial energy expenditures

Variable	Short run	Long run	Variable	Short run	Long run
Constant	−58.00	−64.83	% outpatient	2.95e-3	3.99e-3
	(−8.05)	(−8.45)		(3.61)	(4.50)
Jan. temp	−1.31e-2	−1.79e-2	% lab/ref whs	9.65e-3	1.11e-2
	(−2.90)	(−3.64)		(6.57)	(6.93)
Jan. temp^2	4.20e-4	6.85e-4	% industry	1.36e-2	1.96e-2
	(1.37)	(2.06)		(4.00)	(5.30)
Jan. precip	2.98e-2	4.73e-2	% office	4.21e-3	5.36e-3
	(2.32)	(3.40)		(9.62)	(11.71)
Jan. precip^2	−1.58e-2	−1.94e-2	% retail/service	2.81e-3	3.50e-3
	(−8.45)	(−9.54)		(7.54)	(8.84)
July temp	−2.62e-2	−5.80e-3	% education	2.97e-3	4.23e-3
	(−3.11)	(−0.64)		(5.30)	(7.00)
July temp^2	−5.22e-3	5.23e-3	metropolitan	0.38	0.47
	(3.83)	(3.53)		(13.69)	(15.79)
July precip	2.67e-3	−6.81e-4	log sqft	0.52	0.69
	(0.25)	(−0.06)		(39.06)	(52.44)
July precip^2	5.66e-3	5.05e-3	log # floors	0.13	0.21
	(1.45)	(1.19)		(4.14)	(6.27)
Log electricity price	−0.53	−0.65	log year built	7.83	8.55
	(−16.91)	(−19.35)		(8.22)	(8.43)
Log natural gas price	−9.73e-2	−0.10	months open/year	2.67e-2	2.91e-2
	(−3.21)	(−3.05)		(4.87)	(4.87)
Log fuel oil price	9.01e-2	−0.17	alternative fuel used	−0.53	−0.61
	(0.45)	(−0.79)		(−11.90)	(−12.51)
Log dist. heat price	−1.03e-2	−9.78e-2	% food sale/serve	8.15e-3	1.46e-2
	(−0.07)	(−0.66)		(13.45)	(25.71)
% health	7.09e-3	1.09e-2	% nonref wh/vac	−3.45e-3	−5.90e-3
	(5.87)	(8.33)		(−7.68)	(−12.52)
Ice/vending/water	0.47		ht. pump – heat	0.14	
	(17.05)			(2.06)	
Refrigerator	0.45		tenant controls heat	−0.15	
	(12.62)			(−5.57)	
Air duct – cool	0.12		roof: built up	0.14	
	(3.64)			(4.87)	
Air duct – heat	0.08		roof: glass	−1.79	
	(2.47)			(−5.69)	
Boilers	0.22		roof: metal surface	−0.15	
	(6.16)			(−4.32)	
AC in computer room	0.59		wall: masonry	−0.80	
	(11.00)			(−4.23)	
Ht. pump – cool	−0.12		wall: shingle	−0.14	
	(−1.74)			(−4.33)	
Adjusted R^2	0.96	0.95			
Number of obs.	5,611	5,611			

Note: t-statistics in parentheses.

except for the short-run simulation for the Northwest. Damages rise more rapidly with larger temperature changes.

Larger regions with more population have larger impacts. The populations for each region are reported in Chapter 1 (Table 1.3). The Northeast, Midwest and Southeast have the largest populations. We wish to test whether warmer regions have greater damages. However, the regions with larger populations have larger effects, making it difficult to separate out the independent effect of temperature in Table 7.4. Consequently Table 7.4 is not well suited for detecting the consequences of a region's current temperature. It is clear from Table 7.4, however, that damages are more sensitive to temperature changes than precipitation changes. More precipitation increases damages linearly. The magnitude of these damages depends largely on population, with larger regions leading to larger effects.

Short-run damages tend to be smaller than long-run damages. When owners can adjust their building characteristics to reflect climate, they spend more on energy. These results could be due to a reduction in insulation in cool regions where heating dominates and an increase in cooling capacity in warm regions where cooling dominates. Both building adjustments for heating and cooling reduce the welfare costs to the household. However, both building adjustments result in more energy being used. Because we measure energy expenditures and not the sum of energy and building expenditures, our measures go up in the long run.

The 95 per cent confidence intervals suggest that the residential results are statistically significant. In the long-run model, warming causes long-run damages to the residential sector in every region. These results are significant across all the climate scenarios in all regions except for the Northwest. The short-run estimates follow a similar pattern except that they suggest benefits in the Northwest. For small temperature increases and no precipitation increase, the damages in the residential sector are not significant in the Northeast and Midwest. With larger precipitation and temperature increases, however, every region except the Northwest has significant damages. The Northwest is unusual because it has the narrowest range between winter and summer temperatures of all the regions. With the coolest summer temperatures in the United States, the region has smaller damages in the summer.

The commercial results, presented in Table 7.5, are more complex than the residential results. The commercial study implies that warming will result in energy benefits in the Northeast, Midwest, Northern Plains and Northwest. The greater the warming, the bigger the benefits in all regions except the Northern Plains. In contrast, warming is expected to cause damages in the Southeast, Southern Plains and Southwest. The greater the warming, the larger the damages. As with the residential sector, the magnitude of the impacts is larger in regions with more population. The only noticeable exception to this

Table 7.4   Regional results for residential energy[a] *(billions 1998 USD/yr)*

Region	Precipitation (%)	Temperature 1.5°C	Temperature 2.5°C	Temperature 5.0°C
Northeast				
Short run	0	0.21	0.71	3.20
		(−0.4 to 0.8)	(−0.1 to 1.5)	(1.7 to 4.8)
	7	0.71	1.2	3.72
		(0.1 to 1.3)	(0.4 to 2.1)	(2.1 to 5.3)
	15	1.20	1.70	4.24
		(0.5 to 1.9)	(0.7 to 2.7)	(2.6 to 5.9)
Long run	0	1.42	2.61	6.50
		(0.8 to 2.0)	(1.8 to 3.5)	(4.8 to 8.1)
	7	1.99	3.20	7.14
		(1.4 to 2.6)	(2.2 to 4.1)	(5.6 to 8.9)
	15	2.61	3.81	7.79
		(1.9 to 3.3)	(2.8 to 4.8)	(6.1 to 9.6)
Midwest				
Short run	0	0.20	0.58	2.38
		(−0.2 to 0.6)	(−0.1 to 1.3)	(1.2 to 3.7)
	7	0.50	0.87	2.70
		(0.0 to 0.9)	(0.2 to 1.5)	(1.4 to 4.0)
	15	0.79	1.17	3.01
		(0.2 to 1.3)	(0.5 to 1.9)	(1.8 to 4.3)
Long run	0	1.01	1.85	4.61
		(0.6 to 1.4)	(1.2 to 2.6)	(3.3 to 5.9)
	7	1.35	2.19	4.97
		(0.8 to 1.8)	(1.5 to 3.0)	(3.7 to 6.3)
	15	1.68	2.54	5.33
		(1.2 to 2.2)	(1.8 to 3.3)	(4.0 to 6.7)
Northern Plains				
Short run	0	0.26	0.54	1.71
		(0.0 to 0.5)	(0.2 to 0.9)	(0.9 to 2.5)
	7	0.38	0.66	1.84
		(0.1 to 0.6)	(0.4 to 1.1)	(1.1 to 2.6)
	15	0.50	0.79	1.97
		(0.2 to 0.7)	(0.5 to 1.2)	(1.2 to 2.7)
Long run	0	0.58	1.05	2.56
		(0.4 to 0.8)	(0.7 to 1.4)	(1.8 to 3.4)
	7	0.71	1.19	2.70
		(0.5 to 0.9)	(0.8 to 1.5)	(1.9 to 3.5)
	15	0.85	1.33	2.86
		(0.6 to 1.06)	(0.9 to 1.8)	(2.0 to 3.7)
Northwest				
Short run	0	−0.51	−0.72	−0.83
		(−0.8 to −0.1)	(−1.3 to −0.1)	(−1.8 to 0.1)
	7	−0.46	−0.67	−0.78
		(−0.8 to −0.0)	(−1.3 to −0.0)	(−1.8 to 0.2)
	15	−0.42	−0.64	−0.73
		(−0.9 to 0.1)	(−1.3 to 0.0)	(−1.8 to 0.4)

Table 7.4   continued

Region	Precipitation (%)	Temperature		
		1.5°C	2.5°C	5.0°C
Northwest				
Long run	0	0.14	0.31	1.03
		(–0.2 to 0.6)	(–0.4 to 0.9)	(–0.0 to 2.1)
	7	0.26	0.44	1.16
		(–0.2 to 0.7)	(–0.2 to 1.1)	(0.1 to 2.2)
	15	0.39	0.57	1.29
		(–0.1 to 0.9)	(–0.1 to 1.3)	(–0.1 to 1.3)
Southeast				
Short run	0	1.20	2.34	6.47
		(0.8 to 1.7)	(1.5 to 3.2)	(4.4 to 8.6)
	7	1.37	2.50	6.63
		(0.8 to 1.9)	(1.7 to 3.4)	(4.5 to 8.9)
	15	1.44	2.57	6.71
		(0.5 to 2.4)	(1.4 to 3.8)	(4.5 to 9.1)
Long run	0	1.92	3.43	8.18
		(1.5 to 2.4)	(2.6 to 4.3)	(5.9 to 10.5)
	7	2.12	3.65	8.39
		(1.5 to 2.7)	(2.7 to 4.6)	(6.1 to 10.7)
	15	2.24	3.76	8.53
		(1.3 to 3.3)	(2.6 to 5.0)	(6.1 to 11.1)
Southern Plains				
Short run	0	0.90	1.66	4.19
		(0.6 to 1.2)	(1.2 to 2.2)	(2.7 to 5.7)
	7	1.00	1.77	4.31
		(0.7 to 1.3)	(1.2 to 2.4)	(2.8 to 5.9)
	15	1.10	1.86	3.74
		(0.7 to 1.3)	(1.2 to 2.4)	(2.8 to 5.9)
Long run	0	1.10	1.86	3.74
		(0.8 to 1.4)	(1.3 to 2.5)	(3.0 to 6.0)
	7	1.19	2.02	4.55
		(0.8 to 1.5)	(1.4 to 2.6)	(3.0 to 6.1)
	15	1.30	2.14	4.68
		(0.8 to 1.8)	(1.4 to 2.8)	(3.1 to 6.4)
Southwest				
Short run	0	0.52	0.93	2.31
		(0.4 to 0.7)	(0.6 to 1.3)	(1.4 to 3.3)
	7	0.55	0.98	2.37
		(0.4 to 0.7)	(0.6 to 1.3)	(1.5 to 3.3)
	15	0.60	1.03	2.42
		(0.5 to 0.9)	(0.7 to 1.4)	(1.5 to 3.4)
Long run	0	0.54	0.96	2.23
		(0.4 to 0.7)	(0.6 to 1.3)	(1.3 to 3.2)
	7	0.59	1.01	2.29
		(0.4 to 0.8)	(0.7 to 1.4)	(1.4 to 3.3)
	15	0.65	1.07	2.36
		(0.5 to 0.8)	(0.7 to 1.4)	(1.4 to 3.3)

Note: a. Figures in parentheses are 95 per cent confidence intervals. Estimates are for 2060.

Table 7.5   Regional results for commercial energy[a]

Region	Precipitation (%)	Temperature 1.5°C	2.5°C	5.0°C
Northeast				
Short run	0	−1.46	−2.14	−2.93
		(−1.9 to −1.1)	(−2.7 to 1.5)	(−3.9 to −1.9)
	7	−1.42	−2.10	−2.89
		(−1.9 to −0.9)	(−2.7 to −1.4)	(−3.8 to −2.0)
	15	−1.39	−2.07	−2.87
		(−1.9 to −0.9)	(−2.7 to −1.4)	(−3.8 to −1.9)
Long run	0	−1.10	−1.52	−1.68
		(−1.5 to −0.7)	(−2.7 to −0.8)	(−2.7 to −0.6)
	7	−1.01	−1.45	−1.60
		(−1.5 to −0.5)	(−2.1 to −0.7)	(−2.6 to −0.6)
	15	−0.97	−1.40	−1.56
		(−1.4 to −0.5)	(−2.1 to −0.7)	(−2.5 to −0.5)
Midwest				
Short run	0	−1.20	−1.76	−2.37
		(−1.5 to −0.9)	(−2.2 to −1.3)	(−3.2 to −1.5)
	7	−1.09	−1.64	−2.27
		(−1.4 to −0.7)	(−2.1 to −1.1)	(−3.1 to −1.4)
	15	−0.94	−1.50	−2.14
		(−1.3 to −0.6)	(−2.0 to −0.9)	(−3.0 to −1.3)
Long run	0	−0.91	−1.26	−1.36
		(−1.2 to −0.6)	(−1.8 to −0.7)	(−2.2 to −0.5)
	7	−0.76	−1.11	−1.20
		(−1.2 to −0.4)	(−1.7 to −0.5)	(−2.1 to −0.2)
	15	−0.57	−0.94	−1.03
		(−0.9 to −0.1)	(−1.5 to −0.4)	(−2.0 to −0.0)
Northern Plains				
Short run	0	−0.76	−1.09	−1.35
		(−0.9 to −0.5)	(−1.4 to −0.7)	(−2.1 to −0.6)
	7	−0.70	−1.03	−1.29
		(−0.9 to −0.5)	(−1.4 to −0.6)	(−2.0 to −0.5)
	15	−0.63	−0.96	−1.23
		(−0.9 to −0.4)	(−1.4 to −0.5)	(−2.0 to −0.4)
Long run	0	−0.54	−0.72	−0.59
		(−0.8 to −0.2)	(−1.1 to −0.4)	(−1.4 to 0.4)
	7	−0.47	−0.65	−0.52
		(−0.7 to −0.1)	(−1.1 to −0.1)	(−1.3 to 0.4)
	15	−0.38	−0.57	−0.42
		(−0.7 to −0.0)	(−1.1 to −0.1)	(−1.3 to 0.5)
Northwest				
Short run	0	−0.96	−1.42	−2.10
		(−1.4 to −0.5)	(−2.0 to −0.7)	(−3.1 to −0.9)
	7	−1.25	−1.69	−2.32
		(−1.7 to −0.8)	(−2.2 to −1.1)	(−3.2 to −1.3)
	15	−1.57	−1.99	−2.60
		(−2.0 to −1.1)	(−2.6 to −1.3)	(−3.4 to −1.5)

Table 7.5 continued

Region	Precipitation (%)	Temperature		
		1.5°C	2.5°C	5.0°C
Northwest				
Long run	0	−0.68	−0.98	−1.24
		(−1.2 to −0.1)	(−1.7 to −0.1)	(−2.4 to 0.1)
	7	−1.01	−1.29	−1.52
		(−1.5 to −0.5)	(−2.0 to −0.5)	(−2.6 to −0.4)
	15	−1.38	−1.63	−1.83
		(−1.9 to −0.8)	(−2.4 to −0.8)	(−2.8 to −0.6)
Southeast				
Short run	0	−0.21	−0.11	1.12
		(−0.6 to 0.2)	(−0.8 to 0.7)	(−0.8 to 3.2)
	7	−0.13	−0.02	1.23
		(−0.5 to 0.2)	(−0.5 to 0.5)	(0.0 to 2.5)
	15	−0.05	0.07	1.33
		(−0.6 to 0.6)	(−0.6 to 0.8)	(−0.0 to 2.8)
Long run	0	0.31	0.80	3.21
		(−0.1 to 0.8)	(−0.1 to 1.7)	(0.9 to 5.8)
	7	0.39	0.89	3.30
		(0.1 to 0.7)	(0.5 to 1.3)	(1.7 to 4.6)
	15	0.45	0.96	3.40
		(−0.2 to 1.2)	(0.2 to 1.8)	(1.9 to 5.1)
Southern Plains				
Short run	0	0.28	0.64	2.15
		(−0.1 to 0.7)	(0.4 to 1.3)	(0.6 to 4.1)
	7	0.33	0.67	2.19
		(0.0 to 0.6)	(0.2 to 1.2)	(0.8 to 3.8)
	15	0.37	0.72	2.24
		(0.0 to 0.7)	(0.1 to 1.3)	(0.8 to 3.9)
Long run	0	0.60	1.19	3.52
		(0.2 to 1.1)	(0.5 to 2.0)	(1.4 to 6.0)
	7	0.66	1.25	3.58
		(0.4 to 0.9)	(0.7 to 1.9)	(1.9 to 5.4)
	15	0.70	1.30	3.63
		(0.4 to 1.1)	(0.7 to 2.0)	(1.9 to 5.7)
Southwest				
Short run	0	0.17	0.34	1.05
		(0.0 to 0.4)	(0.0 to 0.7)	(0.2 to 2.0)
	7	0.18	0.34	1.06
		(0.0 to 0.4)	(0.1 to 0.6)	(0.4 to 1.9)
	15	0.18	0.35	1.06
		(0.0 to 0.4)	(0.1 to 0.6)	(0.4 to 1.9)
Long run	0	0.28	0.55	1.57
		(0.1 to 0.5)	(0.2 to 0.9)	(0.6 to 2.7)
	7	0.30	0.55	1.59
		(0.1 to 0.5)	(0.2 to 0.9)	(0.8 to 2.7)
	15	0.30	0.57	1.60
		(0.1 to 0.5)	(0.2 to 0.8)	(0.8 to 2.6)

Note: a. Figures in parentheses are 95 per cent confidence intervals. Estimates are for 2060.

rule is the surprisingly large energy damages in the Southern Plains. Precipitation has a small negative impact on commercial energy expenditures. This effect is largely linear and additive. The precipitation results for the commercial sector consequently parallel the residential energy results.

The short-run results are more beneficial than the long-run results. These results also parallel the findings in the residential sector, where long-run results were more harmful than short-run impacts. The commercial sector appears to follow the same behavior as the residential sector. Warming in heating-dominated places leads to a reduction in insulation and warming in cooling-dominated places leads to an increase in cooling capacity. The winter adjustment reduces the sum of energy and building expenditures. The summer adjustment reduces the discomfort from hot days. Both structural adjustments lead to an increase in energy expenditures in the long run.

The 95 per cent confidence intervals indicate that the long-run results are generally statistically significant. Warming leads to statistically significant benefits in the Northeast, Great Lakes, Northern Plains and Northwest. Warming leads to significant damages in the Southern Plains and Southwest. With precipitation increases and temperature increases of 2.5°C or above, warming also causes significant damages in the Southeast.

To isolate the effect of temperature from the population size of each region, we examined the percentage change in energy expenditures for a selected set of scenarios. These additional calculations are shown in Table 7.6 for both the residential and commercial sectors. Because precipitation has such a small effect, we held the change in precipitation constant at 7 per cent. We consequently examined only three climate scenarios (1.5°C, +7 per cent precipitation; 2.5°C, +7 per cent precipitation; 5°C, +7 per cent precipitation).

The residential results indicate that all regions are damaged by warming. However, the warmer southern regions suffer more damages than their colder northern neighbors. For example, damages in the northern regions (excluding the Northwest) range between 5 and 6 per cent with the 2.5°C scenario and between 7 and 10 per cent for the southern regions (Southeast, Southern Plains and Southwest). With the 5°C scenario, residential energy expenditures increase in the northern regions between 12 and 13 per cent, but in the southern regions, the increase is from 15 to 22 per cent.

The commercial results are even more dramatic. With a 2.5°C warming, the northern regions see a reduction in energy expenditures of between 6 and 8 per cent. In contrast, the southern regions face an increase in energy expenditures of between 5 and 17 per cent. This difference is even larger with a 5°C warming. In this scenario, the northern regions drop their energy expenditures between 4 and 9 per cent and the southern regions increase theirs between 18 and 47 per cent. Warming will have beneficial effects on the commercial sector

Table 7.6   *Percentage change in energy expenditures by region*

Region	Temperature		
	1.5°C	2.5°C	5.0°C
Residential – long run (%)			
Northeast	3	5	11
Midwest	3	5	11
Northern Plains	3	6	13
Northwest	1	2	5
Southeast	4	7	15
Southern Plains	5	8	19
Southwest	6	10	22
Commercial – long run (%)			
Northeast	–5	–8	–9
Midwest	–5	–7	–7
Northern Plains	–4	–6	–4
Northwest	–11	–14	–16
Southeast	2	5	18
Southern Plains	7	12	36
Southwest	9	17	47

Note: Negative numbers reflect benefits and positive numbers reflect damages. Precipitation is assumed to increase 7 per cent.

in the colder northern regions and harmful effects on the commercial sector in the warmer southern regions.

CONCLUSION

This study examines the impact of climate change on energy demand in regions throughout the United States. The study relies on a cross-sectional approach comparing a large sample of households and a large sample of firms in different climate zones. A multiple regression of energy expenditures is used to estimate the sensitivity of energy to climate. The cross-sectional analysis reveals that warmer winters reduce energy expenditures, and warmer summers increase expenditures. The summer effect is larger than the winter effect, suggesting that overall warming will increase energy expenditures in the United States.

The regional effect of climate change is calculated by summing the effects of households and firms within each region. Some of the regions such as the Southeast have conspicuously larger populations and thus have larger effects. Controlling for population, it is apparent that climate change has different impacts on the energy sector in each region. The three southern regions, the Southeast, Southern Plains and Southwest, all have greater damages from warming in both the residential and commercial energy sectors. The greater the warming, the greater the damages. The remaining northern regions all have benefits in the commercial sector and smaller damages in the residential sector from warming. The size of the benefits and the size of the damages increase with warming. Overall, the energy sector suffers sizeable damages from warming because the damages in the residential sector outweigh the benefits in the commercial sector.

Residences and firms are expected to adapt to warmer climates by changing their building expenditures. The evidence suggests that people will reduce insulation against the cold and increase cooling capacity. This is likely to be beneficial to firms and households because it reduces building costs or discomfort in the long run. However, both adjustments lead to an increase in energy expenditures. Consequently, our long-run measure of energy expenditures increases relative to the short-run measure.

The national results reported in this chapter are consistent with but slightly different from other studies in the energy literature. Linder and Inglis (1989) also find large damages from warming, whereas Rosenthal *et al.* (1995) find small benefits. This chapter probably gets similar results to the Linder and Inglis study because we predict the future energy sector will shift toward electricity. The savings in the economy from expenditures on other fuels will be less important by 2060. We also predict a large increase in the penetration of cooling, which also pushes our results toward damages. The assumptions about baseline conditions may also explain the Rosenthal *et al.* results. The Rosenthal study focuses on 2020, a relatively near-term year in which the shift toward electricity and the increase in cooling capacity are not that different from today. Further, the warming that Rosenthal *et al.* consider is relatively mild. It is not surprising that Rosenthal *et al.* find that this small amount of warming is in fact beneficial to the country as a whole.

REFERENCES

Linder, K.P. and M.R. Inglis (1989), 'Potential impacts of climate change on regional and national demands for electricity', Appendix H – Infrastructure, of J. Smith and D. Tirpak (eds), *The Potential Effects of Global Climate Change on the United States: Report to Congress*, EPA-230-05-89-050, Washington, DC: US Environmental Protection Agency.

Morrison, W.N. and R. Mendelsohn, (1999), 'The impact of global warming on US energy expenditures', in R. Mendelsohn and J.E. Neumann (eds), *The Impact of Climate Change on the United States Economy*, Cambridge, UK: Cambridge University Press, pp. 209–36.

Morrison, W.N. and R. Mendelsohn (2000), Assessing the Energy Impacts of Climate Change: An Aggregate Expenditure Model for the United States, New Haven, CT: Yale FES.

Rosenthal, D., H. Gruenspecht and E. Moran (1995), 'Effects of global warming on energy use for space heating and cooling in the United States', *Energy Journal*, 16(2), 77–96.

Appendix: Data definitions and means

DEFINITIONS OF INDEPENDENT VARIABLES: RESIDENTIAL REGRESSIONS

Variable	Definition and mean
age of head	Head householder age; 47.8
basement	1 if home has basement, 0 otherwise; 0.30
black/white	1 if resident is black or white, 0 otherwise; 0.97
cash aid	1 if resident receives cash aid for heat, 0 otherwise; 0.01
central AC	1 if household has central air conditioning, 0 otherwise; 0.36
color TVs	Number of color TVs in household; 1.59
computer	1 if household has computer, 0 otherwise; 0.15
dish/cloth wash/dry	1 if household has dishwasher, clothes washer, or dryer, 0 otherwise; 0.83
# doors/windows	Number of doors and windows in home; 14.4
electric wall heat	1 if household uses electric wall units or radiators to heat, 0 otherwise; 0.22
electricity price	Average electricity price; 0.087
family size	Number of household members; 2.54
# floors	Number of floors in home; 1.4
fuel oil price	Average fuel oil price; 1.02
heat aid	1 if resident receives heating vouchers, 0 otherwise; 0.05
Hispanic	1 if resident is Hispanic/non-black, 0 otherwise; 0.07
home area	Home area – square feet; 1837
income	Average household income for relevant income range; 30410
electricity discount	1 if discounted or interruptible electricity rates, 0 otherwise; 0.01
Jan. temp	Average January temperature (demeaned) – degrees C; 0.5
Jan. precip	Average January precipitation (demeaned) – inches; 2.99
July temp	Average July temperature (demeaned) – degrees C; 23.8

July precip	Average July precipitation (demeaned) – inches; 3.38
ExpEnergy	Annual Energy Expenditures; 1177
kerosene price	Average kerosene price; 1.38
lpg price	Average liquid petroleum gas price; 1.48
metropolitan	1 if metropolitan statistical area, 0 otherwise; 0.32
multiple units	1 if more than 1 unit, 0 otherwise; 0.25
natural gas price	Average natural gas price; 0.55
natural gas available	1 if natural gas is available, 0 otherwise; 0.75
over 65	1 if age of head householder > 65, 0 otherwise; 0.20
poor insulation	1 if household has inadequate insulation, 0 otherwise; 0.20
portable kerosene	1 if household uses portable kerosene to heat, 0 otherwise; 0.004
# rooms	Number of rooms in home; 7.1
tenant controls heat	1 if tenant controls heat, 0 otherwise; 0.15
wall/window AC	1 if household has wall or window ac units, 0 otherwise; 0.32
wood burning	1 if wood is burned as alternative heat source, 0 otherwise; 0.24
year built	Year home constructed; 1961

DEFINITIONS OF INDEPENDENT VARIABLES: COMMERCIAL REGRESSIONS

Variable	Definition
AC in computer room	1 if there is air conditioning in computer room, 0 otherwise; 0.20
air duct – cool	1 if air ducts used for cooling, 0 otherwise; 0.50
air duct – heat	1 if air ducts used for heating, 0 otherwise; 0.57
alternative fuel used	1 if alternative fuel used, 0 otherwise; 0.05
boilers	1 if boilers used for heating, 0 otherwise; 0.27
refrigerator	1 if commercial freezer or refrigerator used, 0 otherwise; 0.32
dist. heat price	Average district heat price; 8.20
electricity price	Average electricity price; 0.095
# floors	Number of floors; 3.0
fuel oil price	Average fuel oil price; 0.81
heat pump – cool	1 if heat pumps used for cooling, 0 otherwise; 0.13
heat pump – heat	1 if heat pumps used for heating, 0 otherwise; 0.13
ice/vending/water	1 if ice, vending or water machines used, 0 otherwise; 0.74

Jan. temp	Average January temperature (demeaned) – degrees C; 1.8
Jan. precip	Average January precipitation (demeaned) – inches; 3.0
July temp	Average July temperature (demeaned) – degrees C; 24.2
July precip	Average July precipitation (demeaned)– inches; 3.5
metropolitan	1 if metropolitan statistical area, 0 otherwise; 0.81
months open/year	Number of months open; 11.5
natural gas price	Average natural gas price; 0.87
% food sale/serve	Percent. food sale and food service; 4.9%
% nonref wh/vac	Percent. non-refrigerated warehouse and vacant; 13.3%
% health	Percent. in-patient and skilled healthcare; 2.4%
% out. Patient	Percent. out-patient healthcare and public safety; 1.1%
% lab/ref whs	Percent. lab and refrigerated warehouse; 1.4%
% industry	Percent. industrial: 0.5%
% office	Percent. office; 20.6%
% retail/service	Percent. retail/services; 20.7%
% educ	Percent. education; 12.1%
roof: built up	1 if roof material = built up, 0 otherwise; 0.45
roof: glass	1 if roof material = glass, 0 otherwise; 0.007
roof: metal surface	1 if roof material = metal surface, 0 otherwise; 0.15
sqft	Building size – square feet; 99760
tenant controls heat	1 if tenant controls heat, 0 otherwise; 0.55
wall: masonry	1 if wall material = masonry/siding, 0 otherwise; 0.001
wall: shingle	1 if wall material = siding/shingles, 0 otherwise; 0.003
year built	Year construction completed; 1960
expenergy	Annual energy expenditures; 158,830

8. Adaptation

Robert Mendelsohn

INTRODUCTION

This chapter focuses on how individuals, firms, communities and governments respond to climate change. How they respond depends on the impact the change is likely to have and their resources, knowledge and organization. Adaptation is defined here as actions undertaken by individuals, firms and governments that either ameliorate the harmful effects of climate change or capitalize on the beneficial opportunities arising from climate change. Adaptation is, in other words, viewed as the *human* response to all the changes induced by climate change. Climate change can create important changes in ecosystems and geophysical processes, of course; and human systems can, in turn, respond directly to the climate change and to the changes in these natural systems. All of these changes must be captured in impact analyses to trace the link between the climate stimulus and all the consequences. We define adaptation solely in terms of the human response, not the natural system response to highlight these human reactions. Incorporating adaptation into impact modeling has been one of the major innovations of impact research over the last decade.

Adaptation is an integral component of climate impact assessment (Fankhauser 1996, Yohe *et al.* 1996, Tol *et al.* 1998, Smit *et al.* 1999, Mendelsohn and Neumann 1999, Mendelsohn 2000, Pittock and Jones 2000). Just as it is important to understand how natural systems will change when climate changes, it is also important to understand how social systems will change. Farmers, coastal dwellers, homeowners, firms and government agencies will all adapt to changing environmental conditions. To understand the consequences of climate change, one must understand all these adjustments. This study consequently goes to great length to incorporate adaptation into all of the reported impact analyses.

The literature has explored the ability of many countries, regions and communities to respond to climate change, but culling widely applicable lessons from the collection of disparate studies has been a challenge. The notion of 'adaptive capacity' is an important organizing principle for assessing how different regions of the world are likely to respond. Yohe and Moss (2000) and Smit *et al.* (2000) argue that adaptive capacity depends on the range of available technological options, resources and their distribution; the structure of critical institutions; the stock of human capital; property rights; the system's access to risk spreading processes; the ability of decision-makers to manage information and make decisions; and the public's perception of attribution. These determinants can be used to organize research and policy across countries with very different levels of adaptive capacity. Differences in adaptive capacity can be especially important when comparing developed and developing countries. Developed countries can substitute technological innovation and capital for climate. For example, farmers in developed countries have access to sophisticated geographic sensing techniques to micromanage each area on a farm. Developing countries have less access to technology or capital and must often settle for substituting labor for climate. Developing countries also have fewer resources. Developed countries, in contrast, do not appear to be constrained by the first two determinants of adaptive capacity. They have the resources and technology to undertake desired adaptation activities. Of course, just because an agent can implement adaptation options does not imply that adaptation will be undertaken or that it will offset all climate impacts. In some cases, adaptation will merely offset some of the damages, not eliminate them. In others, investment in adaptation might be under-provided. The key question for developed countries, therefore, is not whether they have the resources or technology to adapt to climate change. The key question is what will developed countries choose to do. It is here that the remaining determinants of adaptive capacity play a role.

By way of contrast, developing countries may not even have sufficiently strong public institutions to take on the government role of facilitating adaptation. Some of the relevant government agencies may lack the necessary resources. They may also be poorly organized for decisive and large-scale responses to climate change. They might have fewer adaptation options from which to choose. And they may suffer the consequences of multiple stresses so that coping with climate change is not the only or even the number one priority.

A great deal of attention has, of course, been directed at building 'private adaptation' into impact models for sectors in developed economies (for example, see Rosenzweig and Parry 1994 or Mendelsohn and Neumann 1999). Because these actors would enjoy the benefits of private adaptation, there is every reason to believe that private adaptation would be undertaken, especially in market sectors. However, the literature also recognizes that there is an important role for government in managing adaptation, even in the market sectors of developed economies. In agriculture, to take one example, the government monitors and publishes climate data, develops climate forecasts and performs research about how to adapt to climate change. The government can thereby set the stage for private action. The government may also be an active agent of adaptation by reallocating water supplies, modifying water and transportation infrastructure and developing breeding programs for new crops and animals. But does all of this activity make a difference? Do farmers use the information? The institutional and informational constraints can be important determinants of adaptive capacity in developed countries just as they can be in the developing world. Governments in developed economies must have decision-making skills and sufficient bureaucratic structures to implement change; and the implementation of that change must inspire private actors to respond appropriately.

Governments must also resist interfering with adaptation in ways that are harmful in the long run. Governments might, for example, be tempted to focus strictly on addressing equity concerns and try to offset harm done to certain groups or individuals by climate change. Of course, this is an admirable goal, but the method chosen to improve equity can sometimes have unintended deleterious effects. Subsidizing agents that would be harmed by climate change might achieve desirable equity outcomes. In some circumstances, though, the government could also end up paying farmers to grow the wrong crops to get the subsidies. Such a program would be a maladaptation, because it could encourage farmers to increase the damage from climate change by growing inappropriate crops. Insurance programs could have similar inefficient effects. Insurance programs might be perfectly justified as a response to climate variability because they can help individuals and firms smooth out stochastic incomes. When applied to long-term climate change, however, poorly designed insurance programs might have the unintended effect of encouraging farmers to keep growing crops that are no longer appropriate or encouraging homeowners to rebuild dwellings in places that will be more frequently damaged by future flooding. Governments will need to design equity programs carefully paying attention not to create new long-term inefficiencies.

Perhaps it is not as obvious as one might first think that the US government brings very high adaptive capacity to the climate impacts table. There are government agencies capable of discerning and implementing efficient adaptation in every sector. There are sufficient resources in the United States to implement advisable adaptation strategies. The issue for the United States is not whether the country has the means with which to cope with climate change. It is, instead, a question of how much and what type of adaptation will the country choose to make.

This study is concerned with climate change impacts in market sectors. The book does not cover nonmarket sectors; consequently, this chapter focuses on adaptations only in market sectors. Adaptation in nonmarket sectors, although outside the scope of this book, is an important topic that deserves far more research and policy attention. There may be many opportunities for society to respond to changes in ecosystems, health, and aesthetics. One of the greatest priorities in climate research is to explore how society can adapt to impacts to ecosystems, health, and aesthetics.

EFFICIENT ADAPTATION

This study assumes that adaptation will be efficient (Fankhauser 1996, Fankhauser *et al.* 1999, Mendelsohn 2000). That is, whether decisions are made privately or by government, we assume that policies are designed to be socially efficient: they do not waste or misdirect economic resources. As we discuss in this chapter, this is a strong assumption in certain circumstances. The authors in each chapter have assumed that adaptation will be done whenever the benefits exceed the costs and that it will not be done if the costs exceed the benefits. The adaptations considered are efficient in the sense that they hold to this cost–benefit paradigm. The study also assumes, at least implicitly, that all costs and benefits are included in the cost–benefit calculus; this is a topic we return to when discussing externalities.

The adaptations actually adopted over the next century may or may not be efficient. It is possible in certain circumstances that society will choose to engage in some adaptations where the costs exceed the benefits. Similarly, society may not act on all of its efficient opportunities, and may fail to adapt even when benefits exceed costs. By focusing only on efficient adaptation, therefore, this study may be too optimistic.

When is it likely that adaptation will be efficient? One precondition for efficiency is that decision makers have incentives to act when benefits exceed costs and not to act when costs exceed benefits. Firms and households have efficient incentives when each is the sole beneficiary of the choice. We define 'private adaptation' as responses to climate change made by decision makers who are the sole beneficiaries of these responses (Mendelsohn 2000). Whether the adaptation is private or not is a characteristic of the action. If the action has only one beneficiary, it is private. If the action has more than one beneficiary, it is no longer private. An action that has multiple beneficiaries is defined as a 'public adaptation' (Mendelsohn 2000).

Private adaptation has efficient incentives. The decision maker will examine the personal cost of the action and the personal benefits. If the benefits to the individual exceed the costs, the person will proceed and make the adaptation. The adaptation itself provides adequate incentive to proceed. If the costs exceed the benefits, the person will forgo the opportunity. Because the individual takes into account all costs and benefits in the decision, the decision maker faces efficient incentives.

Many adaptations in market sectors are private. That is, the firms or the households making the decision will pay for the adaptation and will be the beneficiary. It is consequently likely that the private adaptations considered in this book will be efficient. However, in every market sector, there are also many public adaptations as well. Managing public adaptation is an important role for government. In agriculture and forestry, the government can forecast future climates, gather and publish climate data, research efficient adaptation strategies, and develop new crops and management strategies to help farmers and foresters adapt to climate change (see Adams *et al.*, 1995). In water, the government can build and replace physical infrastructure that holds back floods, stores and distributes irrigation water, and protects drinking water. The government can build sea walls, develop hurricane-warning systems, and organize land use to help protect coastal structures and coastal populations from sea level rise. The government can research new energy conservation techniques to help buildings adapt to warming. Although this chapter reviews the properties and promise of private adaptation, we press special attention on the role of government. Government must evaluate the efficiency of public adaptation strategies and facilitate efficient private adaptation.

The costs and benefits of private adaptation in market sectors are often quantifiable and familiar to decision makers. Microeconomic models that describe the behavior of firms and individuals in terms of maximizing private net benefits reflect observed economic behavior. Of course, people are not always rational and some observers note many examples where people do not maximize their net benefits (for example, see Rayner and Malone 1998, Hanemann 2000). People are not calculating machines, and many citizens do not make optimal choices facing complex and uncertain situations. Human behavior is not always rational and so future adaptation will not necessarily be efficient.

UNCERTAINTY AND TIMING

Many adaptations are investments with long-lasting consequences that are uncertain. For example, decisions to protect the coastline or to depreciate buildings have uncertain benefits, depending on future development and the path of future storms (Yohe and Neumann 1997). Decision makers may know about the distribution of possible consequences, but they will not know which outcome will occur. Adaptation decisions will often be made under uncertainty. How will actual decision makers behave under uncertainty? One simple paradigm is that decision makers will be risk neutral. They will act to maximize the expected net benefits of each choice. Most of the studies in this book implicitly assume risk neutrality. However, it is also possible that decision makers will be risk averse and so will avoid decisions that might have large negative outcomes on their income or well-being (for example, see Dowlatabadi and West 1998). Careful empirical research on risk aversion is sorely needed in climate research.

Timing is another important dimension of adaptation. Initial climate models compared a climate equilibrium from pre-industrial atmospheric conditions with an equilibrium from doubled CO_2. Early impact models consequently focused on exploring the impact from being in one climate equilibrium *versus* the other. The available climate scenarios encouraged impact researchers to engage in comparative static analysis. Especially in market sectors with extensive capital (forestry and coastal structures), comparative static analysis fails to capture important dynamic considerations. For example, Titus (1990) carefully calculated the total cost required to protect all of America's developed coastline. Although this was an important calculation, it explicitly does not consider efficient dynamic strategies to implement coastal protection. Subsequent sea level literature was able to take advantage of such strategies and substantially reduce the present value of coastal protection (Yohe *et al.* 1996, 1999, Yohe and Neumann 1997).

Early studies of ecological effects were, to take another example, also hampered by the absence of dynamic scenarios (Callaway *et al.* 1994). These early studies consequently could not develop efficient dynamic responses to the gradual unfolding of climate effects on ecosystems. As transient climate and ecosystem scenarios have become available, though, more efficient dynamic adaptation strategies have been developed (Sohngen and Mendelsohn 1998, Mendelsohn and Neumann, 1999). These dynamic strategies have helped reduce the damages and increase the benefits in these capital intensive sectors. Of course, other factors have also been involved. Sea level rise damages have come down because of present value calculations. Timber impacts have gone from damages to benefits because of a shift from gap models to biogeography and biogeochemical ecological models (see VEMAP 1995).

Society can make far more adjustments to a change that occurs over a century than to one that suddenly appears unexpectedly. Rapid changes will often force society to abandon substantial existing capital stock. Such changes are costly. If the changes are slower, the economy can make many changes in the design and replacement phase of projects instead of after construction is complete. Even at the design stage, adaptations are not without cost, but it is well known that integrating changes into a design is often much cheaper than retrofitting. Rather than abandoning perfectly good farm equipment, for example, a farmer could choose to switch to new equipment and thus new crops when the old equipment is wearing out. Erratic change is also difficult for decision makers, sometimes causing them to overreact to changes that are only temporary. For example, river planners may build new infrastructure in response to wet and dry periods. If wet and dry periods follow one another, the planners might overadapt and build new structures that are appropriate only for short times.

There are other advantages to having more time to change. By delaying adjustments until they are needed, the present value of the costs can be reduced. Yohe *et al.* (1999) reduce the present value of the cost of coastal protection almost an order of magnitude simply be delaying construction until needed. The literature generally recognizes that adaptation will be less expensive for predictable slow changes than rapid variations in climate (Parry 1986, Katz and Brown 1992, Smithers and Smit 1997, Downing *et al.* 1997, Smit *et al.* 1999).

It is worth noting, however, at least for public adaptation, that there could be an advantage to rapid climate change. Rapid change might draw the attention of the public and therefore solicit more rapid and firm government responses (Dowlatabadi and West 1998, Reilly and Schimmelpfennig 2000). Extreme events and rapid acceleration of change might force new laws and programs, whereas gradual climate change might lull affected parties into doing nothing. By creating a 'crisis', rapid climate change could galvanize political forces into action. Private adaptation might also be influenced by the strength of the climate signal, so this phenomenon may not be limited to just governmental response.

Impact research has focused on exploring the impact of mean changes in temperature and precipitation because climate models have consistently found that mean conditions change. It is also possible, however, that increasing greenhouse gases will increase climate variance and extreme events. Some studies such as Timmerman *et al.* (1999) find more intensive El Niño/Southern Oscillations (ENSOs) in a CO_2 doubled world, whereas other climate studies predict decreases in interannual climate variation. Because of conflicting evidence, the climate community is not yet willing to predict whether greenhouse gases will increase ENSOs or climate variation (Houghton *et al.* 1996). Nonetheless, the impact community has begun to explore what potential impacts increased variance could have.

Because climate variation increases the frequency and possibly the strength of stochastic extreme events that are hard to anticipate, it is more difficult to adapt to climate variance. Agronomic studies have consistently shown that existing climate variance is costly to farmers (Rosenzweig 1994, Mearns *et al.* 1997). Droughts and sudden seasonal reductions in rainfall have been recorded throughout human history because of the huge costs entailed. Further, cross-sectional evidence in the United States indicates that farms in counties with higher interannual climate variance have lower value (Mendelsohn *et al.* 1999). Climate variance is clearly also important to the water sector. Low runoff years place enormous strains on water systems in semi-arid regions. Brief, high volume runoff periods generate most of the floods that cause damage. Increased climate variance would impose high costs on society precisely because it is difficult to adapt to variance.

Some of the literature uses these observations to argue that adapting to mean climate changes may be easier than adapting to climate variability. With long-run mean changes, one can reorganize a sector for a specific state of the climate, be it a warmer (colder) or drier (wetter) state. These changes can generate high returns because one is organizing the sector specifically for the new state of nature. With climate variability, one cannot design the system for a specific climate outcome because one often will not know in advance which outcome will occur. The primary protection against variability is to develop portfolios that reduce the harm when adverse conditions suddenly appear. But these portfolios tend to have lower expected returns across all conditions. For example, a farmer can make his farm more resilient by planting a variety of crops. By planting many crops, the farmer has purchased robustness: some crops will do well regardless of which weather appears. These changes tend to be costly, however, because the variety of crops earns less than the single crop that performs best in each condition. Robustness is purchased at the expense of high return.

Other studies (for example, Smit *et al.* 2000) argue that adaptation to climate change might be driven mostly by changes in the frequency of extreme events. These authors argue that changes in mean climate will increase the likelihood of extreme events that will cross critical thresholds and trigger significant impacts on human systems. Because these extreme events are notable, they will cause systems to react and make adaptation accelerate. This literature argues that adaptation to climate change will be linked closely to the relative frequency of these extreme events. Although this literature is certainly correct that extreme events are visible, it is not clear that the literature has sufficiently considered how rare extreme events tend to be. If extreme events like serious floods and droughts occur once every 50 or 100 years, it could take a long time before people could determine that frequencies have changed. Even if supposedly rare extreme events occur frequently, such an occurrence does not necessarily mean, and may not be interpreted to mean, that climate has changed. Extreme events may consequently be a poor signal for actors to use to react to climate change.

One interesting proposition in the adaptation literature is that adaptation strategies to climate change could be 'win–win'. Win–win strategies are changes that one ought to do anyway given today's conditions that have the additional benefit of preparing for future climate scenarios. The sustainable development-adaptation literature has argued that development strategies designed to cope with current climate variation will also prepare society for future climate change (Rayner and Malone 1998). For example, if California develops a strategy for coping with droughts today by making efficient water allocation plans (which they did in the last drought), these plans could well serve as a blueprint for a future that may have less water. Developing flexibility is likely to be a prudent strategy to prepare for climate change. However, one must be careful not to assume that everything one might do to cope with climate variability would also work well for changes in mean climate. Some strategies, such as storing temporary stocks of food against a short-term drought, may work well for temporary stochastic setbacks but would become ineffective if the adverse condition is sustained.

EXTERNALITIES

Adaptation may be inefficient when externalities extend the effects of the adaptation beyond the private decision makers to others. If the private individual takes these other individuals into account, she will make efficient decisions. But if the private individual considers only her private costs and benefits, she will misestimate the net social benefit of engaging in public adaptation and will not make socially efficient choices. The private decision maker is likely to take into account how the adaptation will affect herself, but her action may also affect others. Externalities are effects on others that are ignored by private decision makers.

The potential that some adaptation activities might cause externalities has been noted in the literature (Smith and Lenhart 1996, Smith 1997). For example, a farmer might adapt to the new pests that warming brings by spraying insecticide over crops more often. People downwind of the farm may get sprayed and groundwater may become contaminated from the pesticide. These external effects bother off-farm individuals. If the farmer disregards the effects on neighbors, he may use too much pesticide or apply it in careless ways. In another example, building a dam to capture winter runoff may be a desirable adaptation as warmer winters shift snow to rain. However, dams have deleterious impacts on fish and wild water recreation, and these externalities must be taken into account. Because most externalities tend to be negative, that is, the actions impose costs (as opposed to benefits) on other people, externalities tend to imply that people and governments might over-adapt. The socially efficient response, in this case, is a more modest or more careful action than the response dictated by purely private incentives.

PUBLIC ADAPTATION AND THE ROLE OF GOVERNMENT

Many important adaptations require coordinated responses across many people. When there are multiple beneficiaries of engaging in a climate response, it is defined as a 'public' adaptation. These types of goods or services have been labeled 'public' in the economics literature (Samuelson 1954), not because they are performed by government but because they have many beneficiaries. For example, flood control dams or sea walls are public adaptations because they will benefit many people. Public adaptations are not likely to be efficiently produced by individuals because people, on their own, are not likely to take account of how their actions affect others. Public adaptation calls for collective action: groups of people must coordinate in their joint interest. Unfortunately, coordinated responses are often difficult and costly to organize. In a *laissez-faire* world with little government involvement, public adaptations are likely to be underprovided. That is not to say that there are no examples of private collective action. In the economics literature, there are examples of collective action, even without government involvement. For example, radio and TV stations are examples of firms providing a shared service. Swimming, golf, and tennis clubs are shared services. Clubs seem to be able to deliver public goods when they can amass a group of members who are relatively similar to one another. When members are similar, they have shared interests and can agree on a collective action. Thus, we see swimming and tennis clubs quite successfully providing pools and tennis courts to their members.

The groups of affected people defined by climate change impacts are not likely to be homogeneous, however. There is no reason, for example, to expect that all the people that live along a seacoast are going to be alike or that the people who want to draw water from a watershed all have the same demand for that water. When members of a group are heterogeneous, it is more difficult for the group to engage in collective action. Heterogeneous members will have different private incentives. Members with much (little) at stake may want very dramatic (modest) investments. In the coastal example, members with an extensive shoreline or an expensive house near the shore may have much to gain from beach nourishment, which is being done in New Jersey and elsewhere. In contrast, members who own higher land set back from the shore may actually benefit from having the sea advance. Members who must pay a larger (smaller) share of the costs may want more modest (dramatic) actions. If people have to pay for the sea wall in proportion to their current shoreline footage, members with an extensive undeveloped shoreline may prefer more modest actions and members with just a small amount of developed coast may want more done.

In short, conflicting private interests amongst people make collective action difficult to organize privately. Because private entities are expected to under-provide public adaptation, the efficient provision of public adaptation is an important role for government. Governments must get involved in planning and managing public adaptation. Public adaptations should not be left to market forces, because markets fail to efficiently deliver public goods. Although governments are frequently aware that they must consider making climate adaptations, the literature has not placed much emphasis on encouraging efficient government responses. It is tempting to ask the government simply to relieve people from suffering damages from climate change. However, what government agencies must carefully consider is whether the benefits of government action exceed the cost.

Government agencies do not always have an incentive to be efficient. They may be more interested in increasing the size of their agency than in performing efficiently (Niskanen 1971, Brennan and Buchanan 1977). For example, the US Army Corps of Engineers was very enthusiastic about building dams. Although these dams officially had to pass a benefit–cost test, the Corps was famous for stretching the analysis so that they could proceed with the project. If agencies become too enthusiastic about engaging in adaptation, they may do too much adaptation: build too many dams, create too many sea walls and do everything too soon. It is important to encourage government agencies to be aware of climate adaptation; however, society must be careful not to create incentives for agencies to act too swiftly and inefficiently.

An important strength of a democracy is that its governmental agencies are attentive to political forces. However, it should be understood that political processes may place little weight on efficiency. Powerful private interests may use the agencies to subsidize projects of great importance to them at the expense of the public at large. As long as the costs of initiatives are spread across a large public, the common citizen may not pay much attention to these costs (Downs 1957, Tullock 1967). Private entities often successfully press for government actions that serve their individual interests but not the social interest (taking everyone into account). Congress often pressed the Corps of Engineers to build inefficient dams because the dams would benefit their constituents. This model suggests that public adaptation projects could benefit a few greatly but not pass a benefit–cost analysis. For example, one could easily imagine wealthy coastal homeowners or hotels along a coast convincing the government to protect the coastline against sea level rise. If the government protection program is financed by the general public, it would raise taxes a few dollars per household. However, it could possibly save wealthy individuals millions of dollars. In contrast, poorly organized small homeowners may fail to press for government action and find that they are inundated by rising seas without any action being undertaken.

It is difficult to predict whether political forces will cause too much or too little public adaptation by the government. What is clear is that few government agencies have clear mandates to make their adaptation responses efficient. Even agencies that have been given efficient mandates, such as the Corps of Engineers, have found it fairly easy to overcome cost–benefit restrictions with creative bookkeeping. This is an age-old problem of democracy and is not peculiar to climate adaptation, but it is certainly relevant. However, one angle of this problem that is unique to climate change is the emphasis on change. Because climate is changing, the efficient response by government is also changing over time. Unlike many other political problems that are often stationary, climate change is complicated by the need for constantly changing adaptation. For example, at one moment people interested in efficiency may have to fight hard to curb premature government action, whereas in the next moment they might have to fight hard to make the government act in time.

Just because the government may not be perfectly efficient does not mean that it cannot help society move toward increased efficiency. Most of the public adaptations that must happen to mitigate the damages from climate change require government action. Rather than bemoan past inefficient government actions, we need to focus on ways that we can improve government performance. That is, we must consider policies that limit poorly behaved programs and encourage the most essential. There is no reason why analysts cannot work on improving the efficiency of government programs even if ideal outcomes are not always achieved.

Further, there is no question but that public adaptations are important. Flood control, sea walls, land-use planning, dams, public inoculations and research programs are all critical adaptations that are by their nature public. Governments must be prepared to engage in these public adaptations when they are needed. Regardless of whether an effective mitigation control program is undertaken by national governments across the world, climate is expected to warm over the next century. The level of warming is likely to require future adaptation. When the time comes, governments need to have plans in place to engage in the public adaptation that will be required.

ADAPTATION EXAMPLES

Mendelsohn and Neumann (1999) and Chapters 2–7 in this book explore numerous adaptations that could occur in each sector. Across all the sectors, some of the adaptations are private and some are public. Both forms of adaptation are important.

The farmer makes many critical adaptation decisions in agriculture. Faced with rising temperatures and changing precipitation, the farmer must re-examine how he farms. First, the farmer must see if there is a better way of growing his current crop. Clearly he can consider planting earlier in response to warming. The farmer can also consider changing varieties to seek heat resistance, drought resistance, or possibly a shorter growing season. He can consider irrigation if water supplies are available. Quite often, however, changing irrigation options will also require support from the government. He can explore a number of subtle adjustments in tilling practice, fertilizer and harvesting that might help the plants adapt to the new climate. If crop productivity has increased, he can consider expanding cropland. If conditions have worsened, cropland can be reduced. Finally, the farmer can consider changing crops. If the climate is warmer, a different crop may well yield higher profits under the new conditions. All of these changes can reduce damages and increase the benefits associated with warming. These are all private decisions. The farmer will bear the costs of the adaptation and will receive the benefits.

However, the government also has important roles to play in agriculture. The government has funded most of the research exploring what will happen to plants and animals if temperatures rise or if carbon dioxide increases. The government funds the critical measurements of climate that each farmer depends on. The government manages the surface water system that delivers most of the irrigation water in the United States (although groundwater can be more important in some places). The government is likely to be the source of crop research that might tell farmers how best to adjust to climate change. Finally, it could well be the government that develops new crops and breeds that will be better adapted to future climates. Of course, private entities will also contribute to crop research and new crops and breeds. Nonetheless, the government sets the stage for private adaptation in agriculture.

Models of farmer adaptation conceive of farmers making enormous changes over the landscape. Crops would shift north in response to warming. Northern croplands would expand and southern arid croplands might contract slightly. Farmers will adjust their practices to reduce climate sensitivity. Estimates vary depending on whether one relies on agronomic–economic simulations (Chapter 2) or on cross-sectional evidence (Chapter 3). Both models predict that farmers will adjust to the changing conditions. However, the cross-sectional model implies much greater elasticity than the simulation model. For example, the cross-sectional model predicts a much larger increase in northern cropland and less sensitivity to warming than the simulation model. The cross-sectional model predicts that Northern Plains and Midwest croplands will expand by 15 to 30 per cent with a 2.5°C warming and 7 per cent precipitation increase, whereas the simulation model predicts only a 1–2 per cent increase. As discussed in Chapter 3, these projected land-use changes are large but not inconceivable across the Great Plains, where only about 25 per cent of the land is currently devoted to cropland. Much of the increase in cropland could conceivably come from other uses of existing farmland.

Holding cropland constant, the cross-sectional evidence suggests more optimistic results for farmers than the agronomic simulation models. For example, with the central warming scenario and no carbon fertilization, the cross-sectional study suggests a 0–10 per cent increase in crop productivity in the Midwest and a 3–24 per cent increase in crop productivity in the Northern Plains. The agronomic–economic simulation model suggests damages of about 19 per cent in the Midwest and a gain of only 2 per cent in the Northern Plains.

Both models have plausible arguments supporting their different results. The simulation models take into account the details of existing farms and price changes. The models suggest that farms cannot change very much. As productivity increases in the north, prices fall and farmers receive even less income. They consequently do not expand their cropland a great deal. The cross-sectional model assumes that prices are determined world-wide and will not respond much to global climate change. Conditions will improve in northern regions and farmers will make dramatic changes in cropland and crop choice. Simulation models underestimate this flexibility because they take existing conditions as too great a constraint. This study cannot resolve this important debate, but it does illustrate the importance of adaptation in agriculture.

Some analysts question whether the extensive modifications predicted by the cross-sectional models could possibly be undertaken by real farmers (Quiggin and Horowitz 1999, Hanemann 2000). These analysts feel that the forecasted adaptations require rapid adjustments that would impose high adaptation costs. A rapid change in climate over a few years would be more costly than the same change over a decade. Farmers will not be able to make the changes predicted in the Ricardian analysis over a short time period. If climate change comes in small intense bursts, there may well be some additional adjustment costs that the current chapter does not predict. However, if climate unfolds gradually, farmers will have many chances to adjust. Typical farming equipment lasts an average of five years. Over the next 60 years, a farmer is likely to replace his equipment about 12 times. If farmers examine their options whenever equipment is changed, they will be able to make 12 adjustments over this period. Farmers are likely to be able to adapt relatively rapidly to climate change, and the adjustments costs may turn out to be relatively low if they are given sufficient time to make changes. Of course, farmers may make mistakes over this period as they gradually learn what responses will prove to be most effective over the long term. How large these mistakes will be is an unresolved issue in the adaptation literature.

Unlike agriculture, forestry has extensive long-lived capital. It takes many years to adjust forests to different species, rotation lengths and management intensities. Forest decisions must take a long-term perspective and anticipate future events. Harvest strategies must include cutting down trees that will be adversely affected by near-term warming and preserving trees that are growing faster. Foresters have to facilitate adaptation by planting species that are likely to grow well in the future climate and avoiding trees that will be susceptible to dieback. Because foresters harvest and plant only a small percentage (1–2 per cent) of the land base in any given year, these adjustments take many years to have an important cumulative effect. Will forestry in fact be able to be as forward looking as the timber model anticipates?

To get a sense of the importance of forward-looking behavior in forestry, Sohngen and Mendelsohn (1999) did a sensitivity analysis with their national model using the 2.5°C, +7 per cent precipitation scenario. They examined what would happen if regeneration took longer because foresters did a poor job of predicting which trees to plant. They also examined what would happen if trees subject to dieback were not harvested or salvaged. With less forward-looking adaptation, the benefits in timber fall. Delayed planting reduces the present value of benefits in timber by $4–6 billion, or 10 to 17 per cent. Poor harvesting decisions reduces benefits by about $2 billion, or 7 per cent. Adding the two adaptations together, forward-looking adaptation increases total benefits by at least $6–8 billion, or about 20 per cent.

Adaptation varies in the energy sector depending on whether one is discussing heating or cooling (Chapter 6). The cross-sectional evidence suggests that people would spend less on insulation in the long run because warming reduces heating costs. The same evidence suggests that people will adapt to warming in the summer by increasing cooling capacity so that they can cool more. These building adjustments are an important component in long-term adaptation to climate change. Curiously, both adaptations increase energy expenditures. In the energy analysis, energy expenditures consistently are higher in the long-run models than in the short-run models.

Comparing the short- and long-run energy expenditures reveals regional patterns in the data. In the residential data, the three cold northern regions increase energy expenditures by about 3 per cent between the short and long run, but in the southern warmer regions, residential energy expenditures are about 2 per cent higher in the long run. These long-run increases reflect predicted changes to the building stock. In the commercial sector, the northern firms increase their energy expenditures by about 3 per cent in the long run, whereas the southern firms increase their energy expenditures by 4–7 per cent. Northern residential and commercial properties appear to have similar behavior. In contrast, southern commercial buildings respond more than southern residential buildings to warming, suggesting commercial buildings are easier to redesign for warmer climates. Substantial redesign may save these buildings enough energy to make it worthwhile. In any case, the difference between long-run and short-run energy expenditures suggests that changes in buildings are an important component of adaptation in the energy sector.

The water model depends on public adaptation through efficient water allocation. As runoff falls because of warming, the models assume that water will be taken away from low-valued uses and given to high-valued uses. If water were reduced proportionately across all users, damages would rise significantly. For example, if water were valued by low-valued agriculture at $2 an acre-foot and by high-valued agriculture at $200 an acre-foot, a program that reduced one million acre-feet just from low-valued uses would lose only $2 million of value. However, a strategy that shared these reductions equally across both high- and low-valued users would cause reductions of $101 million. Efficient adaptation through water reallocation can be very important in water systems with heterogeneous users. Because water is allocated through public agencies, these adaptations are currently public decisions. Whether these adaptations will be efficient will depend on the institutional arrangements surrounding water allocation and management. If water were allocated through markets, efficient water reallocation would occur automatically. Water markets would turn water allocation into a private adaptation.

Although not considered in the water chapter, another important adaptation for water systems is to change infrastructure. In places where water becomes increasingly scarce, additional interbasin transfer infrastructure (for example, canals, pumping facilities) can be built to move water from low-valued to high-valued basins. Dams can be built to hold water from surplus supply seasons such as warm winters to supply deficient seasons such as the summer season. Underground reservoirs can be constructed to hold water with minimal evaporation. Although private investment can contribute to water structures, private construction of dams and canals is problematic. There are many users or beneficiaries of these structures and it is difficult to design appropriate fees for each user. Further, the environmental externalities of these structures are known to be large. It is likely that this enterprise will have to remain a governmental responsibility. Governments will consequently have to re-examine water infrastructure frequently to make sure that the system is keeping up with climate change.

The analysis of sea level rise must also carefully consider adaptation over time. Managing the coast is a difficult problem because of the extensive long-lived capital and the heterogeneous coastline. Sea level rise, even if it occurs globally, will have dramatically different impacts in different areas because of the slope of the land and the intensity of development. A simple, uniform national strategy will not be efficient. Early impact estimates that assume sea walls should be built across the entire developed coast suggest incredibly expensive programs. Even if sea walls were limited just to more valuable coastline, the cost of building the sea walls all at once would be prohibitive.

Estimates of the cost of construction of such a mighty enterprise range from $70 billion to $110 billion (Yohe *et al*. 1999).

Spreading these expenditures over time so that the sea walls are built as needed can dramatically reduce the overall cost of construction. One interesting observation from the sea level rise chapter is that although one would protect only half the coastline against sea level rise today, one would protect almost all of it by the end of the century. The anticipated increase in development along the coast makes it all sufficiently valuable to protect by 2100. Consequently, building sea walls around the entire country over the next few decades is reacting prematurely and too vigorously to sea level rise. By delaying construction of these sea walls until late in the next century, one can reduce the present value of the costs from about $70 billion to $5.5 billion (Yohe *et al*. 1999).

Coastal adaptations will largely be the responsibility of the government. Sea walls, breakers and land use policies must all be managed by the government. The policy issue is whether coastal management will be efficient or not. Many people are affected by each coastal investment. Some stand to gain tremendous value from expensive protection, whereas others may lose from these protection efforts. Properties right along the coast will benefit, but the properties right behind the coastline will lose the opportunity to become coastline. Coastal owners consequently may want the government to spend huge sums to protect their specific property. But from a social perspective, coastline may not always be at risk. It is possible that current coastal properties will simply be replaced by new coastal properties further inland. Whether society will allow this redistribution to take place is not clear, even if it is the minimum cost strategy. Rolling easements could be effective in encouraging efficient adaptation (Titus 1998). By making the homeowner responsible for removing structures as sea level rises, homeowners will need to account for sea level rise in their investment decisions. This is an excellent example of a government action (the rolling easements) needed to encourage efficient private response.

Although the bulk of adaptation against sea level rise is the responsibility of the government, there is a role for private adaptation as well. In the Yohe *et al*. (1999) study, homeowners with perfect foresight depreciate their buildings in anticipation of inundation. Of course, perfect foresight is a demanding standard. Much of the damage from sea level rise may come from random storms riding on higher seas. It will be difficult for people to perfectly time their depreciation to match a future hurricane. However, even when the sea level rise model assumes imperfect foresight, the estimate of the damages rises from $5.5 billion to just $6.4 billion. Private depreciation of buildings is clearly not the most important adaptation in coastal management.

DISCUSSION

The analyses in this book strongly support the assertion that adaptation is important to climate change. Adaptation does mitigate the damages from climate change by lowering damages and creating benefits. How important is this adaptation? Crude aggregate estimates suggest that adaptation can reduce net damages (increase net benefits) by 20–30 per cent (Tol *et al.* 1998). It is consequently important but it is not a perfect substitute for controlling emissions. As climate change scenarios become increasingly more severe, adaptations are not enough to prevent damages. Society can considerably reduce potential impacts by adjusting to the changing conditions that climate change will impose. However, society will not be able to counteract all effects or prevent severe effects from causing substantial harm.

It is clear that it is important to distinguish between public and private adaptation. We believe that private adaptation, because it provides its own rewards, will most likely prove to be efficient and important. However, the government will still have two important roles. First, the government must set the stage for private adaptation by providing the necessary information and freedom to act. Second, governments must manage public adaptation. It is difficult to forecast whether public adaptation will be efficient or not. It is highly likely that some public adaptation efforts will be wasteful either because governments fail to act or because governments overreact. Encouraging efficient government adaptation is an important institutional challenge of global warming. If we can create institutions to manage adaptation efficiently, it is possible that many billions of dollars of potential climate damages can be averted and many billions of dollars of benefits can be collected.

REFERENCES

Adams, R., K. Bryant, B. McCarl, D. Legler, J. O'Brian, A. Solow and R. Weiher (1995), 'Value of improved long-range weather information', *Contemporary Economic Policy*, 13, 10–19.

Brennan, G. and J. Buchanan (1977), 'Towards a tax constitution for Leviathan', *Journal of Public Economics*, 8, 255–73.

Callaway, M., J. Smith and S. Keefe (1994), The Economic Effects of Climate Change for US Forests, Final Report, Washington, DC: US Environmental Protection Agency.

Dowlatabadi, H. and J. West (1998), 'On assessing the economic impacts of sea level rise on developed coasts', in T. Downing, A. Olsthoorn and R. Tol (eds), *Climate, Change, and Risk*, London: Routledge.

Downing, R., L. Ringus, M. Hulme and D. Waughray (1997), 'Adapting to climate change in Africa', *Mitigation and Adaptation Strategies for Global Change*, 2, 19–44.

Downs, A. (1957), *An Economic Theory of Democracy*, New York: Harper and Row.

Fankhauser, S. (1996), 'The potential costs of climate change adaptation', in J. Smith, N. Bhatti, G. Menzhulim, R. Benioff, M. Budyko, M. Campos, B. Jallow and F. Rijsberman (eds), *Adapting to Climate Change: An International Perspective*, New York: Springer.

Fankhauser, S., J. Smith and R. Tol (1999), 'Weathering climate change: Some simple rules to guide adaptation decisions', *Ecological Economics*, 30, 67–78.

Hanemann, W.M. (2000), 'Adaptation and its measurement', *Climatic Change*, 45, 571–81.

Houghton, J., L. Meira Filho, B. Callander, N. Harris, A. Kattenberg and K. Maskell (eds) (1996), *Climate Change 1995: The Science of Climate Change*, Cambridge, UK: Cambridge University Press.

Katz, R. and B. Brown (1992), 'Extreme events in a changing climate: Variability is more important than averages', *Climatic Change*, 21, 289–302.

Mearns, L., C. Rosenzweig and R. Goldberg (1997), 'Mean and variance change in climate scenarios: Methods, agricultural applications, and measures of uncertainty', *Climatic Change*, 34, 367–96.

Mendelsohn, R. (2000), 'Efficient adaptation to climate change', *Climatic Change*, 45, 583–600.

Mendelsohn, R. and J.E. Neumann (eds) (1999), *The Impact of Climate Change on the United States Economy*, Cambridge, UK: Cambridge University Press.

Mendelsohn, R. and W. Nordhaus (1996), 'Reply to Quiggan and Horowitz', *American Economic Review*, 89, 1046–8.

Niskanen, W. (1971), *Bureaucracy and Representative Government*, Chicago: Aldine–Atherton.

Parry, M. (1986), 'Some implications of climatic change for human development', in W.C. Clark and R.E. Munn (eds), *Sustainable Development of the Biosphere*, Laxenburg, Austria: International Institute for Applied Systems Analysis, pp. 378–406.

Pittock, B. and R. Jones (2000), 'Adaptation to what and why?', *Environmental Monitoring and Assessment*, 61, 9–35.

Quiggin, J. and J. Horowitz (1999), 'The impact of global warming on agriculture: A Ricardian analysis: Comment', *American Economic Review*, 89, 1044–5.

Rayner, S. and E.L. Malone (eds) (1998), *Human Choice and Climate Change, Volume 3: Tools for Policy Analysis*, Columbus, OH: Battelle Press.

Reilly, J. and D. Schimmelpfennig (2000), 'Irreversibility, uncertainty, and learning: Portraits of adaptation to long-term climate change', *Climatic Change*, 45, 253–78.

Rosenzweig, C. (1994), 'Maize suffers a sea change', *Nature*, 370, 175–6.

Rosenzweig, C. and M. Parry (1994), 'Potential impact of climate change on world food supply', *Nature*, 367, 133–8.

Samuelson, P. (1954), 'The pure theory of public expenditure', *Review of Economics and Statistics*, 36, 386–9.

Smit, B., I. Burton, R.J.T. Klein and R. Street (1999), 'The science of adaptation: A framework for assessment', *Mitigation and Adaptation Strategies for Global Change*, 4, 199–213.

Smit, B., I Burton, R. Klein and J. Wandel (2000), 'An anatomy of adaptation to climate change and variance', *Climatic Change*, 45, 223–51.

Smith, J. (1997), 'Setting priorities for adaptation to climate change', *Global Environmental Change*, 7, 251–64.

Smith, J. and S. Lenhart (1996), 'Climate change adaptation policy options', *Climate Research*, 6, 193–201.

Smithers, J. and B. Smit (1997), 'Human adaptation to climate variability and change', *Global Environmental Change*, 7, 129–46.

Sohngen, B. and R. Mendelsohn (1998), 'Valuing the market impact of large-scale ecological change: The effect of climate change on US timber', *American Economic Review*, 88, 686–710.

Timmerman, A., J. Oberhuber, A. Bacher, M. Esch, M. Latif and E. Roeckner (1999), 'Increased El Niño frequency in a climate model forced by future greenhouse warming', *Nature*, 398, 694–7.

Titus, J.G. (1998), 'Rising seas, coastal erosion, and the takings clause: How to save wetlands and beaches without hurting property owners', *Maryland Law Review*, 57, 1279–399.

Titus, J. (1990), 'Strategies for adapting to the greenhouse effect', *APA Journal*, Summer, 311–23.

Tol, R., S. Fankhauser and J. Smith (1998), 'The scope for adaptation to climate change: What can we learn from the impact literature', *Global Environmental Change*, 8, 109–23.

Tullock, G. (1967), *Towards a Mathematics of Politics*, Ann Arbor: University of Michigan Press.

VEMAP (1995), 'Vegetation/Ecosystem Modeling and Analysis Project: Comparing biogeography and biogeochemistry models in a continental-scale study of terrestrial ecosystem responses to climate change and CO_2 doubling', *Global Biogeochemical Cycles*, 9(4), 407–37.

Yohe, G. and R. Moss (2000), 'Economic sustainability, indicators and climate change', in *Climate Change and its Linkages with Development, Equity, and Sustainability*, *Proceedings of the IPCC Expert Meeting*, Colombo, Sri Lanka, IPCC and WMO, pp. 67–94.

Yohe, G. and J.E. Neumann (1997), 'Planning for sea level rise and shore protection under climate uncertainty', *Climatic Change*, 37, 111–40.

Yohe, G., J.E. Neumann and P. Marshall (1999), 'The economic damage induced by sea level rise in the United States', in R. Mendelsohn and J.E. Neumann (eds), *The Impact of Climate Change on the United States Economy*, Cambridge, UK: Cambridge University Press, pp. 178–208.

Yohe, G., J. Neumann, P. Marshall and H. Ameden (1996), 'The economic cost of greenhouse-induced sea level rise for developed property in the United States', *Climatic Change*, 37, 243–70.

9.   Synthesis

Robert Mendelsohn and Joel B. Smith

This book contains empirical results measuring the impact of climate change on the United States economy, focusing on quantified regional impacts in each market sector. The sectors include the most important climate-sensitive aspects of the economy: agriculture, coasts, energy, forestry and water. The methods used to measure climate impacts include both experimental-simulation studies and cross-sectional empirical approaches. The methods were developed in Mendelsohn and Neumann (1999) but are adapted to regional analysis in this book.

The book does not contain analyses of the nonmarket impacts of climate change. Impacts such as health effects, ecosystem changes, aesthetic consequences and pollution effects are important to the quality of life but are excluded here because analyses of these sectors have not yet incorporated efficient adaptation and in many cases the nonmarket impacts have not been carefully quantified. Their exclusion should not be interpreted as a judgment that nonmarket effects are not important. Rather the judgment is that economic analyses of the nonmarket sectors have not yet reached the same level of understanding or quantification compared with the market sectors. This study is consequently limited to market impacts only.

HISTORICAL ESTIMATES

To give some perspective on the estimated results in this book, we present results from other studies in Table 9.1. Table 9.1 reports estimates of the national impacts from a doubling of CO_2, which is roughly what this study was intending to measure. These estimates have been updated from the original published accounts using the GDP deflator so that they can be expressed in 1998 rather than 1990 dollars. Most of these estimates from the literature are not directly comparable with the studies in this book because previous authors measured impacts of climate change on a 1990 economy. As stated in the introduction, this study and Mendelsohn and Neumann (1999) break with this tradition and measure the impact of climate change on the economy that

Table 9.1   *US welfare impacts on market sectors from doubling of CO_2*
             (billions 1998 USD/year)

Economy	Nordhaus 1990	Cline 1990	Fankhauser 1990	Tol 1990	Mendelsohn-Neumann 1990	Mendelsohn-Neumann 2060
Agriculture	−1.3	−20.7	−9.9	−11.8	13.3	48.9
Timber	–	−3.9	−0.8	–	4.0	4.0
Water	–	−8.3	18.4	–	−4.4	−4.4
Coastal	−14.4	−8.3	−10.6	−10.0	−0.1	−0.1
Energy	−0.6	−11.7	−9.3	–	−3.0	−4.8
Total	−16.3	−52.8	−49.1	−21.8	9.9	43.5
% GDP	−0.3	−0.9	−0.8	−0.4	0.2	0.2

Sources: Nordhaus 1991, Cline 1992, Fankhauser 1995, Tol 1995, Mendelsohn and Neumann 1999.

is likely to be in place when climate change occurs. That is, we attempt to measure the impact of climate change in 2060 because climate change will affect this future economy, not the economy we know today. To help readers understand how this might affect the impacts, we provide two estimates from Mendelsohn and Neumann (1999); one estimate is for a 1990 economy and the other is for a 2060 economy.

The results in Table 9.1 are striking. Although previous authors could not agree on the importance of impacts in each sector, they clearly agreed that market impacts in the United States were negative, although not necessarily large. Nordhaus (1991), Cline (1992), Fankhauser (1995) and Tol (1995) estimated net market damages from the doubling of greenhouse gases ranging from 0.3 per cent to 0.9 per cent of GDP. Including nonmarket impacts, these authors estimated the damages in the United States from the doubling of greenhouse gases would be equal in magnitude to 1.0–1.5 per cent of GDP (Pearce *et al.* 1996). These results are reflected in the IPCC Second Assessment (Pearce *et al.* 1996) and reflect the state of the art in impact assessment through the mid-1990s.

The new set of impact methods developed in Mendelsohn and Neumann (1999), however, result in very different estimates. In contrast to the damages predicted by the earlier studies, the new studies estimate net market benefits for the United States of 0.2 per cent of GDP. Further, Mendelsohn and Neumann estimate that these climate impacts grow proportionately with GDP as the economy develops.

Mendelsohn and Neumann obtain different estimates of American impacts because they include the full potential of efficient adaptation and they provide broader coverage of each sector. For example, adaptation allows firms and farmers to change their crops and trees by planting more productive species and reducing poorly growing species. Adaptation allows planners to protect coastal structures when needed and reallocate scarce water supplies. Broader coverage includes the benefits of carbon fertilization on both crops and trees. Broader coverage includes the benefits of reduced heating as well as the costs of increased cooling. These improvements in impact research change the results for the United States. The new results suggest that the net impacts from climate change are likely to be beneficial to the United States in the twenty-first century. These new methods are included in this book as well.

NATIONAL ESTIMATES

The national results from the empirical studies in this book are reported in Table 9.2. The results differ slightly from Mendelsohn and Neumann (1999) because of changes in the agricultural and energy sectors. In this book, the results of the cross-sectional study (Chapter 3) are included with the agro-economic results (Chapter 2). In the Mendelsohn and Neumann study, only the agro-economic results were included in the final synthesis. In this synthesis, we extrapolated from the climate scenarios done in the timber study, Chapter 4. Those climate scenarios are all based on GCMs. We extrapolated from these scenarios to the nine uniform scenarios that were done in all the other sectors. This extrapolation is imperfect, especially at high temperature changes, because the GCMs do not predict uniform scenarios and so they are not directly comparable. In this book, the energy sector includes a detailed seasonal model that turns out to be more climate sensitive than the annual model in Mendelsohn and Neumann.

However, the results of this book support the same general conclusions in Mendelsohn and Neumann. This book estimates that the average net effect to the United States economy across all precipitation scenarios for a 1.5°C warming is $31 billion of net benefits; with 2.5°C warming, the average effect is $21 billion of net benefits; and with a 5.0°C warming, the average effect is $13 billion of net damages. These impact estimates are for 2060, when the GDP is assumed to be $21.8 trillion. These estimates consequently imply an impact on the US economy of 0.14 per cent at 1.5°C, 0.10 per cent at 2.5°C and –0.06 per cent at 5.0°C. These new estimates are about an order of magnitude smaller than the estimates in the IPCC report (Pearce *et al.* 1996). Further, there are net benefits with mild warming and net damages only with relatively large temperature increases.

Table 9.2 also reveals that there is a wide range of estimates of the impact in each scenario. Not only are we uncertain which scenario will apply, but we are also uncertain what will happen if that scenario occurs. The range of

Table 9.2   National annual impacts of climate scenarios in 2060 (billions 1998 USD/year)

Sector	0% precipitation	+7% precipitation	+15% precipitation
	Climate scenario: 1.5°C		
Agriculture[a]	30.0	30.9	31.4
	(25.4 to 35.5)	(25.2 to 37.5)	(25.0 to 37.8)
Forestry	0.9	3.8	6.7
	(0.9 to 0.9)	(3.7 to 3.9)	(6.5 to 6.9)
Energy	−1.7	−3.1	−4.5
	(−4.7 to 1.3)	(−6.3 to 0.0)	(−7.9 to −1.2)
Coastal	−0.1	−0.1	−0.1
Water	−2.6	−0.4	2.7
Total	26.5	31.0	36.1
	(18.9 to 35.0)	(22.1 to 40.9)	(26.2 to 46.1)
	Climate scenario: 2.5°C		
Agriculture[a]	25.5	25.8	26.1
	(16.8 to 32.8)	(16.0 to 33.4)	(16.0 to 28.5)
Forestry	1.5	4.2	6.9
	(1.4 to 1.5)	(4.0 to 4.3)	(6.6 to 7.2)
Energy	−5.3	−6.9	−8.3
	(−10.1 to −0.5)	(−11.9 to −1.8)	(−13.5 to −3.1)
Coastal	−0.2	−0.2	−0.2
Water	−4.8	−3.1	0.6
Total	16.7	19.8	25.1
	(3.1 to 28.8)	(4.8 to 32.6)	(9.5 to 33.0)
	Climate scenario: 5.0°C		
Agriculture[a]	14.1	16.1	17.0
	(−6.5 to 23.5)	(−6.6 to 24.5)	(−6.6 to 25.7)
Forestry	1.5	9.1	7.8
	(1.4 to 1.5)	(8.8 to 9.3)	(7.8 to 7.8)
Energy	−21.3	−25.7	−26.9
	(−32.3 to −15.0)	(−34.8 to −16.5)	(−36.6 to −17.2)
Coastal	−0.4	−0.4	−0.4
Water	−11.3	−9.0	−5.4
Total	−19.9	−9.9	−7.8
	(−49.1 to −1.6)	(−42.0 to 8.0)	(−41.2 to 10.6)

Notes:
Positive numbers imply benefits and negative numbers imply damages. Numbers in parenthesis represent range of effects across methods. All estimates are for 2060, when US GDP is predicted to be $21.8 trillion.
a.   Agriculture estimates come from both Chapters 2 and 3.

uncertainty presented comes solely from looking across different impact methods. In addition to methodological causes, the uncertainty can also vary because of statistical variance and problems with measurement. The true uncertainty surrounding the estimates is even larger than the ranges in Table 9.2. With a uniform 1.5°C warming and 15 per cent precipitation increase, the aggregate net effects across the economy just from using different impact methods range from net benefits of $26 billion to $46 billion. With a 2.5°C warming and 7 per cent precipitation increase, impacts range from benefits of $5 billion to $33 billion. Finally with a 5°C warming and no precipitation increase, effects range from damages of $49 billion to $2 billion.

One of the most important sectors in the analysis is clearly agriculture. Because past studies have estimated that agriculture has the largest market impacts, this study relies on two methods to value climate impacts on agriculture. The agronomic–economic simulation model in Chapter 2 calculates changes in yields of each crop for the United States and then consumer and producer surplus. The Ricardian empirical analysis in Chapter 3 relies on cross-sectional analysis to impute what future changes would cost. Both methods make assumptions about what will happen to future world prices. The simulation model predicts that global prices will fall with at least mild warming, whereas (partially accounting for potential changes in global production) the cross-sectional model assumes that prices will remain unchanged. The actual impact will depend on how prices will change once the world market is taken into account.

The study finds that the agricultural sector is more sensitive to temperature than precipitation. Although production increases with higher precipitation levels, this effect is relatively small for the country as a whole, except at the 5°C increase. As seen in Table 9.2, raising temperatures 1.5°C increases overall welfare significantly ($31 billion with a 7 per cent precipitation increase). These benefits fall slightly with a 2.5°C increase, suggesting that warming above 1.5°C is harmful. The benefits fall substantially with a 5.0°C warming, although the effects remain beneficial compared with a no climate change scenario.

As temperatures rise, energy and water impacts increase noticeably. Using the 2.5°C warming, 7 per cent precipitation increase scenario in Table 9.2, energy damages for the country are almost $7 billion, but with the 5°C warming, damages rise to $26 billion. These negative impacts turn the net national impacts to damages. The large damages in energy are the result of sizeable increases in cooling costs that more than offset the heating savings. Water damages also are largest at 5°C, especially with no precipitation increase, amounting to $11 billion, because of sharp reductions in runoff. Forestry impacts are beneficial for the country in every scenario because of increased productivity and increased acreage of more productive species.

Annual coastal effects are relatively small because coastal protection costs are spread across an entire century.

REGIONAL ESTIMATES

Although these national estimates are interesting, the focus of this book is on the regional impacts of climate change. The studies in each sector took special care to estimate how impacts were distributed across seven regions in the United States. Although nine climate scenarios were evaluated in this study, we focus on three scenarios to discuss the range of regional effects. The results from these three scenarios are displayed in Table 9.3; the results from the remaining six climate scenarios are shown in the appendix to this chapter. We label the case with a 2.5°C warming and a 7 per cent precipitation increase as the 'central scenario'. We also examine two more extreme scenarios: a 'mild scenario' with a 1.5°C warming and a 15 per cent precipitation increase and a 'harsh scenario' with a 5.0°C warming and a 0 per cent precipitation increase. In all three cases, we present the estimated outcome from each scenario. By examining these three scenarios, the reader can begin to appreciate the sensitivity of each region to climate change.

One broad hypothesis suggested by earlier impact studies is that the effects would be more beneficial in the cooler northern regions and more harmful in the warmer southern regions of the country. This general hypothesis suggests that the three cooler northern regions, the Northeast, Midwest and Northern Plains, should have more beneficial net impacts than the three hotter southern regions, the Southeast, Southern Plains and Southwest. The Northwest is an anomaly because it is a northern region and yet it has a moderate climate. Using the results in Table 9.3, we can test this general hypothesis.

With the mild climate change scenario, the northern regions enjoy a slightly larger share of the national net benefits compared with the south. The northern regions have $19 billion of net benefits (53 per cent in this discussion with the Pacific Northwest omitted) and the southern regions have $12 billion of net benefits (33 per cent). This is close to their share of GDP, the northern regions with 56 per cent and the southern regions with 44 per cent. There are two explanations for these relatively neutral interregional results. First, carbon fertilization dominates this scenario since the temperature change is so mild. Since every region benefits from carbon fertilization, the effects are spread evenly. Second, the scenario results in large price reductions in agriculture. These benefits are enjoyed by all consumers and so are distributed evenly across regions in proportion to GDP.

With the remaining two climate scenarios, the central hypothesis of the book is more clearly confirmed. Northern regions benefit more than southern

Table 9.3   *Estimated regional impacts of climate change in 2060 (billions*
              1998 USD/year)

Region	Agriculture	Forestry	Energy	Coast	Water	Total
1.5°C warming with +15% precipitation: Mild scenario						
Northeast	3.1	1.5	−0.7	−0.0	0.0	3.9
Midwest	7.5	1.3	−0.5	0.0	0.1	8.4
Northern Plains	5.3	1.1	−0.2	0.0	0.2	6.5
Northwest	2.2	0.1	1.5	−0.0	1.0	4.8
Southeast	6.7	1.1	−2.0	−0.1	0.2	5.8
Southern Plains	3.3	0.4	−1.7	0.0	0.2	2.2
Southwest	2.7	1.1	−0.9	0.0	1.1	4.0
National	31.4	6.7	−4.5	−0.1	2.7	36.1
2.5°C warming with +7% precipitation: Central scenario						
Northeast	3.2	2.2	−0.4	−0.1	0.0	4.9
Midwest	6.5	1.3	−0.2	−0.0	−0.1	7.5
Northern Plains	3.9	0.8	−0.1	−0.0	−0.3	4.4
Northwest	2.0	−0.3	1.6	−0.0	−1.8	1.5
Southeast	5.7	−1.0	−3.5	−0.1	−0.5	0.6
Southern Plains	2.0	0.3	−2.9	0.0	−0.2	−0.8
Southwest	2.1	1.0	−1.4	0.0	−0.2	1.4
National	25.8	4.2	−6.9	−0.2	−3.1	19.8
5.0°C warming with 0% precipitation increase: Harsh scenario						
Northeast	1.8	2.6	−2.6	−0.2	−0.1	1.6
Midwest	3.6	1.0	−1.6	0.0	−0.5	2.4
Northern Plains	2.7	0.5	−1.2	0.0	−1.2	0.8
Northwest	1.7	−0.6	1.6	−0.0	−5.7	−3.1
Southeast	3.6	−2.8	−9.5	−0.2	−0.5	−9.4
Southern Plains	0.5	0.1	−6.7	−0.0	−0.9	−7.0
Southwest	0.5	0.6	−1.5	−0.0	−2.5	−2.7
National	14.1	1.5	−21.3	−0.4	−11.3	−19.9

Note: Coastal scenario assumes 33 cm sea level rise in 1.5°C scenario, 67 cm in 2.5°C
scenario and 100 cm in 5.0°C scenario. Impacts are beneficial if positive and harmful if
negative. Expected values average results across all methods.

regions from warming. With the central scenario, the three northern cool
regions have beneficial impacts of $17 billion whereas the three warm south-
ern regions now have benefits of only $1 billion. Agricultural benefits dominate

net impacts in the northern regions. The southern regions enjoy smaller agricultural benefits in this scenario but they are also beginning to be affected by much higher energy costs. With the harsh scenario, the northern regions have net benefits of $5 billion but the southern regions have net damages of $19 billion. In the northern regions, the benefits in agricultural and forestry offset the damages largely in energy and water. In the southern regions, agricultural benefits shrink and energy damages increase substantially. Water and forestry losses also accumulate in the southern regions.

The study is consistent with the conclusion that the effect of warming in a region depends on the initial climate of a region and the magnitude of the warming. The warmer (cooler) the initial climate, the more harmful (beneficial) is warming. The larger the warming, the smaller (larger) are the additional benefits (damages). By comparing the expected impacts in the mild, central and harsh scenarios, one can begin to understand the sensitivity of each region to climate. In the mildest scenario, the Midwest and Southeast appear to be the most sensitive regions because they enjoy the largest benefits. However, all the regions enjoy sizeable benefits from this scenario. In the central scenario, the Midwest has by far the largest benefits, although all the northern regions enjoy benefits over $4 billion. In the harsh scenario, the Midwest continues to benefit the most, but all the southern regions and the Northwest experience large damages. Regional sensitivity clearly depends on the severity of the scenario. With the mild scenario, benefits are widespread. With the central scenario, benefits are concentrated in the northern regions. Finally, with the harsh scenario, damages are concentrated in the southern regions.

Increased precipitation has a positive but declining effect on the economy. The independent effect of precipitation is clear when comparing Table 9.3 and the appendix. With a 2.5°C warming, the net national impact is a $17 billion benefit with no change in precipitation, a $20 billion benefit with a 7 per cent increase in precipitation, and a $25 billion benefit with a 15 per cent increase in precipitation. More precipitation is especially beneficial to forestry and water. The higher precipitation increases tree growth and offsets the evaporation losses from higher temperatures. Energy damages increase slightly with higher precipitation, probably because of the effect of higher humidity. Interestingly, precipitation has little effect on national agricultural results. Except with high temperatures, agriculture is surprisingly insensitive to higher precipitation.

CONSUMER VERSUS PRODUCER IMPACTS

In agriculture (Chapter 2) and forestry (Chapter 4), climate change has an effect on the market prices of food and timber. We can examine both producer and consumer surplus in both sectors. That is, we can examine the effect of climate on productivity, prices and the welfare of both producers and consumers. This approach has been followed in national studies of climate change effects (Adams *et al.* 1995, 1999; Sohngen and Mendelsohn 1998, 1999) but never in regional studies. With regional studies, it is clear that producer surplus and consumer surplus have entirely different regional distributions. Producer surplus depends on where the goods are supplied. For timber, the producer surplus lies in regions with productive forestland: the Southeast (55 per cent) and the Northwest (25 per cent). For agriculture, the producer surplus occurs in regions with productive farmland: Midwest (30 per cent), Northern Plains (15 per cent), Southeast (15 per cent), Southern Plains (14 per cent) and Southwest (14 per cent). With consumer surplus, however, the effects are distributed in proportion to the population (consumers) and GDP: Northeast (25 per cent), Midwest (21 per cent), Southeast (21 per cent) and Southwest (18 per cent). Consequently, regions with large populations, such as the Northeast, can have large climate impacts even when they have little forestland or farmland. The distribution of indirect effects on consumers through the market plays an important regional role. Table 9.4 displays the producer and consumer surplus effects in agriculture and forestry for the three climate scenarios.

The producer surplus effects depend on the size of each sector and the sector's climate sensitivity. Regions with substantial farmland (Midwest, Northern Plains, Southeast and Southwest) and forestland (Southeast and Pacific Northwest) were expected to have large producer surplus effects. Regions that were already warm were expected to be more sensitive (South). The results reported in Table 9.4 suggest the magnitude of agriculture producer surplus impacts has more to do with the climate sensitivity of a region than to the size of the sensitive sector. Similar results apply to forestry. Although the Southeast has the largest impacts as expected, it is also quite sensitive to warming. Further, the Northeast also exhibits large effects even though it is currently relatively unimportant in forestry, whereas the Pacific Northwest has relatively small impacts despite its importance in timber. Producer surplus impacts thus appear to depend a great deal on the sensitivity of a region to climate change.

Consumer surplus impacts for both sectors are felt in the regions with the largest populations (Northeast, Midwest and Southeast). Consumer surplus effects are distributed through prices to all consumers nationwide. Consequently, regions with more people tend to enjoy a large share of the national benefits. The market consequently distributes climate impacts more evenly across the nation. Given the magnitude of the consumer surplus benefits in agriculture and forestry, the regional distribution of net climate impacts is far more equitable than what producer effects alone would suggest.

Table 9.4   Producer and consumer surplus effects in agriculture and forestry in 2060 (billions 1998 USD/year)

Region	Agriculture		Forestry	
	PS	CS	PS	CS
1.5°C warming with +15% precipitation: Mild scenario				
Northeast	−2.12	7.97	0.03	1.51
Midwest	2.80	7.48	0.00	1.30
Northern Plains	3.30	0.87	0.79	0.33
Northwest	0.45	0.90	−0.15	0.24
Southeast	−1.53	6.08	−0.24	1.30
Southern Plains	2.57	2.05	0.09	0.35
Southwest	−3.25	3.84	0.02	1.10
National	2.24	29.1	0.57	6.13
2.5°C warming with +7% precipitation: Central scenario				
Northeast	−0.96	7.81	1.22	0.98
Midwest	1.43	7.32	0.41	0.85
Northern Plains	1.74	0.86	0.46	0.23
Northwest	0.38	0.88	−0.48	0.14
Southeast	−0.52	5.96	−1.82	0.87
Southern Plains	0.25	1.97	0.15	0.25
Southwest	−3.08	3.76	0.22	0.72
National	−0.84	28.50	0.17	4.00
5.0°C warming with 0% precipitation increase: Harsh scenario				
Northeast	−0.47	4.19	2.30	0.30
Midwest	−1.49	3.93	0.78	0.25
Northern Plains	0.54	0.46	0.48	0.06
Northwest	0.64	0.47	−0.69	0.03
Southeast	0.44	3.20	−3.06	0.27
Southern Plains	−0.90	1.06	0.05	0.07
Southwest	−3.62	2.10	0.40	0.22
National	−4.86	15.30	0.24	1.20

Notes: Impacts are beneficial if positive and harmful if negative. PS refers to producer surplus and CS to consumer surplus. Agricultural results are from Chapter 2 and timber results are from Chapter 4.

PER CAPITA IMPACTS

To show how regional effects vary for individuals, Table 9.5 presents the climate impacts on a per person basis. Regional impacts are divided by population size. Of course, this represents just an average effect per person in each region. Actual effects for individuals will vary depending on their role in each sector. With the mild scenario, every region shows net gains, with an average annual benefit in the United States of almost $125 per person. The people in the Northern Plains and Northwest are the biggest winners, with annual net gains of $743 and $535, respectively. With the central scenario, national net benefits fall to about $68 per person. People in the Northern Plains still enjoy relatively large benefits of $500 per person, but the benefits in the southern regions fall sharply. With the harsh scenario, the average American loses about $70 per person. The Pacific Northwest is hard hit with damages of almost $350 per person because of losses to their water system. The Southern Plains area is also hard hit with damages of the same magnitude, but these effects come from high energy costs. Although the Southern Plains have the highest *per capita* damages, all the southern regions are damaged by high energy costs in the harsh scenario. People in the northern regions continue to benefit, but only by small amounts as beneficial and harmful effects across sectors counterbalance each other.

The analysis shows that the geographic distribution of effects in the United States is clearly not uniform. Impacts across regions vary widely, depending

Table 9.5   Estimated aggregate market impacts per person in 2060 (1998 USD/person/year)

Region	Climate scenario		
	Mild	Central	Harsh
Northeast	49.2	61.8	20.3
Midwest	113.0	101.0	32.8
Northern Plains	742.8	500.4	96.4
Northwest	535.2	164.3	−342.6
Southeast	96.2	10.5	−154.4
Southern Plains	108.1	−38.5	−348.9
Southwest	104.4	35.6	−71.6
National	124.5	68.4	−68.5

Notes: Positive numbers imply net benefits and negative numbers net damages. Estimates are for 2060 with an assumed national population of 290 million.

on the region's productive acreage of farmland and forests, population, and economic activity. Impacts also vary across region, depending on initial climate and climate scenario. With the mild warming scenario (1.5°C), benefits are more uniformly distributed. With the central warming scenario (2.5°C), benefits are concentrated in the northern regions. With the harsh warming scenario (5.0°C), damages are concentrated in the southern regions.

DISCUSSION

Although the analysis did not examine impacts within regions, there is reason to expect that effects will not be uniform here as well. Certain pockets in a region may be warmer or cooler, wetter or drier. They will have different responses from the rest of the region. Climate change itself is not likely to be uniform. Changes in precipitation especially could vary widely on a local scale. Ecological impacts may be different in the southern edge of a region than in the northern edge. Economic activity and populations vary widely across regions. For all these reasons, one should expect that the experience of every household could vary within a region. Nonetheless, the broad regional patterns that this research estimates should bear out.

This research measures the impact of climate changes associated with the increase in greenhouse gases in the atmosphere. A range of climate scenarios is explored to provide a sense of the range of possible outcomes. However, the tested scenarios do not capture all possible outcomes. Individual regions could experience very different climate outcomes. Climates may change across seasons. Interannual variance could increase or fall with changes in El Niño events or fluctuations in the patterns of winds or ocean currents. Extreme climate events such as storms and hurricanes could change. These specific types of climate change were not examined in this book. If new climate research can tie changes in greenhouse gases to interannual climate fluctuations, to specific geographic patterns, to seasonal variation or to extreme climate events, the impact studies ought to be redone to include these effects.

Baseline economic conditions may not follow what was assumed in this study. Development could occur more rapidly than expected in some sectors and regions and more slowly in others. Technological adaptations to climate change may mitigate some damages and create new benefits. There is consequently a great deal of uncertainty associated with forecasting damages into the next century. Despite this uncertainty, we are forced to rely on these long-term forecasts to guide current policy. The long lags between actions and consequences associated with greenhouse gases require a forward-looking approach.

There are many uncertainties that should be associated with every aspect of these results. The climate scenarios and the baseline scenarios are both uncertain. What the climate or the economy will actually look like by 2060 is not known. This study does not address this climate and baseline uncertainty. Readers should turn to climate science sources (such as Houghton *et al.* 2001) to determine which climates are more likely and to economic projections (such as World Bank 1987 and Nakicenovic *et al.* 2000) to determine which baseline changes are possible. This study focuses on estimating climate change impacts given the assumed scenario. Even these conditional impact estimates are uncertain, however. Alternative methods lead to slightly different estimates. All the estimates generate only expected outcomes. The data and methods support a wide range of possible outcomes.

The results in this book imply that climate change is not a great threat to the US economy in the twenty-first century. The results in fact suggest that climate change for this century could be beneficial, if the warming turns out to be relatively mild. Even with more severe warming scenarios up to 5°C, the warming is likely to be only mildly harmful to the economy. The declining benefits with higher degrees of warming make it apparent that continued warming beyond the twenty-first century could begin to impose damages to the US economy. In addition, increased frequency and intensity of extreme events could also increase damages or reduce benefits, even in the twenty-first century.

This book does not address noneconomic impacts of climate change such as the effects on natural ecosystems, health or aesthetics. If these impacts were carefully quantified, the effects of climate change could be more harmful. It is consequently urgent that empirical studies be undertaken to measure the magnitude of these additional effects. Nonmarket studies are urgently needed to quantify the value of the environmental changes that are expected to occur over the twenty-first century. Studies need to be conducted on health impacts which include both stimuli and public health responses. Research is also needed to measure American values for climate and how Americans will react to warmer seasons.

One must be careful not to extrapolate from the US results to low latitude countries. The studies reported in this book are all carefully calibrated to American conditions. That is, they measure climate impacts in the temperate zone for a highly developed country. Developing countries in lower latitudes are in subtropical and tropical climate zones. Their economies rely upon less capital and technology. Further, developing countries have limited financial and other resources for adaptation. Developing countries are consequently expected to be at much greater risk to climate change than the United States. Additional empirical studies are especially needed in the low latitude countries to obtain a clearer estimate of the size of damages to expect in developing countries.

Finally, it is important to do new impact studies over time. As our economy grows, climate changes, and we experience future impacts, our understanding of climate impacts will improve. Estimates of future impacts should be regularly updated so that greenhouse gas decisions can be based on the best available information.

REFERENCES

Adams, R.M., R. Fleming, B.A. McCarl and C. Rosenzweig (1995), 'A reassessment of the economic effects of climate change on US agriculture', *Climatic Change*, 30, 147–67.

Adams, R.M., B.A. McCarl, K. Segerson, C. Rosenzweig, K.J. Bryant, B.L. Dixon, R. Conner, R.E. Evenson and D. Ojima (1999), 'Economic effects of climate change on US agriculture', in R. Mendelsohn and J.E. Neumann (eds), *The Impact of Climate Change on the United States Economy*, Cambridge, UK: Cambridge University Press, pp. 18–54.

Cline, W. (1992), *The Economics of Global Warming*, Washington, DC: Institute of International Economics.

Fankhauser, S. (1995), *Valuing Climate Change – The Economics of The Greenhouse*, London: Earthscan.

Houghton, J.T., Y. Ding, D.J. Griggs, M. Noguer, P.J. van der Linden, D. Xiaosu and K. Maskell (eds) (2001), Climate Change 2001: The Scientific Basis, Cambridge, UK: Cambridge University Press.

Mendelsohn, R. and J.E. Neumann (eds) (1999), *The Impact of Climate Change on the United States Economy*, Cambridge, UK: Cambridge University Press.

Nakicenovic, N., J. Alcamo, G. Davis, B. de Vries, J. Fenhann, S. Gaffin, K. Gregory, A. Grubler, T.Y. Jung, T. Kram, E.L. La Rovere, L. Michaelis, S. Mori, T. Morita, W. Pepper, H. Pitcher, L. Price, K. Raihi, A. Roehrl, H.-H. Rogner, A. Sankovski, M. Schlesinger, P. Shukla, S. Smith, R. Swart, S. van Rooijen, N. Victor and Z. Dadi (2000), Emissions Scenarios. A Special Report of Working Group III of the Intergovernmental Panel on Climate Change, Cambridge, UK: Cambridge University Press.

Nordhaus, W. (1991), 'To slow or not to slow: The economics of the greenhouse effect', *Economic Journal*, 101, 920–37.

Pearce, D.W., W.R. Cline, A.N. Achanta, S. Fankhauser, R.K. Pachauri, R.S.J. Tol and P. Vellinga (1996), 'The social costs of climate change: Greenhouse damage and the benefits of control', in J.P. Bruce, H. Lee, and E.F. Haites (eds), *Climate Change 1995: Economic and Social Dimensions of Climate Change*, Cambridge, UK: Cambridge University Press, pp. 179–224.

Sohngen, B. and R. Mendelsohn (1998), 'Valuing the market impact of large-scale ecological change: The effect of climate change on US timber', *American Economic Review*, 88, 686–710.

Sohngen, B. and R. Mendelsohn (1999), 'The impacts of climate change on the US timber market', R. Mendelsohn and J.E. Neumann (eds), in *The Impact of Climate*

Change on the United States Economy, Cambridge, UK: Cambridge University Press, pp. 94–132.

Tol, R.S.J. (1995), 'The damage costs of climate change toward more comprehensive calculations', *Environmental and Resource Economics*, 5, 353–74.

World Bank (1987), *World Development Report 1987*, New York: Oxford University Press.

Appendix

Table A9.1   Estimated regional impacts of climate change in 2060 (billions 1998 USD/year)

Region	Agriculture	Forestry	Energy	Coast	Water	Total
1.5°C warming with 0% precipitation increase						
Northeast	3.14	0.74	0.47	−0.04	0.00	4.31
Midwest	6.80	0.29	0.45	0.00	−0.12	7.42
Northern Plains	5.42	0.61	0.23	0.00	−0.29	5.97
Northwest	2.10	−0.26	1.01	−0.01	−1.92	0.92
Southeast	6.43	−0.85	−1.61	−0.05	−0.14	3.77
Southern Plains	2.72	0.12	−1.44	0.00	−0.24	1.16
Southwest	2.61	0.25	−0.76	0.00	0.13	2.23
National	29.99	0.89	−1.66	−0.09	−2.58	26.55
1.5°C warming with +7% precipitation						
Northeast	3.42	1.14	−0.14	−0.04	0.00	4.39
Midwest	7.23	0.80	0.00	0.00	−0.03	8.00
Northern Plains	5.41	0.87	0.04	0.00	−0.03	6.29
Northwest	2.22	−0.09	1.23	−0.01	−0.48	2.88
Southeast	6.60	0.12	−1.88	−0.05	0.00	4.79
Southern Plains	2.90	0.28	−1.59	0.00	−0.04	1.55
Southwest	2.63	0.68	−0.81	0.00	0.17	2.67
National	30.89	3.80	−3.14	−0.09	−0.41	31.04
2.5°C warming with 0% precipitation increase						
Northeast	2.82	2.59	0.17	−0.06	−0.01	5.51
Midwest	6.26	1.02	0.30	0.00	−0.20	7.38
Northern Plains	4.31	0.54	0.11	0.00	−0.56	4.40
Northwest	2.14	−0.64	1.41	−0.01	−3.22	−0.32
Southeast	5.41	−2.79	−2.79	−0.12	−0.20	1.20
Southern Plains	1.90	0.12	−2.68	−0.00	−0.45	−1.11
Southwest	2.03	0.62	−1.39	−0.01	−0.11	1.14
National	25.5	1.45	−5.32	−0.20	−4.75	16.71

Table A9.1   *continued*

Region	Agriculture	Forestry	Energy	Coast	Water	Total
2.5°C warming with +15% precipitation						
Northeast	2.69	1.80	−1.02	−0.06	0.00	3.41
Midwest	7.04	1.48	−0.64	0.00	−0.01	7.87
Northern Plains	3.93	1.03	−0.30	0.00	0.02	4.68
Northwest	1.89	−0.02	1.85	−0.01	−0.15	3.56
Southeast	5.56	0.89	−3.68	−0.12	0.10	2.76
Southern Plains	2.52	0.45	−3.01	0.00	0.00	−0.05
Southwest	2.06	1.28	−1.51	−0.01	0.65	2.47
National	26.09	6.90	−8.31	−0.20	0.61	25.10
5.0°C warming with +7% precipitation						
Northeast	1.90	2.51	−3.19	−0.15	−0.02	1.06
Midwest	4.16	2.86	−2.10	0.00	−0.33	4.59
Northern Plains	2.90	1.52	−1.37	0.00	−1.05	2.00
Northwest	1.81	−0.15	1.73	−0.02	−5.13	−1.75
Southeast	3.97	0.14	−9.78	−0.19	−0.33	−6.18
Southern Plains	1.06	0.62	−7.32	−0.01	−0.79	−6.44
Southwest	0.74	1.57	−3.66	−0.02	−1.34	−2.71
National	16.07	9.05	−25.67	−0.38	−8.99	−9.91
5.0°C warming with +15% precipitation						
Northeast	1.85	3.26	−3.80	−0.15	0.00	1.16
Midwest	4.83	2.52	−2.59	0.00	−0.20	4.56
Northern Plains	2.26	0.89	−1.59	0.00	−0.63	0.92
Northwest	1.90	−0.15	1.94	−0.02	−3.48	0.19
Southeast	4.10	−0.67	−9.99	−0.19	−0.14	−6.88
Southern Plains	1.61	0.48	−7.15	−0.01	−0.49	−5.55
Southwest	0.98	1.47	−3.72	−0.02	−0.44	−1.73
National	17.02	7.79	−26.89	−0.38	−5.38	−7.84

Notes: Coastal assumes 33 cm in 1.5°C scenario, 67 cm in 2.5°C scenario and 100 cm in 5.0°C scenario. Impacts are beneficial if positive and harmful if negative.

Index

Index

Global warming and the
American economy : a
regional assessment of
climate change impacts

About the Author

Gregory R. Woirol received his PhD in economics from the University of California, Berkeley. He is currently professor emeritus of economics at Whittier College, Whittier, California. While at Whittier College he received the Nerhood outstanding teaching award as well as recognition for academic advising and service. His scholarship awards include grants from the Ford Foundation, National Science Foundation, and Haynes Foundation. His publications include *In the Floating Army: F. C. Mills on Itinerant Life in California, 1914*, *The Technological Unemployment and Structural Unemployment Debates*, and over a dozen articles in the areas of U.S. economic history and the history of economic thought.